CONVERSATION ANALYSIS

Second Language Acquisition Research
Theoretical and Methodological Issues
Susan Gass and Jacquelyn Schachter, Editors

Tarone/Gass/Cohen • Research Methodololgy
in Second-Language Acquisition

Schachter/Gass • Second Language Classroom
Research: Issues and Opportunities

Birdsong • Second Language Acquisition
and the Critical Period Hypothesis

Monographs on Research Methodology

Gass/Mackey • Stimulated Recall Methodology
in Second Language Research

Yule • Referential Communication Tasks

Markee • Conversation Analysis

CONVERSATION ANALYSIS

Numa Markee
University of Illinois at Urbana-Champaign

LEA LAWRENCE ERLBAUM ASSOCIATES, PUBLISHERS
2000 Mahwah, New Jersey   London

The final camera copy for this work was prepared by the author, and therefore the publisher takes no responsibility for consistency or correctness of typographical style. However, this arrangement helps to make publication of this kind of scholarship possible.

Lawrence Erlbaum Associates, Inc., Publishers
10 Industrial Avenue
Mahwah, NJ 07430

Cover design by Kathryn Houghtaling Lacey

Library of Congress Cataloging-in-Publication Data
Markee, Numa.
Conversation analysis / Numa Markee
     p.   cm. — (SLA research)
  Includes bibliographical references and index.
ISBN 0-8058-1999-1 © : alk. paper). — ISBN 0-8058-2000-0 (pbk. : alk. paper).
1. Conversation analysis. 2. Second language acquisition I. Title. II. Series.

P95.45.M35   2000
302.3' 46—dc21

           99-39744
            CIP

Books published by Lawrence Erlbaum Associates are printed on acid-free paper, and their bindings are chosen for strength and durability.

Printed in the United States of America
10 9 8 7 6 5 4 3 2 1

For Susan

CONTENTS

Foreword

This series is born of our belief that to adequately understand conclusions drawn from second language acquisition research, one must understand the methodology that is used to elicit data for that research. The concern with research methodology is common in all fields, but it takes on particular significance in second language research given the interdisciplinary nature of the field and the varying perspectives of second language researchers. Within a single common field, we have psychologists talking to linguists; we have sociolinguists concerned with variation talking to sociolinguists concerned with pragmatics; we have ethnographers talking to generative grammarians. Although all this is healthy for the long-term outcome of the field, it is problematic in that researchers bring with them research traditions from their own disciplines. Again, this is ultimately healthy but can lead to serious misunderstandings, in the short term, of the value of a particular elicitation instrument. As a result, research traditions are attacked through their methodologies without a full understanding of what linguistic or psycholinguistic or sociolinguistic knowledge or abilities a particular instrument is intended to tap. This series of monographs is an attempt to bring these issues to light.

The series consists of monographs devoted to particular data-collection methods of instruments. Each monograph probes a specific research method or tool, discussing the history of the instrument as well as its current uses. A major feature of each monograph is an exploration of what the research instrument does and does not purport to tell us about second language acquisition or use. Each monograph addresses the kinds of research questions for which the method or instrument is best suited, its underlying assumptions, a characterization of the method or instrument, and an extended description of its use, including the problems associated with its use. It is hoped that the series as a whole will reflect the state of the research in second language acquisition. It is only through a deeper understanding of the strengths and weaknesses, and the advantages and disadvantages of particular research tools, that the field of second language acquisition can get beyond issues of methodology and begin to work together as a collective whole.

—Susan Gass
—Jacquelyn Schachter
Series Editors

ACKNOWLEDGMENTS

I express my thanks to a number of friends and colleagues who have provided invaluable assistance and support during the writing of this book. In particular, I express my deep appreciation to the general editors of the series in which this book is published, Susan Gass and Jacquelyn Schachter, and Judith Amsel, the executive editor at Lawrence Erlbaum Associates, for their unfailing courtesy and Job-like patience as they waited for me to produce the manuscript. The help of Sara Scudder of Lawrence Erlbaum Associates and Geoffrey Muckenhirn of the Language Learning Laboratory at the University of Illinois at Urbana-Champaign was also crucial during the production of the camera ready copy of the manuscript. This book would never have seen the light of day without the constant help and encouragement of all these individuals.

I also acknowledge an important intellectual debt to Richard Young, whose ideas about interactional competence helped me frame the discussion of sequencing, turn-taking and repair in Part II of this book in a satisfyingly unified fashion. I was first exposed to these ideas in a talk (Young, 1997) given under the auspices of the University of Illinois' SLATE Speaker Series and have had a number of valuable opportunities since then to discuss in greater detail what the parameters of interactional competence might be. One of the most important of these opportunities includes an invitation extended by Richard Young and Cecilia Ford to discuss my ideas with their students at the University of Wisconsin at Madison's English Language and Linguistics Colloquium. During this presentation, I received many valuable suggestions from colloquium participants for ways in which I could revise and complexify my analyses of the "Coral" collection data (see chapter 7 and appendix B), which had been previously published as Markee (1994). Similarly, I wish to thank David Olsher and the students in the Applied Linguistics Department at UCLA for giving me the opportunity to present a preliminary analysis of the "Auschwitz" collection data (see chapter 8 and appendix C). Feedback from Elinor Ochs and other colleagues at UCLA helped me understand more clearly that such data could be used to complexify current notions of understanding and learning in second language acquisition studies. Finally, I acknowledge the fact that the data and analyses contained in chapter 4 are based in part on previously published material (Markee, 1995).

LIST OF ABBREVIATIONS

ACD   Analysis of conversational data
CA   Conversation analysis
SLA   Second language acquisition
L2   Second language
NS   Native speaker
NNS   Non-native speaker
UG   Universal grammar
LAD   Language acquisition device
LSS   Lexicalized sentence stem
Q   Question turn
A   Answer turn
C   Commenting turn
CQ   Counter Question turn
CQ(D)   Counter Question turn done as a display question
CQ(R)   Counter Question turn done as a referential question
MS   Main sequence
IS   Insertion sequence
NTRI   Next turn repair initiator

I: ISSUES AND DEFINITIONS

Overview of SLA Studies

1.0. INTRODUCTION

This book is about using conversation analysis (CA) as a methodological resource for analyzing and understanding second language acquisition (SLA) behaviors. Its premise is that, although considerable progress has been made in understanding the big picture of how second language (L2) learners use talk to learn new language, not only has theory far outstripped empirical verification but the details of how learners actually deploy talk to learn on a moment-by-moment basis have largely been ignored. To develop a photographic analogy, many pictures that depict the vast sweep of the SLA landscape are available; but there are few photographs that depict the fine details of this landscape. In part, this situation is due to the difficulty of demonstrating how learning occurs. Language acquisition is a long drawn-out, multi stage process, whose products may only become accessible to researchers over periods of time lasting weeks, months, or even years. Furthermore, language-learning processes may not always be reflected as observable behaviors. However, researchers must recognize that this situation is also an artifact of the predominantly nomothetic epistemology that dominates the field of SLA studies.

The preference (whether esthetic or scientific) for a theory-driven, experimental, and quantitative approach to knowledge construction privileges the development of the big picture of SLA at the expense of a data-driven, microanalytic, and qualitative approach to knowledge construction. However, this is not to say that language-learning behaviors can never be observed in action nor analyzed on a moment-by-moment basis. The premise of this book is that CA represents one way of demonstrating how micro-moments of socially distributed cognition instantiated in conversational behavior contribute to observable changes in participants' states of knowing and using new language. My purpose in writing this book, therefore, is to fill in some of the empirical gaps left by proponents of big picture SLA and also to demonstrate the potential of using the microanalytical power of CA as a methodological resource for SLA studies. In so doing, I not only confirm some of the proposals of mainstream SLA research concerning the role of conversation in SLA but also reconstitute the way in which SLA researchers have traditionally conceptualized notions such as understanding and learning new language.

The book is divided into three parts. Part I lays out the range of issues that are the subject of this book. In this preliminary chapter, I begin by briefly defining the field of SLA studies. I then review in some detail three influential hypotheses in the SLA literature, namely, the discourse hypothesis, the social interaction hypothesis, and the interactionist hypothesis. In chapter 2, I first sketch out when and how CA emerged and then define CA. Having set the theoretical stage in this fashion, I proceed to develop a methodological critique of current SLA studies from a conversation-analytic perspective. Finally, chapter 3 concludes Part I with a practical discussion of how to do CA.

Parts II and III lay out the insights into language use and language-learning behaviors that can be constructed by using CA as a methodological resource for doing SLA research. More specifically, in chapters 4, 5 and 6, which constitute Part II, I develop a model of interactional competence (Young, 1997) that provides an account of the sequential, turn-taking, and repair organizations to which participants orient in different speech exchange systems. In chapters 7 and 8, which constitute Part III, I then show empirically how members orient to these three types of conversational organization as potential resources for language learning. That is, in chapter 7, I provide a moment-by-moment microanalysis of the conversational behaviors one learner deploys to understand and learn (at least in the short term) the meaning of the word *coral*. In chapter 8, I use exactly the same methodology to show how another learner, interacting in a very similar environment and under very similar conditions, fails to understand and learn the meaning of the phrase "We cannot get by Auschwitz." Therefore, I end this book by arguing that because both learners use similar kinds of strategies to try to understand and learn these problem items, the empirical analysis in this final chapter problematizes current notions of what it means to understand and learn new language.

1.1. TOWARD A DEFINITION OF SLA STUDIES

SLA researchers have borrowed ideas from many different sources (among others, linguistics, psychology, education, sociology). Consequently, SLA studies may be understood as an interdisciplinary field that seeks to explain how a broad range of psycholinguistic, sociolinguistic, or neurobiological factors affect the acquisition of second (and, indeed, subsequent) languages by child and adult learners. The range of issues that potentially falls under the purview of SLA research is consequently extremely large, encompassing the domains of both linguistic and communicative competence (see, e.g., Gass, 1998; Gass & Selinker, 1994; Hatch, Shirai, & Fantuzzi, 1990, for further discussion and exemplification of this issue).

This breadth not only reflects the inherently interdisciplinary nature of the field but also its rapid intellectual growth in a comparatively short period of time. SLA research has grown from an initially modest and exclusive concern with pedagogically related issues of contrastive and error analysis into a theoretically motivated, arguably independent field in its own right (Sharwood-Smith, 1991, cited in Gass, 1993). This means that findings from SLA research may, but need not necessarily, have direct pedagogical applications. For example, Gregg (1996) viewed this discipline as a purely theoretical field. In contrast, Foster (1998), Hatch (1978, 1979) and Hatch et al. (1990), among others, argued that it is ultimately desirable for the theoretical SLA literature to connect with pedagogical issues. As these last authors remarked, "Since foreign and second language acquisition includes formal and informal instruction, the effect of teaching — and the different types of programs that promote particular types of teaching — should be made explicit in any theory of SLA" (p. 698).

For the purposes of this book, I align myself with this latter position and argue that SLA studies can make important contributions not only to theories of language learning but also to theories of language teaching, which, as Richards (1990) argued, must be based on empirical accounts of effective language teaching behaviors.

I now discuss in more detail three SLA hypotheses that are particularly relevant to this book: the discourse hypothesis, the social interactionist hypothesis and the interactionist hypothesis.

1.2. THE DISCOURSE HYPOTHESIS

The discourse hypothesis (Hatch, 1978) initially emerged as a result of Hatch's interest in establishing the kinds of relation that exist between form and function in language use and describing the strategies that L2 learners use to differentiate between various functions of the same form. Hatch was also motivated to explore the possibilities offered by a discourse-analytic approach to SLA because she believed that "one learns how to do conversation, one learns how to interact verbally and out of this interaction syntactic structures are developed" (p. 404; see also Wagner-Gough & Hatch, 1975). That is, Hatch wanted to gain insights into the then little researched area of how learners learn second languages, not just what they learn.

How might a discoursal approach help SLA researchers make connections between the how and the what of SLA? Hatch cited the following piece of talk between H (an adult native speaker of English) and T (a 2 1/2- year-old L2 learner of English) to illustrate how such connections can be made (note that the transcription convention used in this excerpt is to align all of T's talk in the left-hand column, and all of H's talk in the right-hand column):

Excerpt 1.1

```
1  T:     * this
2         * broken
3 H:      *                broken
4  T:     * broken
5         * This /az/ broken
6         * broken
7 H:      *                Upside down
8  T:     * upside down
9         * this broken
10        * upside down
11        * this broken
```
            (excerpt from Itoh, 1973, cited in Hatch, 1978, pp. 409–410)

More specifically, this excerpt shows how the vertical constructions of T's and H's collaborative talk (see lines 1–2, 4–6) become elaborated and transformed into the horizontal constructions in T's talk (see lines 8–11) through a process of scaffolding (see line 3 and, in particular, line 7); (Slobin, 1982). In other words, one way in which syntactic structure may develop out of conversation, at least in children learning an L2, is through a collaborative process of incorporation of linguistic material by L2 novices from the previous, often adjacent, turns of native speakers.

However, Hatch was careful not to assume that the same kinds of insights would necessarily also hold for adult L2 learners. Indeed, she noted that, although the talk of children and adults is in some ways structurally quite similar — for example, both have difficulties in identifying or nominating discourse topics and developing ideas in syntactically acceptable ways — child–child, child–adult and adult–adult discourse are also qualitatively quite different from each other in important ways (Hatch, 1978; Peck, 1978, 1980).

For example, the function of vertical and horizontal constructions is less clear in adult conversations than it is in child talk. Whereas children seem to use such constructions primarily as a means of constructing syntax, adults seem to use them either to get needed vocabulary or to orient to normal conventions of conversational politeness. Moreover, adult non–native speaker (NNS) learners make extensive strategic use of various repair strategies as a means of getting needed clarifications from native speaker (NS) interlocutors. These clarifications enable adult learners to get important content words they have missed and thus help them either to identify topics nominated by their NS interlocutors or nominate topics of their own. This behavior may be explained by the fact that, unlike conversations involving children, the talk that occurs during adult conversations is rarely about objects in the immediate environment. When adult NNSs attempt to nominate the complex topics typical of adult talk, therefore, it seems that they often have to expend a great deal of time and effort on trying to get the vocabulary they need from their NS interlocutors. For their part, NSs do a lot of paraphrasing in an attempt to confirm their understanding of the learner's topic nominations.

As Hatch (1978) suggested, these kinds of findings imply that adult talk-in-interaction may be particularly useful for the acquisition of L2 vocabulary. Furthermore, she also explicitly allowed the possibility that conversation may not be as useful a resource for the acquisition of L2 syntax by adults as it seems to be for children. This issue is, of course, ultimately an empirical question, which can therefore only be settled by empirical research (see Gass & Varonis, 1989; Mackey, 1999; Swain & Lapkin, 1998, for recent papers on this. See also Sato, 1986. This work, based on insights from Hatch, 1983, suggested that conversation may be an efficient resource for highlighting syntactic structures such as adverbs and lexical past verbs, but less efficient for highlighting verbal inflections).

1.3. THE SOCIAL INTERACTION HYPOTHESIS

Hatch's ideas on the role of input in SLA proved to be a seminal influence on the subsequent work of Krashen and Long and their respective associates. For example, Krashen (1980) suggested that exposure to comprehensible input (also known as "i+1") or input that is slightly beyond a learner's current level of competence in the L2 was both a necessary and sufficient mechanism for explaining SLA. In contrast, Long (1983b, 1983c, 1996) argued that although exposure to comprehensible input is certainly necessary, it is not by itself sufficient to ensure acquisition. Arguing that NNSs cannot just be passive recipients of i+1 if they wish to acquire new language, Long suggested that learners must actively get the raw linguistic data they need from NSs by engaging their interlocutors in social interaction. Extending this hypothesis, Swain (1985, 1995) further argued that learners must also produce comprehensible output in order to move their interlanguage from a semantic to a syntactic analysis of the L2 input.

1.3.1. The Conversational Resources Used by Learners to Obtain Comprehensible Input

What conversational resources do L2 learners use in order to get comprehensible input from NS interlocutors? Long argued that NNSs induce conversational partners to provide comprehensible input by initiating a range of repairs, including comprehension checks, clarification requests, confirmation checks, verifications of meaning, definition requests, and expressions of lexical uncertainty (Porter, 1986). The idea that speakers' repair strategies function as a resource for SLA in both naturalistic and instructed contexts has since gained widespread currency in the SLA literature. Indeed, as Pica (1987) noted:

> what enables learners to move beyond their current interlanguage receptive and expressive capacities when they need to understand unfamiliar linguistic input or when required to produce a comprehensible message are opportunities to modify and restructure their interaction with their interlocutor until mutual comprehension is reached. Although there is no direct proof that the immediate comprehension and production gains experienced as a result of interactional restructuring generalize to the learner's interlanguage repertoire, i.e., lead directly to acquisition, there is a great deal of indirect evidence and convincing theoretical claims to support the contributions of interactional modification moves to the acquisition process and to encourage their use by classroom participants (p. 8).

Pica also provided some useful illustrations of what clarification requests, confirmation checks and comprehension checks actually look like. For example, there are two clarification requests in Excerpt 1.2 (see lines 2 and 5), one confirmation check in Excerpt 1.3 (see line 3) and one clarification request (see lines 7 and 8) and one comprehension check in Excerpt 1.4 (see line 11).

As Pica noted, these repair types can be initiated either by the NNS learner or by the NS interlocutor. Thus, whereas all the repairs in Excerpts 1.2 and 1.3 are initiated by the NS, both the NNS and the NS initiate one repair each in Excerpt 1.4. Note that similar conversational adjustments have also been observed in NNS–NNS interactions (Long & Porter, 1985; Pica & Doughty, 1985; Porter, 1986).

Excerpt 1.2

Learner (NNS English)	Interlocutor (NS English)
1 and they have the chwach there	
2 *	the what
3 the chwach ___ I know someone	
4 that-	
5 *	what does it mean
6 like um like American people they	
7 always go there every Sunday	
8	yes?
9 you know___every morning	
10 that there pr- that- the American	
11 people get dressed up to go to um	
12 chwach	
13	oh to church____I see

(Pica, 1987, p. 6).

Excerpt 1.3

Learner (NNS English)	Interlocutor (NS English)
1 like us three months ago that the	
2 SEPTA doft doft doft	
3 *	dropped?
4 No you lo- you lend me I am	
5 you	
6	oh owes_____debt
7 debts okay they debt million of dollars	
8	oh yeah yeah

(Pica, 1987, p. 6).

Excerpt 1.4

Learner (NNS English)	Interlocutor (NS English)
1 ... so this young woman doctor	
2 hope this young man doctor drive	
3 car, go home ... Now this young	

4		woman boyfriend very angry ... he	
5		want have a very no- good idea for	
6		this girl	
7	*		which girl? the one who
8	*		can't speak?
9		can't speak girl. and why? because	
10		this this girl very angry also.	
11	*	you know what I mean	
12			yes

(Pica, 1987, pp. 6–7).

The occurrence of such conversational adjustments are thought to promote communication and to fulfill an implicit teaching function (Hatch, 1983), provided that these adjustments address gaps in learners' knowledge structures and that learners assume responsibility for these gaps and do not blame their interlocutors for their occurrence (Faerch & Kasper, 1986). Based on these theoretical ideas and empirically based insights, psycholinguistically based rationales for task-based, small group-mediated teaching methodologies have begun to emerge (see Long 1985b, 1989, 1991, in press; Pica, 1987; Pica, Kanagy, & Falodun, 1993; Skehan, 1998) that complement previous pedagogical justifications for such activities. According to this perspective on SLA, then, it is the large number of repairs and other tokens of negative evidence that potentially make comprehensible talk that is initially too complex for NNSs to understand (Carroll & Swain, 1993; Gass, 1997; Gass & Varonis, 1985a; Long, 1983c, 1996; Oliver, 1995; Scarcella & Higa, 1981).

1.3.2. Familiarity

A related strand of research has focused on how the construct of familiarity, which has a number of different dimensions, may affect the comprehensibility of input. For example, it was shown that familiarity with one's interlocutor, with other speakers of the target language, and with non-native varieties of speech in general has a positive impact on comprehension (Gass & Varonis, 1984). In contrast, when NNS interlocutors do not share a linguistic or cultural background, little conversational restructuring occurs (Varonis & Gass, 1985). In addition, familiarity with the task that is to be completed may decrease the amount of restructuring that occurs in NNS–NNS conversation (Gass & Varonis, 1985a).

Continuing this line of research, Plough and Gass (1993) showed that there is a higher incidence of overlaps, sentence completions, confirmation checks and clarification requests in NNS dyads whose members are familiar with each other than in unfamiliar dyads, although unfamiliar partners used more echoes than familiar partners did. With reference to task familiarity, these researchers also found that whereas partners who were familiar with a task produced more confirmation checks and clarification requests than task-unfamiliar partners, task-unfamiliar dyads interrupted each other more often than conversationalists who were familiar with the task. Plough and Gass cautioned, however, that these results did not receive strong empirical support. They concluded that the optimal conditions for the negotiation of input are met when conversationalists are involved in the talk and interacting in a nonthreatening environment.

Other research on input has focused on who plays the dominant role in restructuring both NS–NNS interaction and NNS–NNS talk in terms of different levels of communicative competence, that is, how familiar different participants are with the L2. Thus, early research on this topic found that NSs were responsible for initiating more confirmation checks, comprehension checks and clarification requests than NNSs. This behavior was explained in terms of NSs' higher levels of communicative competence in English (Beebe & Giles, 1984; Scarcella, 1983). But more recent research has shown that NNSs who possess specialist content knowledge become the dominant conversational partners with NSs who do not have such specialist knowledge (Woken & Swales, 1989; Zuengler 1989; Zuengler & Bent, 1991).

1.3.3. Task Types

Also important is research on the technical attributes of task types. In this respect, not all tasks are equally good at generating acquisitionally useful varieties of talk. For example, free conversation is a notoriously unreliable tool for getting learners to negotiate their interlocutors' speech (Long, 1989). Some of the characteristics of tasks that seem to be most relevant include whether a task involves a one-way or two-way exchange of information; is convergent or divergent; is closed or open; is planned or unplanned.

One-way (also frequently referred to as information gap) tasks involve only one party to a conversation possessing information that is necessary to the solution of a problem. In contrast, two-way (also known as jigsaw) tasks are structured in such a way that all participants possess information that is necessary to the ultimate solution of the problem. The crucial difference between these kinds of tasks is that two-way tasks are said to force all participants to contribute to the talk and thus to engage in conversational modifications of each others' talk. In contrast, one-way tasks only set up the possibility that all parties will contribute to the talk and modify their conversational exchanges (Doughty & Pica, 1986; Long, 1980, 1989).

Convergent tasks involve learners reaching consensus on a mutually acceptable solution to a problem, while divergent tasks involve learners developing their own individual viewpoints on a problem, which they must defend against other learners' positions. Convergent tasks have been found to generate more conversationally modified talk than divergent tasks (Duff, 1986). Long (1989) has also suggested that closed tasks (i.e., tasks that require learners to arrive at a single correct solution or restricted set of solutions) yield a greater quantity and variety of negotiation than open tasks (i.e., tasks that have no single predetermined solution). However, this hypothesis has yet to be tested empirically. Finally, the amount of planning that learners do before they perform a task seems to be related to the syntactic complexity of the language that students ultimately produce (Crookes, 1989; Ortega, 1999). In a pedagogical context, this suggests that it is desirable for teachers not to insist that learners should produce language spontaneously at all times. Rather, teachers should provide learners with opportunities to work out what they are going to say and how they are going to say it.

Drawing on this body of research, Pica et al. (1993) argued that jigsaw tasks force interlocutors to exchange conversationally modified input slightly more efficiently than information gap tasks do. However, both these task types are much more efficient at ensuring this result than opinion gap tasks are. I examine the former comparison first.

Jigsaw and information gap tasks share several important characteristics. More specifically, both task types require conversationalists to exchange needed information, and both are convergent and closed. However, these tasks differ in one crucial respect: Whereas jigsaw tasks are necessarily two way, information gap tasks may be either two way or one way. This suggests that jigsaw tasks are slightly better than information gap tasks at ensuring that learners repair their speech during the course of solving a problem.

Moving on now to the comparison between jigsaw tasks and information gap tasks on the one hand and opinion gap tasks on the other, jigsaw tasks and information gap tasks are clearly qualitatively different from opinion gap tasks in that opinion gap tasks may be either one way or two way, do not require speakers to exchange information, and are highly divergent and open. Opinion gap tasks are therefore thought to be less likely to force interlocutors to modify their speech than jigsaw tasks and information gap tasks.

Of course, as Pica et al. (1993) readily admitted, few studies have actually demonstrated that negotiated talk produced by learners engaged in jigsaw and information gap tasks demonstrably promotes SLA. Indeed, results from an empirical study of a "real" classroom (as opposed to students interacting in a laboratory setting) by Foster (1998) suggest that the situation is much more complicated than Pica et al. and others allow. More specifically, aggregate scores obtained by Foster provided general support for Pica's et al. position that tasks with the specific attributes discussed previously will yield more conversational modifications than tasks that do not possess these desirable characteristics. However, when individual scores were analyzed, considerable variation was observed in the extent to which individual students produced any significant amounts of language at all during the completion of either one-way or two-way tasks; negotiated meaning; or produced output that had been semantically, syntactically, morphologically, or phonologically modified. Interestingly, what seemed to be the most important factor in accounting for this variability was not so much whether tasks were constructed in a particular way as whether interlocutors were configured in pairs or small groups. By and large, a dyadic configuration resulted in more conversational modification of the input than did a small group configuration.

Finally, Foster and Skehan (1996) showed that there are different accuracy, complexity, and fluency effects for three different task types carried out under three different planning conditions. More specifically, Foster and Skehan devised three kinds of tasks for this study. Personal tasks involved pairs of learners in an exchange of personal information, during which students told their partners how to get to their house in order to turn off a gas oven that had inadvertent-ly been left on. Narrative tasks involved dyads inventing a story on the basis of sets of pictures that did not suggest an obvious story line but shared common characters. And in the decision-making tasks, students had to role-play the decisions of a judge deciding how to punish different crimes appropriately.

The accuracy, complexity, and fluency effects for each task under the conditions of no planning, undetailed planning, and detailed planning were then measured. Accuracy effects were determined by dividing the total number of correct clauses by the number of clauses produced by each subject. The maximum value that could be achieved in this column was 1.00. Complexity effects were measured by dividing the total number of clauses by the total number of communi-cation units (c-units) for all subjects, thus reflecting the number of clauses per c-unit. In this column, the minimum value students could

TABLE 1.1
Accuracy, complexity, and fluency for three tasks and three planning conditions

	Personal	Narration	Decision Making
Accuracy			
Unplanned	.64	.61	.63
Undetailed planning	.76	.66	.73
Detailed planning	.69	.58	.71
Average for task	.70	.62	.69
Complexity			
Unplanned	1.11	1.22	1.23
Undetailed planning	1.16	1.42	1.35
Detailed planning	1.26	1.68	1.52
Average for task	1.18	1.43	1.37
Fluency			
Unplanned	32	120	91
Undetailed planning	20	29	26
Detailed planning	15	14	30
Average for task	22	54	49

Note. From P. Foster & P. Skehan, 1996, cited in Skehan (1998, p. 109). Reprinted with the permission of Cambridge University Press.

obtain was 1.00. Finally, fluency effects were measured by aggregating the total seconds of silence per subject for each 5-minute task. The results of this research are summarized in Table 1.1.

Table 1.1 shows that students produced more accurate language when they were engaged in personal and decision-making tasks than when they were telling a story. Furthermore, learners produced more complex language when they were telling a story or making decisions than when they were doing personal tasks. Finally, students were most fluent during the personal task and least fluent during the narration and decision-making tasks.

The planning conditions associated with each task type were also found to have different effects on the accuracy, complexity, or fluency with which each task was accomplished. Thus, the more planned a task was, the more complex and fluent the language that was produced. However, with respect to accuracy, it turned out that the most accurate performance was associated with the undetailed planning condition. Furthermore, whereas there was only a comparatively small increase in complexity and fluency as a result of planning for the personal task, there was a dramatic improvement on these two measures when students were able to plan how they would perform the decision-making and narrative tasks. It therefore seems that the technical attributes of tasks are not the only variables that are implicated in modifying the quality of interaction.

1.4. THE INTERACTIONIST HYPOTHESIS

Research on how the linguistic environment shapes the input that is available to learners has always been a particularly vibrant area in SLA studies. However, researchers working within a social interaction paradigm were quick to recognize that this research had to be related to other areas of SLA studies if satisfactory explanations for such a complex phenomenon as L2 learning were ever to be devised. Following Larsen-Freeman and Long (1991), I call all such proposals interactionist models of L2 learning.

1.4.1. A Metaphor for L2 Learning

Before I discuss what one of these models looks like, I stress that interactionist models are relatively "messy" representations of how L2 learning is constructed. Speaking to this issue, Hatch et al. (1990) suggested that although it is often conceptually necessary for researchers initially to develop theories of SLA that focus on a small part of the overall language acquisition picture, it is nonetheless important to recognize that these theoretical modules overlap considerably. Given the current state of SLA studies, interactionist models of SLA are bound to be quite messy, because the modules involved are often based on very different theoretical assumptions that do not co-exist easily. Nonetheless, this is the best that can be done at the present time. To explain how interactionist models of SLA might work, therefore, Hatch et al. developed an overhead transparency metaphor that illustrates both the potential and the problems associated with interactionist accounts of language learning.

More specifically, because light can shine through several transparencies at once, transparencies representing different theoretical perspectives can be laid on top of each other to illuminate a particular problem from different points of view. In this way, it is possible to begin analyzing how people make complaints by using a conversation analysis transparency to analyze how participants open and close complaints sequences and how they orient to the practices of turn-taking and repair in order to do complaining. Another transparency (say a service encounter script transparency) can be added to highlight how participants constitute themselves as actors in this speech event, the roles they adopt, and the props they use in order to support their arguments. Other transparencies (e.g., a lexical transparency to deal with vocabulary issues, an intonation and stress transparency to deal with sentence-level and suprasegmental phonology, a syntactic transparency to deal with non-formulaic utterances, etc.) can be added on an as-needed basis.

This metaphor is obviously attractive in that it enables researchers to appeal to a broad range of perspectives in order to explain how SLA works. But the picture of SLA that is constructed in this way also clearly runs the risk of becoming unreadable because mutually incompatible transparencies are laid over each other. With these caveats in mind, I now draw on Gass' (1997) discussion of the interactionist model of L2 learning shown in Fig. 1.1 to illustrate how research on input, interaction, and L2 learners might be integrated into a single conceptual whole.

1.4.2. An Interactionist Model of L2 Learning

As Gass (1997) remarked, all the input to which learners are exposed does not automatically become available to them. Consequently, the dotted line in Fig. 1.1 represents the fact that only some of the data about an L2 actually filters through to learners at any given time. The first step in the acquisition process addresses the following issue: Learners must apperceive, or consciously notice, that there is a gap

INPUT

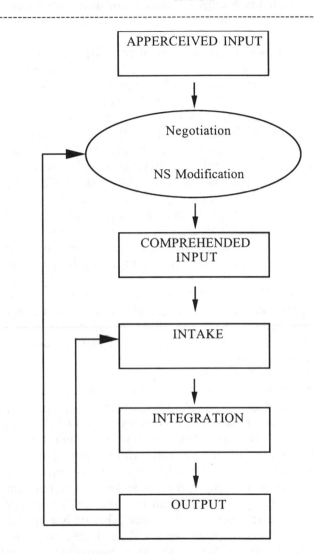

FIG 1.1 An interactionist model of second language acquisition (adapted from Gass, 1997). Reprinted with the permission of Lawrence Erlbaum Associates.

between their present knowledge of the L2 and information contained in the input that they are hearing or reading (Schmidt, 1990, 1993; Schmidt & Frota, 1986).

Learners may notice this gap for many different reasons. For example, having enough time to process the L2 may enable learners to notice aspects of its structure that had previously gone over their heads. Learners may also notice an item if it is particularly frequent in the input (Larsen-Freeman, 1976), or, conversely, because its occurrence is so rare that it sticks out from the surrounding language. Learners may also notice a gap in their knowledge due to a variety of affective factors, such as social or psychological distance, status, motivation, or attitude (see Krashen 1977, 1980, 1982; Schumann, 1976). Learners may also notice a gap based on their prior knowledge of how the L2 works in general or how similarly a particular L2 (e.g., Italian) functions in comparison with a typologically close third language (e.g., Spanish). Learners may also notice language because it is made salient in a particular way, for example, by its position in the input, by stress, by its relation to previously known language, or by frequency criteria. Finally, learners may notice gaps if they pay attention to language that is developmentally accessible to them. To summarize, Gass (1997) proposed that the principal function of apperceived input is to "act as a priming device that prepares the input for further analysis" (p. 4).

The second step (which is mediated by the kinds of conversational modifications of the input discussed in section 1.4.1) involves a preliminary analysis of the input. As Gass observed, the most familiar version of the issues treated here is Krashen's (1980) notion of comprehensible input. However, Gass' notion of comprehended input is qualitatively different from comprehensible input in at least two ways. First, the term *comprehended input* represents a hearer's perspective on what makes input understandable, whereas the term *comprehensible input* suggests that input becomes understandable as a result of whatever the speaker does to modify his or her speech. For the purposes of this book, given that CA is based on a hearer's perspective on how talk is done, this is a particularly significant difference. Second, the notion of comprehension is not an either-or construct. According to Gass (1997), "Comprehension represents a continuum of possibilities ranging from semantics to detailed structural analyses" (page 5). Consequently, comprehension is thought to range from a comparatively shallow, semantically based process, during which learners are able to get the general gist of a message, to a deeper, syntactically based analysis of the structure of the language contained in the input.

The third step, intake, involves the assimilation of apperceived input into learners' preexisting frames of knowledge about the L2. It is at this stage of the model that psycholinguistic processing of apperceived data occurs. However, the nature of the underlying knowledge systems that enable learners to process new input is a matter of some debate. Indeed, the transition from comprehended input to intake is an example of the inherent messiness" of interactionist models of SLA to which I referred in section 1.4.1.

There are at least three theories that address the question of what language is and how it is organized: universal grammar (UG), the information-processing model, and connectionism. I discuss only the first two of these models. In UG, language is seen as an autonomous system of abstract knowledge about the rules of grammar that govern all possible human languages (Chomsky, 1975). These rules consist of so-called universal principles and variable parameters that constrain core grammar. An example of a universal principle is subjacency, which constrains how wh-elements may be moved across bounding nodes in different languages. Parameters, on the other hand, are principles that vary across languages. So, for example, whereas some languages (e.g., Spanish or Italian) are [+ pro-drop] languages (i.e., verbs do not need to have subjects explicitly stated), others (e.g., French or German) are [- pro-drop] languages (i.e., subjects must precede verbs). Furthermore, individual parameters seem to cluster together. Whereas Spanish or Italian allow subject–verb inversion in declarative sentences, French and German do not. Interestingly, this observation about Spanish and Italian and German and French may be generalized to a universalist statement that no [+ pro-drop] language ever allows subject–verb inversion in declarative sentences.

To summarize, from a first language (L1) acquisition perspective, these are very powerful claims. They provide a possible explanation for the relative ease and speed with which L1 acquisition occurs in all normal children. More specifically, it is claimed that all normal human beings are "pre-wired" at birth with an abstract knowledge of what language is and that the bulk of the work of language acquisition is automatically done for the child by a so-called language acquisition device (LAD). An important function of this LAD is to specify the child's innate knowledge of the universal constraints on what a possible grammar is for his or her native language. From this perspective, therefore, input is comparatively unimportant. All that is needed are a few samples of the L1, which then act as a catalyst for subsequent internal processing by the LAD.

Some researchers, notably Gass (1997), maintain that mentalist and social interactionist perspectives on the role and relative importance of input can be reconciled within an interactionist framework for SLA. The problem, however, is that some writers working within the UG tradition, in particular Gregg (1993, 1996), will have nothing to do with such a hybrid position. A potentially more promising alternative to UG, which might therefore be used to explain how apperceived input becomes intake, is the information processing perspective proposed by McLaughlin (1987), Skehan (1998), and others. According to this view, language may be as much memory-based as it is rule driven (Bolinger, 1975). Although NSs certainly have access to a rule-driven system to generate completely new sentences when they have to, they much more frequently access memorized chunks of language, particularly when they are under the normal communicative pressure of doing ordinary conversation. According to Skehan (1998), the differences between these two systems are as follows.

The rule-based system is probably quite compact in its organization. Furthermore, it is likely to be parsimoniously organized, generative, restructurable, and amenable to feedback. Consequently, this system is capable of great analytic precision. However, because the processing demands of this form-focused system are also quite high, NSs and, even more so, NNSs, will not always have the opportunity to use this system in order to encode or decode talk. For this reason, under normal communicative pressure, speaker-hearers may have to rely on an exemplar-based system in order to communicate.

This second system is likely to be highly redundant, to be meaning-focused, and to have limited generative potential. This means that it is not well suited to the expression of precise new meanings. In addition, it is probably not very efficient because learning can only proceed by accumulating context-bound chunks of language, which are unlikely to be amenable to feedback. However, the huge advantage of this system is that the processing demands on speaker-hearers and, in particular, on L2 learners, are comparatively quite low. In other words, it is principally designed to provide fast, easy access to large stocks of relatively fixed, prefabricated phrases.

Skehan suggested that in L1 acquisition, these two systems interact in this way: Initially, language learning is primarily lexical; that is, the child builds up a stock of unanalyzed chunks of language that are deployed in appropriate linguistic contexts. Subsequently, as the child matures, lexical knowledge becomes syntacticized. The child analyzes his or her stock of exemplars in order to express more precise, personal meanings. Finally, in the last stage of language learning, analyzed language becomes relexicalized in order to make it easily deployable in everyday talk. This gives rise to a dual-mode system, which combines the advantages of both rule- and exemplar-based systems. More specifically, according to Pawley and Syder (1983), (cited in Skehan, 1998, p. 36), when speaker-hearers use expressions such as

I'm sorry to keep you waiting
I'm so sorry to have kept you waiting
Mr X is sorry to keep you waiting all this time

they are producing analyzed talk that nonetheless also incorporates significant amounts of lexicalized chunks of language. More specifically, these sentences may all be derived from a "base" lexicalized sentence stem (LSS), which may be represented as

NP be-TENSE sorry to keep-TENSE you waiting

Thus, according to an information processing account of language, L1 speaker-hearers are constantly accessing this dual system of representing language in order to express themselves fast as well as accurately. In an L2 learning situation, learners may fossilize if they are not pushed in some way to syntacticize initially lexicalized input. If they move on to analyze lexical chunks, L2 learners will also proceed to develop a dual system of language storage and use. It is by appealing to this dual processing system that learners turn apperceived input into intake (see chapter 7 for a possible example of a learner orienting to such a structure).

The fourth step in Gass' (1997) model, integration, interacts rather closely with intake. According to Gass, after apperceived input has been processed to become intake, this new knowledge may either become incorporated into the learner's interlanguage, or it may be put into storage for subsequent integration at a later date. More specifically, a learner may do one of four things. First, he or she may confirm or reject a hypothesis about how the L2 works during the intake phase and incorporate this new knowledge into his or her grammar in the subsequent step of integration. Second, the learner may seem not to use the input at all. This occurs when the information contained in the input has become intake and has thus already been integrated into the learner's grammar. What is important about this possibility is that this kind of input is useful for strengthening or reconfirming prior hypotheses. Furthermore, it enables learners to automatize retrieval of L2 knowledge for production.   Third, the learner may store incompletely processed input until an opportunity presents itself for further clarification.   Last, the learner may not use a particular piece of input at all.   That is, the input exits the system and is not used further, perhaps because the learner did not succeed in understanding the input in any personally meaningful way.

Finally, the fifth step in the model is output (Swain, 1985, 1995).   Output is commonly understood to be an integral part of the acquisition process because learners can get feedback from interlocutors on the validity of the hypotheses they have formed during the intake step of the model (hence the feedback loop from output to intake in Fig. 1.1).   In addition, output is thought to play an important role in forcing learners to switch from a semantic to a syntactic mode of L2 processing.   That is, it may force learners to analyze the syntactic structure of the message they wish to express, thus ultimately contributing to the goal of speaking precisely, accurately, and appropriately.   Thus, because production entails a knowledge of syntax (however preliminary), there is a feedback loop to the enabling factor of negotiation, which is what allows learners to obtain comprehended input in the first place.

1.5.   CONCLUSION

In this chapter, I have outlined three important hypotheses in SLA studies.   The discourse hypothesis and the social interaction hypothesis speak most directly to the themes of this book, whereas the interactionist hypothesis goes some way toward synthesizing different strands of SLA research into a greater whole.   In the next chapter, I consider what CA is and examine how the use of CA might lead to reconceptualizing some of the basic assumptions about SLA processes that I have just discussed in this chapter.

Chapter 2

Conversation Analysis:
A Resource for Reconceptualizing
SLA Studies

2.0. INTRODUCTION

In the previous chapter, I reviewed some of the important hypotheses that constitute SLA studies. In this chapter, having first given a brief historical sketch and definition of CA, I examine some of the implicit assumptions that inform current SLA research from a CA perspective. I, therefore, rebutt some criticisms that have been made of CA and then proceed to problematize how mainstream SLA studies have been constructed to date.. This critical examination of basic tenets in SLA provides the theoretical underpinnings for the kind of conversation-analytic respecification of SLA studies that is worked out in later chapters of this book.

2.1. TOWARD A DEFINITION OF CA

The term *conversation analysis* has been used to describe work that is informed by a broad range of disciplinary perspectives, including pragmatics, speech act theory, interactional sociolinguistics, ethnomethodology, the ethnography of communication, variation analysis, communication theory, and social psychology (Schiffrin, 1991). For my purposes, however, I restrict the use of this term to describe only the kind of work that has been carried out within an ethnomethodological tradition. In this, I follow the practice of Stubbs (1983), who noted that CA is almost always used as a synonym for an ethnomethodological orientation to what I more generally call the *analysis of conversational data* (ACD). Thus, according to this distinction, ACD subsumes CA and, indeed, all the other disciplinary perspectives previously mentioned.

What, then, is CA? Historically, CA began life in the late 1960s and early 1970s as a subdiscipline of sociology. Like SLA, which is beginning to claim autonomy from applied linguistics, there are signs that CA is seceding from sociology and is also establishing itself as a separate discipline in its own right (Schegloff, 1987, 1991a, 1992a). Initially, CA researchers focused on describing the organizational structure of mundane, ordinary conversation, which may be defined as the kind of casual, social talk that routinely occurs between friends and acquaintances, either face-to-face or on the telephone. More specifically, researchers described this organizational structure in terms of sequences, turn-taking and repair practices (Goodwin, 1981; Jefferson, 1974, 1978, 1987; Sacks, Schegloff, & Jefferson, 1974; Schegloff, 1968, 1990, 1992b, in press; Schegloff, Jefferson, & Sacks, 1977; Schegloff & Sacks, 1973). Other representative work also carried out in the area of ordinary conversation includes studies of the sequential organization of various speech acts (Davidson, 1984; Drew, 1984; Pomerantz, 1975, 1978a, 1978b, 1984a, 1984b, Psathas, 1986; Schegloff, 1972), the construction of syntax-for-conversation (Goodwin, 1979; Lerner, 1991; Schegloff, 1979, 1996), reference (Sacks & Schegloff, 1979), and the structure of joke and story telling (Goodwin, 1984; Sacks, 1974; Stubbs, 1983).

These lines of research continue to be major foci of conversation-analytic work today. However, as Drew and Heritage (1992) noted, since the late 1970s there has been increasing interest in analyzing the structure of talk used to construct institutional contexts, including (among others) news, medical, courtroom and classroom contexts. Although the term *conversation analysis* continues to be used as the name of the field, the domains of CA now include both ordinary conversation and institutional talk (for useful collections of papers on institutional talk in L1 contexts, see Atkinson & Heritage 1984a; Boden & Zimmerman, 1991; Button, 1991; Button & Lee, 1987; Drew & Heritage, 1992a. For parallel examples of CA work on institutional talk that uses L2 data, see Firth, 1995, 1996; Firth & Wagner, 1997; Gaskill, 1980; Lerner, 1995; Liddicoat, 1997; Markee, 1994, 1995; Marriot, 1995; Schwartz, 1980; Wagner, 1996). For this reason, the more encompassing term *talk-in-interaction* (Schegloff, 1987) is widely used to refer to the full range of speech exchange systems just identified, which therefore all fall within the analytical purview of CA.

I now situate CA explicitly within the intellectual tradition of ethnomethodology, as it is the ethnomethodological foundations of CA that set it apart from other ACDs (Button, 1991; Heritage, 1987; Taylor & Cameron, 1987). According to Roger and Bull (1988):

The term "ethnomethodology" was coined by Garfinkel (1974). In combining the words "ethno" and "methodology," Garfinkel was influenced by the use of such terms as "ethnobotany" and "ethnomedicine" to refer to folk systems of botanical and medical analysis. What is proposed is that any competent member of society (including the professional social scientist) is equipped with a methodology for analysing social phenomena; the term "ethnomethodology" thus refers to the study of ways in which everyday common-sense activities are analysed by participants, and of the ways in which these analyses are incorporated into courses of action. The most prominent development within ethnomethodology is undoubtedly that which has become known as conversation analysis, which examines the procedures used in the production of ordinary conversation. The influence of conversation analysis is being increasingly felt in disciplines outside sociology, notably psychology, linguistics[1] and anthropology. (p. 3)

More specifically, ethnomethodology is the product of a marriage between two seemingly incompatible intellectual perspectives, the *hermeneutic-dialectic* and the *logico-analytic* (Heritage, 1987; Mehan, 1978; Mehan & Wood, 1975). From the former, it borrowed its theoretical interest in folk ways of making sense of the world; from the latter, it took its empirically based methodology. As Mehan (1978) commented:

one of Garfinkel's (1967) seminal contributions was to translate the idealistic and subjectivistic notions associated with the phenomenological branch of the hermeneutic-dialectic tradition into the realm of the social by exhorting researchers to find in the interaction between people, not in their subjective states, the processes that assemble the concerted activities of everyday life. (p. 60)

Based on these characterizations, I define CA as a form of ACD that accounts for the sequential structure of talk-in-interaction in terms of interlocutors' real-time orientations to the preferential practices that underlie, for participants and consequently also for analysts, the conversational behaviors of turn-taking and repair in different speech exchange systems.

2.2. CA: EPISTEMOLOGICAL AND METHODOLOGICAL CONSIDERATIONS

The "rules of evidence" used by conversation analysts are not as well understood as those used by experimental researchers or, indeed, by ethnographers. Therefore, I briefly review what "counts" as evidence in CA and what kinds of claims are made by conversation analysts (see also Jacobs 1986, 1987).

2.2.1. Making Arguments in CA

The methodology of CA is qualitative and thus subject to the usual evaluation criteria for such research. Beyond this, however, CA attempts to explicate in emic terms the conversational practices that speakers orient to (i.e., the rules of talk they deploy for each other and, by extension, for analysts) by "unpacking" the structure of either single cases or collections of talk-in-interaction. Such cases provide the primary evidence for the asserted existence of particular conversational mechanisms identified by analysts. In short, a case is only convincing to the extent that it is directly motivated by the conversational data presented for analysis. As Benson and Hughes (1991) stated:

> the point of working with "actual occurrences," single instances, single events, is to see them as the products of "machinery" that constituted members' cultural competence enabling them to do what they do, produce the activities and scenes of everyday life ... the explication, say, of some segment of talk in terms of the "mechanism" by which that talk was produced there and then, is an explication of some part of culture. (p. 130)

2.2.2. The Role of Ethnographic Information in CA

CA is epistemologically quite close to ethnography, as both these approaches focus on the particular rather than the general and also seek to develop a participant's rather than a researcher's perspective on whatever phenomenon is being studied. Developing a participant's perspective involves developing a rich description of context. However, conversation analysts and ethnographers do not necessarily understand context in the same way (indeed, this is one of the most contentious issues in CA today. For an overview of the arguments, see Duranti & Goodwin 1992; Hopper,1990/1991).

For ethnographers, understanding members' practices involves developing a "thick description" of their local knowledge (Geertz, 1983). Developing such a description entails developing a detailed profile of members' cultures and biographies through a variety of data collection techniques. Typical data include video and audio tapes of behavior, transcripts, interviews, and retrospective talking-aloud protocols. These various kinds of data are then often triangulated (i.e., cross-checked against each other) in an effort to document the multiple perspectives of different participants (e.g., students, teachers and researchers) on a given event.

Some conversation analysts (see Bilmes, 1992, 1993; Cicourel, 1992; Mehan, 1993; Moerman, 1988) incorporate ethnographic information into their analyses (though not all do so to the same extent; see Wilson, 1991), claiming that such information is necessary for a complete understanding of talk-in-interaction. In contrast, researchers who work within the "purist" tradition of CA (e.g., Schegloff, 1987, 1990, 1991a; 1992a) make no appeal to ethnographic accounts of members' cultures or biographies to make an argument unless there is internal evidence in the conversational data to provide a warrant for the introduction of such data.[2]

For example, in Excerpt 2.1,[3] five observable facts in the talk of L9, L10 and L11[4] combine to warrant an analysis that appeals to the specific biographical details that L10 and L11 are Chinese speakers, whereas L9 comes from a different language background. First, L10 translates the word *coral* into Chinese (see lines 407 and 410). Second, L11 orients to this translation (see line 409). Third, L9 does not understand what the Chinese word means (see line 412). Fourth, as Chinese speakers, L10 and L11 can (and actually do) translate *sanku* back into English (see 413–414). Finally, L9 indicates that she understands what this Chinese word means by reference to its English equivalent (see line 415).

Excerpt 2.1

```
407  L10: *  oh I see (+) I see the chinese is uh (+) sanku
408          (++)
409  L11: *  unh?
410  L10: *  sanku
411          (+)
412  L9:  *  what
413  L10: *  c//orals//
414  L11: *  //corals//
415  L9:  *  corals oh okay
416  L10:    yeah
             (NM: Class 1, Group 3)
```

Absent such a warrant, analysts are said to be as well placed to analyze observed talk-as-behavior as the individual(s) who first produced it because they are using the same evidence that the participants were displaying to each other as they co-constructed the conversation in the first place. From a purist perspective on CA, then, context means the immediate sequential environment of a turn. It is this local environment (sometimes referred to by discourse analysts as the *co-text* of talk) that provides participants with a metric with which to judge the appropriateness of the talk that is produced in next turn. In this sense, therefore, conversation is highly context-dependent. At the same time, conversation may without contradiction also be said to be context-free (Sacks et al. 1974), in that socioeconomic status, gender, biographies or other such ethnographic data are not used a priori to explain how members organize and make sense of the talk that they construct for each other.

For these reasons, the production of additional texts by the original participants to explain or comment on what they "really" meant in the primary text is avoided, because such texts can only serve to confuse the analysis. This is because self-report data do not explicate the original behaviors so much as reconstruct and re-interpret them (see also Lantolf, 1994a, who comes to a similar conclusion), and these reconstructions are not necessarily more accurate or insightful than the original interpretations of the observed behavior.

2.2.3. Four Defining Characteristics of CA

Four important implications follow from this discussion. First, CA is profoundly agnostic about the value of explanations that are derived from etic theories of social action because these explanations are not grounded in members' constructions of their own naturally occurring behaviors. Second, conversation analysts do not, therefore, develop arguments about the structure of conversation on the basis of quantitative analyses of frequency data. This is because such analyses cannot reveal anything about how participants orient to the underlying preferential structure of conversation.[5] Instead, conversation analysts seek to demonstrate that conversation could not be conversation if such universal interactional resources for making meaning as turn-taking or repair did not exist.

Third, in order to demonstrate the existence of such resources, conversation analysts use prototypical examples which give discursive form to the phenomenon being analyzed. However, such examples are not by themselves sufficient to make a convincing argument. Analysts must be able to corroborate their claims by pointing to a convergence of different types of textual evidence or by showing that a single structure identified by the analyst plays a role in different types of cases.   Note that the use of convergent evidence is a particularly important resource for countering the charge that an analysis is merely an artifact of the examples collected and chosen for presentation to readers.   So indeed is the use of related data.   For example, it can be shown that reading a turn as an invitation is cotextually warranted by an invitation-relevant presequence that enquires into the potential availability of the invitee and by a following acceptance or rejection sequence which brings the business to a close.   Finally, analyses must be subject to critical falsification.   That is, analysts must demonstrate that potential counterexamples and different accounts for the same data set have been anticipated and that other researchers can replicate findings with different transcripts.

2.2.4. Summary

CA is radically different from other forms of ACD that are relatively more familiar to SLA specialists.   Most importantly, it avoids developing its arguments on the basis of any a priori theory, be this nomothetic (see Long, 1980; Long & Sato, 1983; Pica, 1983a, 1983b; Pica & Doughty, 1985; Pica, Young, & Doughty, 1987 for work of this kind), formal (Chomsky, 1965, 1975, 1980, 1986; Gregg, 1993, 1996; White; 1989) or constructivist (see Coughlan, 1995; Hall, 1993, 1995a; 1995b, 1997; Lantolf, 1994b; Lantolf & Appel, 1994; Ohta, 1995; van Lier, 1988, 1996, all of whom work within the Vygotskyan paradigm of sociocultural theory).

        Although CA is most different from the dominant nomothetic tradition of SLA research, it nonetheless also differs from more main-stream qualitative approaches to SLA.   In particular, CA tends to avoid appealing to ethnographic data (as used by Douglas & Selinker, 1994; Hawkins, 1985; van Lier, 1988, 1996), thereby formulating the notion of context much more strictly than is commonly the case in SLA work (see, e.g., the work of Selinker & Douglas, 1985, 1989 in this area). Clearly, therefore, CA has the potential to provide a far-reaching epistemological critique of mainstream SLA studies, whether in the experimental or ethnographic tradition.   Before I develop such a critique, however, let me first deal with some objections to the use of CA as a methodological resource for SLA studies.

2.3. SOME POTENTIAL OBJECTIONS TO THE USE OF CA AS A METHODOLOGICAL TOOL FOR SLA STUDIES

There are three principal objections to using CA as a methodological tool for understanding SLA processes. The first two have been most forcefully articulated in the rebuttals of Firth and Wagner (1997) by Kasper (1997), Long (1997)[6] and Gass (1998), whereas the third has been advanced by Crookes (1990). The first objection is that CA is a behavioral discipline while SLA studies is a cognitive discipline. More specifically, CA is suspicious of individual cognitive constructs (e.g., knowledge, understanding, learning, etc.). In contrast, SLA theory seeks to describe and explain the cognitive processes that underlie language learning. It is therefore not clear what CA has to offer SLA studies, because the two disciplines have such seemingly incompatible outlooks on the nature of the phenomenon that is to be explained. The second, clearly related, objection is that CA is designed to account for language use, not its acquisition. As such, any insights that CA might provide into the structure of conversation is peripheral to the central concerns of SLA studies. The third objection is that the turn is not a suitable unit of analysis for SLA studies.

2.3.1. Are CA and SLA Studies Incompatible?

Although it is perfectly true that CA is fundamentally a behaviorally oriented discipline that focuses on language use, I wish to argue that this does not therefore automatically disqualify CA as a methodological tool for studying the kinds of learning processes that are central to SLA studies. Furthermore, I do not accept that the turn is not a viable unit of analysis for researchers interested in SLA. Let us first examine Gass' (1998), Kasper's (1997), and Long's (1997) objection that CA and SLA studies have mutually incompatible outlooks on how the phenomenon of language acquisition might be analyzed.

    In my view, what separates SLA researchers from conversation analysts is not so much whether language is best described in terms of cognition or behavior as whether cognition is understood exclusively as an individual or as both an individual and a socially distributed phenomenon that is observable in members' conversational behaviors. Early CA work on the sequential organization of talk, turn-taking, and repair (see Goodwin, 1981; Jefferson, 1974, 1978; Sacks et al. 1974; Schegloff, 1968; Schegloff et al. 1977; Schegloff & Sacks, 1973) specifies the rule-governed nature of members' observed, real-time conversational practices that constitute their interactional compe-

tence. This interactional competence interacts with members' individual and collective ability to analyze and deploy syntax-for-conversation in order to achieve socially relevant, locally occasioned acts of
communication (Goodwin, 1979; Lerner, 1991; Sacks et al. 1974;
Schegloff, 1979, 1996).

Although the precise nature of members' grammatical
knowledge is not specified by these authors, it is clear that conversationalists constantly monitor and analyze the grammatical phrase
structure of interlocutors' unfolding turns in order to take their own
turns and to interject repair initiations at appropriate moments in the
talk (Sacks et al. 1974). As Gass' (1997) model of the phases of
language learning (discussed in chapter 1) shows, conversational repair
is viewed by SLA researchers as the sociopsychological engine that
enables learners to get comprehended input. This understanding of the
nature of repair in SLA is broadly consistent with more recent work by
Schegloff (1991a) in CA, who argued that repair can be analyzed as an
example of socially distributed cognition. By extension, the same
claim can be made for sequencing and turn-taking.

This development potentially clears the way for a convergence
of perspectives between SLA researchers and conversation analysts on
the utility of CA as a methodological resource for SLA studies.
However, this convergence has radical implications for mainstream
SLA. More specifically, it seems clear that the idea that cognition is
not solely an individual but also a socially distributed phenomenon that
is observable in members' conversational behaviors must oblige social
interactionist researchers in SLA to reconsider the idea that cognition
is exclusively instantiated in the minds of individuals. Of course, this
position has already been championed by Vygotskyan researchers, who
argue that learning first occurs interpsychologically as a result of
interaction between mentor and novice, only later becoming
appropriated intrapsychologically by the novice (Aljaafreh & Lantolf,
1994). I develop this idea further in CA terms in chapters 7 and 8.

2.3.2. Is CA Unsuitable as a Resource for SLA Studies?

This section examines the second objection raised by Gass (1998),
Kasper (1997) and Long (1997), namely, that CA focuses on language
use, not acquisition, thus making it of marginal use to SLA researchers.
This objection is clearly prompted by these writers' fear that if Firth
and Wagner's argument for broadening the present scope of SLA
studies were to be widely adopted, it would in effect no longer be SLA
studies but a new field called second language studies, which would no
longer necessarily be committed to addressing the traditional
acquisitional issues of SLA studies as its primary intellectual goal.

I am sympathetic to these concerns. Thus, as an SLA specialist, I accept that issues of language use are subsidiary to questions of language acquisition in SLA studies. However, as a conversation analyst, I also agree with Firth and Wagner (1997, 1998) that the boundaries between language acquisition and use are in fact quite indistinct — a point that should be quite familiar to SLA colleagues because it lies at the heart of sociolinguistic critiques (Halliday, 1973; Hymes, 1972) of generative notions of competence and performance (Chomsky, 1965). Furthermore, as argued in the previous section, when researchers investigate the structure of conversational practices such as sequencing, turn-taking, and repair, they are in fact also investigating processes of socially distributed cognition; these processes surely lie at the heart of sociolinguistically influenced approaches to SLA studies. Consequently, I believe that a strong case can be made that SLA studies would be greatly enriched by incorporating into its methodological arsenal conversation analyses of the sequential and other resources that speakers use to modify each others' talk and thereby to comprehend and learn new language.[7] Finally, it is worth pointing out that this type of research would of course play directly into the research program outlined by Long (1985a) on the role played by comprehensible input in SLA.

2.3.3. Is the Turn a Suitable Unit of Analysis for SLA Studies?

Finally, let us examine Crookes' (1990) objection that the turn is not a suitable unit of analysis for SLA studies. According to Crookes, SLA researchers have used at least five different kinds of units to describe the structure of L2 discourse, sometimes singly, sometimes in combination: T-units, c-units, turns, tone units, and utterances. Crookes argued that, of these five categories, the utterance is the most suitable analytic category for use with L2 discourse data. The reason that he cited in support of this position is that, if they are to be useful, analytic categories must have a high degree of instrumental validity, that is that researchers' analytical categories must reflect the psychological processes that underlie individual language learners' speech production. He concluded:

> On these grounds, the turn may be eliminated from consider-
> ation. Since its boundaries are determined by the processes of
> speaker interaction, it does not reflect the psychological
> processes of an individual's speech production alone, but is
> additionally influenced by the many social variables which

determine the flow of multi-party discourse. (It also becomes meaningless when monologue is considered). (pp. 191–192)

There are three theoretical and empirical problems with this objection. First, Crookes' own preference for the category of utterance reflects a speaker's, not a hearer's, perspective on who controls the production of talk-in-interaction. However, as Sacks et al. (1974) and many other conversation analysts have amply demonstrated, this position is empirically not sustainable. Second, by adopting — as I believe is necessary — a hearer's perspective on talk-in-interaction, speech production cannot be understood solely from an individual, cognitive perspective, even if the object of study is how individuals learn new language. This is because talk-in-interaction is fundamentally collaborative in nature (Sacks et al. 1974). Consequently, in order to be logically consistent, researchers must view the conversational resources that individuals potentially draw on to learn new language as collaboratively achieved micro-moments of cognition. Just as communicative competence is said to subsume linguistic competence (Hymes, 1972), so these collaboratively achieved micromoments of cognition are best understood as socially distributed phenomena that subsume at least some individual cognitive processes in SLA.

Finally, Crookes' assertion that a turn-taking account of speech production is vitiated by the many social variables that determine the flow of multiparty discourse is also suspect. Invoking the principle of "ethnomethodological indifference" (Garfinkel & Sacks, 1970), conversation analysts maintain that the putative effects of social variables on the structure of talk are not a matter of a priori theorizing. Rather, they are an empirical matter, whose relevance to speakers has to be located in speakers' own conversational practices (Schegloff, 1972, 1987, 1991b, 1992a). In practice, empirical research has shown that speakers seem to orient to a turn-taking machinery that is remarkably unaffected by external social variables (see Sacks et al. 1974).

For these reasons, I maintain that the turn is a particularly valuable analytical category for L2 ACDs. There can surely be no better yardstick for determining the validity of turns as a unit of analysis than demonstrating that the existence of such units can be empirically located in the participants' own conversational behaviors.

2.4. RESPECIFYING SLA STUDIES

Having dealt with these objections to the use of CA as a methodological tool for SLA studies, let me now offer an ethnomethodologically motivated critique of mainstream SLA. In common with many other disciplines in the social sciences, mainstream SLA relies on the idea that if an explanation of how the world functions is to be scientifically adequate, it must be based on ways of knowing that are compatible with a rationalist approach to constructing scientific knowledge (see, e.g., Gregg, Long, Jordan, & Beretta, 1997). Furthermore, if (as often happens) a folk explanation diverges from a scientific explanation, then the former is to be discounted as irrational and, therefore, as scientifically inadequate. As Heritage (1987) remarked:

> a radical gulf is thus created between rational actions with their self-subsistent reasons and non-rational actions in which the actors' reasoning is discounted in favour of causal normative explanations of conduct ... [The effect of this epistemology is] to marginalize the knowledgeability of social actors to a remarkable degree and to treat the actors, in Garfinkel's memorable phrase, as 'judgemental dopes' (Garfinkel, 1984, p. 68) whose understanding and reasoning in concrete situations of action are irrelevant to an analytical approach to social action. (p. 229)

The rationalist position on the scant value of members' knowledge about the world derives from Talcott Parsons, whose theories of social action dominated postwar sociology for 20 years. In contrast, ethnomethodologists such as Garfinkel argue that rationalist explanations of the world are not in any sense more insightful or indeed useful than those of social actors.[8] As Heritage explained:

> Garfinkel proposed that, if mundane social actions were premised on the characteristic features of scientific rationality, the result would not be successful activity but, rather, inactivity, disorganization and anomie (Garfinkel, 1952, 1984, pp. 270–271). A scientifically adequate orientation to the events of the social world is thus far from being an ideal strategy for dealing with the flow of ordinary events. Its imposition as a standard with which to evaluate actors' judgements is therefore wholly unwarranted and, Garfinkel insisted, it is both unnecessary and inhibiting in analysing the properties of practical action (Garfinkel, 1984, pp. 280–281). Moreover, if ideal conceptions of rational action are dropped from the picture, the way is open to begin investigations based on the properties of the actors' actual knowledge in the making of reasonable choices among courses of action, i.e.

"the operations of judgement, choice, assessment of outcomes, and so on that he does in fact employ" (Garfinkel, 1952, p. 117, cited in Heritage, 1987, p. 231).

Of course, the implications of such criticisms are potentially open to serious misinterpretation. Let me therefore immediately nip in the bud any suggestion that ethnomethodologists subscribe to an "anything goes" approach to doing science, in which potentially any and all explanations are equally valid.[9] As already noted, CA is empirically based, has clearly defined methodological procedures for developing participant-relevant analyses of talk-in-interaction, and is concerned with the possibility of replication. Furthermore, the rules for developing such analyses are just as, if not more, rigorous than those followed by experimental researchers.

For example, it is common practice in experimental research to treat the behaviors of so-called "outliers" as atypical of the sample. Consequently, these outliers are often discarded from the final analysis. In CA, however, all participants' behaviors are viewed as making sense to the individuals concerned, and thus must be accounted for in the analysis. So, for example, in his analysis of sequencing in conversational openings, Schegloff (1968) initially developed an analysis that accounted for 499 out of 500 cases in his database. However, Schegloff did not ignore the solitary apparent exception to his analysis. Instead, he went on to reanalyze the entire corpus to yield the 499 cases plus the apparent exception as alternative specifications of the phenomenon under study at a more general level of organization.

Having established that ethnomethodology represents a serious, though undoubtedly heretical, approach to doing science, it is clear that the adoption of CA as a methodological resource for SLA studies necessarily entails a fundamental respecification of the SLA research enterprise.[10] This respecification has at least three dimensions: developing an emic alternative to rationalist science, developing a critical attitude toward quantified data, and using highly detailed transcripts of talk-in-interaction as primary data.

2.4.1. Developing an Emic Alternative to Rationalist Science

Most SLA writers have until recently treated the rationalist norms of the dominant nomothetic paradigm as intellectually unproblematic. One of the most important of these norms is that an experimental, quantitatively oriented methodology holds the principal key to scientific progress. However, this is not necessarily true. For example, Foster's (1998) work on conversational modifications (which, incidentally, is not informed by ethnomethodological ideas) presents two alternative pictures of the same phenomenon. These two pictures are hard to reconcile. On the one hand, Foster's study shows that, in aggregate, certain task types seemed to prompt learners to modify their speech more frequently than other types did. However, when the speech of individual learners was examined, it became clear that there was tremendous individual variation in the number of repairs that were initiated by learners during different tasks. A small minority of learners did the lion's share of initiations, whereas the majority initiated few or no repairs at all. Furthermore, the organizational factor that seemed to explain whether learners engaged in negotiation work at all seemed to be whether learners were working in pairs rather than in small groups, not the characteristics of the tasks that they had to solve.

These results demonstrate that an experimental, quantitatively oriented methodology inevitably loses important details of individual behavior. For some researchers, of course, this is an acceptable price to pay to get generalizable results that contribute to the theoretical evolution of SLA studies as a scientific discipline. However, Foster's paper raises the possibility that the results of mainstream SLA research on the psycholinguistic properties of different task types or the acquisitional function of conversational repairs could merely be artifacts of an experimental, quantitative methodology. In order to address this crucial issue, SLA theory construction needs more input from emically focused research on the contextual and interactive dimensions of talk-in-interaction (Firth & Wagner, 1997). This input would allow an assessment of whether the results of quantitative and qualitative SLA research ultimately converge or diverge.

2.4.2. Developing a Critical Attitude Toward Quantified Data

The second point is closely related to the first. Even though quantification has provided many important insights into SLA processes, there is an urgent need for SLA researchers to develop a more critical attitude toward the use of certain types of quantified data than is currently the case. For example, as as I noted previously (Markee, 1994), an experimental approach to SLA studies fundamentally depends on clear definitions of terms. Furthermore, any analytical categories that are based on these definitions must not overlap. After all, from an experimental perspective, the whole point of positing such categories is to investigate whether the distributions of these categories are statistically significant (thus allowing researchers to generalize beyond the sample studied) and whether these distributions are consistent with researchers' theoretically motivated predictions.

However, the functional subcategories of repair that are commonly used in mainstream SLA research are notorious for their ambiguity and lack of discreteness. Consider, for example, the categories of comprehension checks and clarification requests proposed by Long and Porter (1985) and Porter (1986). Porter (1986) gives the following examples of these categories in Excerpts 2.2 (see line 2) and 2.3 (see line 1).

Excerpt 2.2
Comprehension check

```
1 L:    To sin- uh ... to sink
2 N:  * Do you know what that is?
3 L:    To go uh-
5 N:    To go under ...
        (p. 207)
```

Excerpt 2.3
Definition request

```
1 L:  * ... what is the meaning of research?
2 N:    Um, study?  You study a problem and find an answer.
        (p. 207)
```

From a participant's intersubjective perspective, there is no evidence that members orient to these categories as distinct constructs at all. The participants in both these excerpts orient to a need to resolve lexical trouble that occurs in their conversation. Although in functional terms the initiations of repair work may look different, in sequential terms, the participants end up doing definition work that is spread over a number of turns (see, in particular, Excerpt 2.2).[11] Arguably, therefore, the general category of "definition talk," whose defining organization is ultimately sequential rather than functional, seems better motivated by the data than the two more specific speech acts proposed by Porter. This conclusion poses severe methodological problems for SLA researchers working within an experimental framework because repair subcategories must not overlap if subsequent statistical manipulations of the data are to have any validity or reliability.

These kinds of considerations also underlie Aston's (1986) critique of what he called the "more the merrier approach" to analyzing repair. Aston also pointed out that it is difficult to differentiate empirically between subcategories of repair. In addition, he noted that decontextualized experimental research on conversational modifications implies that students should be taught to negotiate meaning at any and every opportunity. Citing Garfinkel's (1967) breaching experiments, Aston remarked that this kind of behavior would quickly be perceived as irritating.[12] This notion is empirically supported by the talk in Excerpt 2.4 although in this instance, it is a learner, L11, who becomes annoyed with the teacher's repeated repair initiations. More specifically, L11's asterisked turn at line 541 illustrates the social consequences of the teacher's excessive repair initiations at lines 524 and 538.

Excerpt 2.4

```
520 L11:    ok (+) excuse me (+) uh: what what does it mean hab- (+) habi-
521         (+)
522 T:      habitats
523 L11:    habitats
524 T:    * yeah (+) you had that word as well (+) what do you think it means
525         (++)
526 L10:    <hhh>//hh//
527 T:              //you// all spoke about habitats didn't it
528 L10:    uh:m
529 T:      the //m//ost important (1) habitat
530 L10:        //I//
531         (++)
532 L10:    I think (+) the habitats is the:[əm] (+) e//nvironment uh// and the
533 L9:                                          //environment//
534 L10:    environment and uh (1) uhm
535         (++)
536 L9:     is it is //it the: nearest environment//
537 L10:             //for for (+) for the fish// you (mea be:) (hh)
538 T:    * <h> yeah what would be another word for a habitat then (+) it's like
539         (1)
540 T:      //it's  hli-//
541 L11:  * //I ha//ve no idea ((in an exasperated tone))
            (NM: Class 1, Group 3)
```

Notwithstanding these kinds of criticisms of experimental research, Long (1997) continued to articulate the received position in SLA studies when he criticized the lack of quantification in most sociolinguistically oriented naturalistic ACDs. More specifically, it seems that Long believes that the inclusion of descriptive statistics would automatically improve the quality of qualitative research. But, as I have shown, this position ignores the methodological weaknesses of quantification. Furthermore, insisting on the virtues of quantified data in this way is rather like saying that American football would be a much better game if only it were played with a round ball, as in soccer, rather than with the oval-shaped ball that is used in American football. Finally, this criticism misses the point that naturalistic researchers may avoid using even the simplest statistics (e.g., percentage scores) because to use them would be inconsistent with developing an emic analytical perspective on the phenomenon being studied.[13]

Speaking to this issue in the context of analyzing mundane conversation, Schegloff (1993) pointed out that developing an index of sociability that is based on quantifying the number of laughter tokens that subjects produce per minute completely ignores the issue of when it is sequentially appropriate for conversationalists to laugh. Laughter at inappropriate times or, conversely, the lack of laughter at appropriate moments in the talk, are accountable events that may hold serious consequences for participants. For example, in its most extreme form, inappropriate laughter may be interpreted as a manifestation of emotional instability, even mental illness. Less drastically, laughing at the wrong moment may be judged as rude and have adverse effects on a member's social relationships with his or her peers. Quantitative techniques are thus ill-suited to capturing these subtleties and, when applied to conversational data, tend to distort their communicative import.

In the context of SLA studies, similar criticism may be leveled against Foster and Skehan (1996), who defined fluency in terms of continued performance and repair avoidance. On the basis of these definitions, they develop a statistically based index of fluency which reflects an interaction between a particular task type and the amount of planning time that is available to students to prepare for the task (see Table 1.1 in chapter 1). However, the conceptualizations of fluency and planning used by Foster and Skehan are theoretically problematic on three counts.

First, the notion of continued performance as an indicator of fluency completely ignores the fact that there are times when it is imperative for speakers to stop talking. Conversationalists who insisted on continuing a prior conversation about the weather during the middle of a funeral service would not be judged fluent but rather insensitive. Indeed, if they persisted in this behavior, they would likely be asked to leave. Second, Foster and Skehan's definition of fluency wrongly assumes that normal discourse is free of trouble when, in point of fact, all interaction — including repaired talk itself — is not only potentially repairable but is actually repaired quite regularly in order to transact the business at hand both successfully and fluently (Schegloff et al. 1977). Thus, repaired talk, and the associated pauses and silences that are often a signal that a repair is in progess, is not by itself indicative of a lack of fluency.

Finally, although a distinction can be made between spontaneous and prepared speech, particularly when these notions are tied to technical specifications of different speech exchange systems, the idea that conversation is ever unplanned is also problematic. All talk is designed to achieve a particular goal at a particular moment in a particular conversation. Furthermore, it is designed for a particular recipient. Thus, the notion of "recipient design" (Sacks et al. 1974) is inextricably bound up with the idea of moment-by-moment planning.

2.4.3. Using Highly Detailed Transcripts of Talk-in-Interaction as Primary Data

Since CA rarely quantifies members' conversational practices, except in the most general, participant-relevant terms, it is clear that suitably transcribed audio or video recordings of talk become the primary data for analysis and discussion. As Heritage (1988), noted, four basic assumptions govern CA work and are therefore reflected in how talk-in-interaction is transcribed:

- Conversation has structure.
- Conversation is its own autonomous context; that is, the meaning of a particular utterance is shaped by what immediately precedes it and also by what immediately follows it.
- There is no a priori justification for believing that any detail of conversation, however minute, is disorderly, accidental or irrelevant.
- The study of conversation requires naturally occurring data.[14]

I already discussed the first two points in earlier parts of this chapter. I concentrate now on fleshing out the implications for SLA studies of the last two elements of this position. For reasons of organizational convenience, I begin with Heritage's fourth point, noting that a preference for naturally occurring data requires researchers to be extremely sensitive to the social context of data collection. I then address the implications of Heritage's third point, that is, if no detail of conversation is disorderly, accidental, or irrelevant, then clearly, extremely fine-grained transcriptions will be required to capture the complexity of talk-in-interaction. This principle also implies that the use of sampling procedures should be avoided because such techniques are likely to exclude vital details from the analysis. Based on this discussion, I finally sketch out what a CA-inspired methodology for SLA studies might look like.

Data collected in laboratory settings[15] inevitably reflect a member orientation to a speech exchange system that is demonstrably different from that of ordinary conversation (Schegloff, 1993). Thus, there can be no expectation that results obtained in laboratory settings will necessarily generalize to other settings. To make statements about how mundane conversation or ordinary classroom talk is organized, it is best to gather such data directly from these settings (see also Foster, 1998, who makes the same general point).

Speaking to this issue, Firth and Wagner (1997) argued that SLA data gathered under laboratory conditions are tainted because researchers attribute stereotypical roles such as NS and NNS to their subjects. These psycholinguistically defined roles do not take into account other sociolinguistically defined roles (father, friend, wife, etc.) that might be more relevant to participants in ordinary conversation.[16] The attribution of such psycholinguistically defined roles to speakers is said to entail a number of other theoretical problems, which led Firth and Wagner to suggest that the scope of SLA studies should be broadened to include the study of naturally occurring lingua franca talk, that is, interactions between L2 speakers who are communicating in a shared L2 for instrumental reasons, such as conducting business.[17]

As I noted previously, Gass (1998), Kasper (1997), and Long (1997) all objected, perhaps justifiably in some ways, that broadening the scope of SLA studies to this extent would effectively remove the A from SLA studies. However, Liddicoat (1997), who is in substantial agreement with Firth and Wagner's position, made a subtler point in suggesting that the reason why NSs are massively constituted as interviewers and NNSs as interviewees in so many transcripts of NS–NNS talk is due to the fact that the overwhelming majority of SLA conversational data — be they naturalistic or gathered in laboratory settings — instantiate various kinds of institutional talk, not ordinary conversation. Liddicoat therefore claims that many broadly accepted findings in SLA studies, such as the reported dominance of NSs in NS–NNS conversation and NSs' preference for other-initiated repairs of NNSs' talk, are nothing more than the products of the specialized speech exchange systems to which members are orienting at the time they are being recorded. For this reason, Liddicoat joins Firth and Wagner in calling for naturalistic, ordinary conversational data.

I accept that it would be desirable for SLA researchers to have access to such data in order to study naturalistic, non instructed SLA processes, but I believe that a broader lesson should be drawn than either Firth and Wagner or Liddicoat envision. It is necessary to understand how speech exchange systems differ from each other. For this reason, a model of interactional competence needs to be developed that distinguishes between the conversational practices to which members orient in different speech exchange systems. This is the subject of Part II of this book. For now, however, I address the more immediate implications of Heritage's third point.

As even a cursory inspection of the excerpts displayed in this and the preceding chapter demonstrates, CA transcripts (see Excerpts 2.1–2.3) are more detailed than those normally found in the SLA literature (see Excerpts 1.1–1.4). The wide spread adoption of such fine-grained transcriptions would enable SLA researchers interested in understanding the effects of conversational repairs on language learning to investigate whether the moment-by-moment sequential organization of such talk has any direct and observable acquisitional consequences. In other words, fine-grained transcripts may potentially allow SLA researchers to show empirically that learning occurs or does not occur as a direct result of learners first getting comprehended input and later producing comprehended output (Markee, 1994). As I noted in this article, SLA researchers have shown little interest to date in pursuing such a line of enquiry despite the fact that this line of research would be consistent with the research program on the function of comprehensible input as a resource for SLA proposed by Long (1985a) and Pica (1987).

Finally, I develop the idea that the use of sampling procedures should be avoided because such techniques are likely to exclude vital details from the analysis. For example, if lines 93–136 of the data set reproduced in Excerpt 2.5 appeared in a 5-minute sample of talk taken from a 50-minute lesson, it might be concluded, on the basis of the co-constructed talk at lines 135–136, that L15 had understood the meaning of the phrase "we cannot get by Auschwitz."[18]

Excerpt 2.5

```
093 L15:   excuse me ((L7's name)) do you understand what's this (+) we cannot get
094        by auschwit[ʃ] ((reading)) I don't understand what we can't get by (1.5)
095 L7:    oh <hh> (+) uh we-
096 L15:   we can't get by I'm not su- I don't understand what is the meaning
097 L7:    we have every reason to be afraid of ((unintelligible)) ((L7 is reading; her
098        turn trails off into an unintelligible mutter))
099 L15:   we cannot get by (+) what's the meaning ((L15's turn overlaps the end of
100        L7's turn))
101 L7:    (+) what is auschwitz (+) it is a::
102 L15:   I think it's a place because::
103 L7:    ((unintelligible)) a ((unintelligible)) right,
104 L15:   yeah I guess that (+) I already understand that
105 L7:    //concentra//tion camp,
```

```
106 L15:   //((unintelligible))//
107        (+)
108 L7:    is that the one
109 L15:   yeah it cannot get by what is this
110 L7:    we cannot get by ((reading)) <h> I think (+) you cannot s:kip like you
111        cannot (+) you have to go through it, (+) you cannot get by (+) like (+)
112        you have to go through it, say (+) we cannot get by <hh> 'cause
113        (1)
114 L15:   yes I understand
115        //you (+) why  he would <hh> because uh (++) the reason why//
116 L7:        //have every reason to be afraid of ((unintelligible))//
117 L15:   he doesn't want t- a united germany is //be//cause that
118 L7:                                            //oh//
119 L7:    because (+) you know the concentration camp, (+) then hitler he he tried
120        to kill (+) in nazi germany,
121 L15:   yeah?
122 L7:    ok (+) and the jewish (+) //right,//
123 L15:                             //yeah?//
124 L7:    ok (+) so (+) say (+) he: he said we cannot get by that we- we never will
125        forget about this (+) //to the end//
126 L15:                         //he says it's// (+) history:
127 L7:    uh huh (+) see, (+) //says this is really terrible//
128 L15:                       //says it's-it's like-// he doesn't wa:nt to: (+)
129        //a u//nited germany
130 L7:    //I mean//
131 L15: * like=
132 L7:  * =I guess (+) he says (+) this is  terrible
133 L15: * oh=
134 L7:  * =a lot (+) they killed a lot of people right,
135 L15: * uh=
136 L7:  * =we cannot get (+) by (+) auschwitz <hh> this means that <hh> he=
137 L15:   =we can't forget we can't forget
           (NM: Class 2, Phase 2, Group 2).
```

However, as shown in the complete collection of Auschwitz-related talk reproduced in appendix C, L15 participates in a total of eight lengthy episodes of such talk. Thus, the exchange shown in Excerpt 2.5, which occurs during the sixth episode shown in appendix C, represents a tiny proportion of the total work that L15 actually does during a 50-minute lesson to understand the meaning of the phrase "we cannot get by Auschwitz." As I argue in chapter 8, there is good reason to believe that L15 never understood what this phrase meant in the context of a debate on German reunification despite all the work that she did to understand this phrase. Thus, a reliance on the kinds of sampling procedures that are so often used in SLA work on L2 interactions would have led to important errors of interpretation because such an analysis would have been based on an incomplete picture of participants' behaviors.

2.5. CONCLUSION

I do not propose that CA holds the key to formulating yet another
theory of SLA. I do claim that CA can help refine insights into how
the structure of conversation can be used by learners as a means of
getting comprehended input and producing comprehended output. CA
is therefore in a position to contribute to research on two of the
modules in Gass' (1997) model of SLA (see Fig. 1.1 in chapter 1).

More specifically, CA-oriented research in SLA would link up
rather directly with the work of Hatch (1978) and later social
interactionists such as Gass and Varonis (1985a, 1985b, 1989, 1994),
Long (1980, 1981, 1983b, 1983c, 1989), Long and Porter (1985),
Pica and Doughty (1985), Pica et al. (1986), Pica, Holliday, Lewis,
and Morgenthaler (1989), and Plough and Gass (1993). Given Hatch's
own caution in specifying the role of conversational modifications in
SLA, it is perhaps ironic that the utility of conversationally modified
input as an important resource for the acquisition of L2 syntax by
adults rapidly became a theoretical given in the SLA literature. The
research that was done to test this hypothesis was mostly experimental
and unfortunately largely circumvented any significant body of prior
qualitative work on how learners use conversational modifications and
whether such modifications can be shown to result in learning a second
language. CA-oriented SLA work could fill this gap. However, in
filling this gap, this kind of research would now take on an
epistemologically unusual or, as some will undoubtedly argue,
unwarranted, hypothesis-confirming character rather than fulfilling the
hypothesis-generating role traditionally assigned to qualitative research
by experimentalists.

My own position on these issues is as follows. First, I am not
particularly concerned with committing epistemological heresy if this
yields interesting insights into the role of conversation as a resource
for SLA. In this regard, I strongly believe that there is still much to be
learned from further qualitative work in this area. Some 20 years after
Hatch initially formulated the discourse hypothesis, detailed analyses
of how SLA processes are instantiated in the moment-by-moment
talk-in-interaction of adult L2 learners are still exceedingly rare.

Second, although many of the results of experimental
researchers on the function of conversationally modifed input as a
resource for the acquisition of syntax by adult L2 learners are likely to
be quite robust, I nonetheless prefer to use a CA methodology in order
to return to some of the ideas that Hatch sketched out in 1978. In
particular, I would like to further explore how adults learn to deploy
new vocabulary (and indeed syntax) by doing conversation.

In part, this interest is prompted by methodological concerns. It is undoubtedly far easier to demonstrate how participants achieve the acquisition (or, indeed, the non acquisition) of L2 vocabulary in real time than it is to show how they construct new syntax. However, it would be a mistake to maintain that CA has nothing to say about how learners pragmatically construct syntax from talk-in-interaction. As I show in chapters 7 and 8, even when learners focus on vocabulary, they inevitably have to pay attention to, and also deploy, a broad range of semantic and syntactic resources in order to understand and learn the meaning of unknown words or phrases.

What, then, would a CA-oriented methodology for a social interactionist approach to SLA studies look like? I propose that such a methodology should be:

- based on empirically motivated, emic accounts of members' interactional competence in different speech exchange systems;
- based on collections of relevant data that are excerpts of complete transcriptions of communicative events;
- capable of exploiting the analytical potential of fine-grained transcripts;
- capable of identifying both successful and unsuccessful learning behaviors, at least in the short term;
- capable of showing how meaning is constructed as a socially distributed phenomenon, thereby critiquing and recasting cognitive notions of comprehension and learning.

Chapter 3 provides a practical review of how CA researchers set about doing conversation analyses of talk-in-interaction. The remainder of the book demonstrates how such an ethnomethodologically respecified SLA methodology works and the kinds of insights it can provide into the processes of L2 learning. More specifically, Part II lays out the theoretical ground by sketching out what CA has to say about the construct of interactional competence (bullet 1). Part III analyzes two collections of definition talk. The first analysis instantiates a case of successful learning behavior, whereas the other, which uses identical methodological procedures that are applied to similar, but more complex data, illustrates a case of unsuccessful learning behavior (bullets 2–4). This analysis therefore not only problematizes mainstream SLA's traditional understanding of comprehension and learning as exclusively cognitive constructs (bullet 5) but also suggests how such notions might be reanalyzed more fruitfully in socially situated, behavioral terms.

NOTES

1. CA is also the intellectual heir of the work of the structuralist linguist Zelig Harris (1951), who pioneered research into the discourse level of language.

2. Ethnographic evidence may certainly draw a conversation analyst's attention to the existence of an interesting phenomenon. For example, Hawkins (1985) established through retrospective talking-aloud protocols that, although NNSs' answers to NSs' questions might be conversationally appropriate, this did not mean that the NNSs had necessarily understood what the NSs had said to them. In Markee (1994), I drew on Hawkins' insight to establish that one participant had not understood talk addressed to her at particular moments in the interaction. However, I did so by using only the real-time conversational evidence that speakers displayed to each other (and, therefore, to the analyst) as they constructed their conversation.

3. See appendix A for the conventions used to transcribe this and other CA excerpts in this book. Excerpt 2.1 is the fifth excerpt in a collection of eight excerpts that are thematically related to L10's attempts to understand and learn the word *coral*. This collection is reproduced in full in appendix B and constitutes the complete database for the analysis of successful learning discussed in chapter 7.

4. In all transcripts made from my own recordings, I use abbreviations such as L9 (Learner 9) or T (Teacher) as a means of keeping the participants' identity confidential. Note that this convention is a matter of convenience and in no way implies that other social roles that participants might construct in and through their talk are of no consequence to the analyst (for discussion of these issues, see Firth & Wagner, 1997).

5. This does not mean that CA researchers never report regularities in behavior (see Heritage & Greatbatch, 1986; Jefferson, 1988) nor that they always eschew simple statistical data such as percentages (see Heritage & Roth, 1995; Markee, 1995). Furthermore, as Schegloff (1993) was at pains to point out, neither does it mean that CA researchers should not follow up their initial studies with experimental research (see Wilson & Zimmerman, 1986, for an example of such a follow-up study). But experimental research should only be carried out once a thorough qualitative understanding of the issues has been achieved.

6. See also Long (1983a) for an earlier critique of Mehan's (1978) work on constitutive ethnography.

7. Indeed, Susan Gass (personal communication, November 30, 1998) seems to accept this argument, noting that "my reading of K[asper] and L[ong] (and my own 1998 rebuttal [of Firth & Wagner]) is not so much a rejection of CA, but a rebuttal to F&W's proclamation about what SLA should be."

8. Thus, as Hatch (1978) pointed out, it might be worth while to take seriously adult learners' insistence that vocabulary (rather than grammatical) learning is a primary goal of SLA.

9. See also the exchange between Firth and Wagner (1997) and Long (1997) on the issue of CA's relationship to rationalist approaches to doing science.

10. In developing this critique of mainstream SLA studies, I am not advocating that SLA researchers should stop doing experimental research. This would be akin to throwing the proverbial baby out with the bath water. Experimental researchers have made many crucial contributions to SLA studies and will doubtless continue to do so. The issue here is that, contrary to Gregg et al. (1997), there is more than one way of doing good science.

11. It is interesting to note that experimental research is in one sense uninterested in the acquisitional *consequences* of repairs. More specifically, no evidence was presented by Porter (1986) that the learners in Excerpts 2.2 and 2.3 actually understood, much less learned, what the words "sink" and "research" mean.

12. During these experiments, Garfinkel instructed his students to repair all possible ambiguities that occurred in conversation. These experiments had such disastrous social consequences for the experimenters that they had to be discontinued.

13. Long also claimed that quantified data are more useful than qualitatively described data in advancing the theoretical agenda of SLA studies. I believe the issue is not whether one type of research is more useful than another, so much as what each approach can contribute to the SLA debate. Some questions are better addressed via experimental studies, whereas others are more suited to a qualitative treatment.

14. See also Hopper (1988), Hopper, Koch, and Mandelbaum (1988), Jefferson and Schenkein (1978), Levinson (1983, pp. 318–325), McLaughlin (1988), and Zimmerman (1987) for other comprehensive accounts of CA. For a summary of the transcription conventions widely used by conversation analysts, see Atkinson and Heritage (1984b).

15. Of course, the distinction between a laboratory and a naturalistic setting is not at all clear-cut because the observer's paradox may be a factor in the way in which participants behave in so-called naturalistic settings. Apart from this issue, however, if data collection involves the use of subjects who do not know each other, occurs in an unfamiliar location, and is designed to test performance on completely unfamiliar tasks, then the research location will likely be constructed by participants as a laboratory situation (Liddicoat, 1997). Conversationally, this phenomenon will manifest itself as some variety of talk that is not ordinary conversation, which is clearly problematic if one is trying to study ordinary conversation. Conversely, if data collection involves the use of participants who already know each other, occurs in a familiar place, and entails members engaging in familiar tasks, then the research location will likely be constructed naturalistically by participants; that is, they would be expected to construct their relationships through the practices of ordinary conversation.
        However, even if an attempt is made to distinguish between naturalistic and laboratory settings in this way, there are still plenty of data collection situations that involve a certain amount of ambiguity. For example, participants may know each other and may perform tasks with which they are already familiar, but be recorded in an unfamiliar setting (e.g., a video studio), which may have an adverse impact on the naturalness of the ensuing talk. Thus, the notions of naturalistic and laboratory settings probably represent the ends of a naturalness continuum, which merge into each other in infinite shades of grey.

16. See, Goodwin (1979), who shows how one conversationalist's interactive construction of a sentence simultaneously constructs two of his interlocutors as friends and the remaining participant as his wife.

17. In this context, see also Gass' (1998) rebuttal of these criticisms.

18. This excerpt was recorded in 1990. The learners are discussing the then current issue of whether East and West Germany should reunite,

using information from an article by the left-wing West German writer Günter Grass. In this article, Grass argued that Germany's Nazi past, symbolized by the concentration camp Auschwitz, precluded reunification.

Doing Conversation Analysis: Practical Issues in Recording, Transcribing and Analyzing Data

3.0. INTRODUCTION

I ended the previous chapter by outlining what I believe a CA-oriented methodology for a social interactionist approach to SLA studies should look like. In this short chapter, I backtrack a bit to provide readers who are not trained conversation analysts with a basic, rather practical review of current CA methodological practices. In so doing, I am of course not claiming that anybody who reads this chapter will thereby become instantly qualified to undertake CA research. Learning to become a skilled CA researcher minimally entails completing at least one year of course work in CA (Hopper, 1988), ideally followed up by a continuing apprenticeship with an established CA practitioner. Nonetheless, this chapter provides readers who are not familiar with how CA research is done with a more informed sense of how conversation analysts record, transcribe, and analyze conversational data.

3.1. RECORDING DATA

The analysis of talk-in-interaction minimally requires the use of audio or, preferably, video, recordings of participants' talk to capture the tremendous complexity of conversational behavior. These recordings constitute the primary source of data used by conversation analysts. In the early days of CA, audio recordings were the preferred medium. This choice was in large part dictated by the expense and bulkiness of video equipment in the late 1960s and early 1970s, and it is no accident that a lot of early CA studies used telephone conversations as their principal source of data (see, e.g., Schegloff, 1968). One of the best known examples of telephone talk is the *Two Girls* transcript, excerpts from which may be viewed and heard on the World Wide Web (WWW) at http://www.sscnet.ucla.edu/soc/faculty/schegloff/prosody/.

By focusing on talk that occurs during telephone calls, researchers were able to circumvent two problems rather neatly. First, the expense involved in conducting CA research was reduced to manageable levels because audio was already a mature recording technology. Second, because telephone partners do not have access to each others' facial expressions and gestures, audio recordings are well suited to capturing how participants display their mutual understandings to each other by voice alone. However, with the advent of cheaper and better video equipment, video recordings are now the medium of choice, as they allow researchers to see how phenomena such as the direction of participants' eye gaze, facial expressions, and gestures are coordinated with, and indeed are part of, the structure of talk-in-interaction (see Goodwin, 1979, for a seminal early example of research based on video recordings).

3.1.1. Gathering usable data

When audio or video recordings are made of talk-in-interaction that involves a small number of participants — for example, three or four people talking at the dinner table — the recording problems are relatively simple. Typically, one audio cassette recorder or video camera with an external microphone for better sound quality is used to capture the interaction. "High tech" solutions may use radio microphones or specialized directional microphones supported by booms above or to the side of participants. Obviously, this approach is expensive and may not be within financial reach of many researchers. Fortunately, however, whereas high tech solutions yield clearer data when properly used, there is no reason why lower tech solutions should not also yield acceptable recordings.

Other types of talk-in-interaction are more difficult to record adequately and therefore need to be recorded somewhat differently. For example, in classroom situations where small group work is the principal form of learning activity, recording the interaction with a single video camera (even with an external microphone) does not yield usable data. Although the teacher's announcements and other teacher-to-whole-class interactions (e.g., question and answer routines) may be adequately recorded, the various groups' intragroup conversations yield a babble of untranscribable noise.

In order to record these kinds of interactions, each group must be separately recorded. Depending on the researcher's financial and technical resources, separate recordings of each group can be made by using a stations approach (i.e., having one tape recorder per group) or by recording each student separately.[1] The latter solution is preferable, particularly when students are required to move around the classroom, as a stations approach is not well suited to capturing the talk that occurs as students move from one station to another. Again, there are both high and low tech solutions available to capture individual speakers' contributions during concurrent intragroup talk. Each participant can be equipped with a radio microphone. Alternatively, each individual may be given a Walkman-sized cassette recorder and lapel microphone that records their talk. Because the equipment is highly portable and can be battery-operated, this solution has the added advantage of allowing participants to move around a classroom without having to worry about tripping over cables, etc. Whichever solution is used, the availability of multiple audio recordings means that such technically significant information as the difference between pauses and in-drawn or exhaled breaths, the specific number of laughter tokens, the precise onset and resolution of overlaps, the content of muttered commentaries, and other such fine details can be distinguished and therefore transcribed with a high degree of confidence. A Real Audio file of a recording made using the Walkman recorder solution may be heard on the WWW at http://deil.lang.uiuc.edu/class.pages /EIL367/RealAudio/Coral14.ram. The accompanying transcript may be found in PDF format at http://deil.lang.uiuc.edu/class.pages /EIL367/RealAudio/Coralcollection.pdf.

This multiple recordings technique also has the advantage of providing plenty of insurance. For example, if one group member's recorder jams, is turned off, or yields unintelligible data for any reason,[2] the other members' recorders continue to pick up the talk in the group. The disadvantage of this technique is that it yields vast amounts of data, which therefore take longer to transcribe because so much more detail is hearable on the tapes.[3] Furthermore, because the resulting transcript for each group is produced from a mosaic of overlapping data, it is possible to introduce errors that do not occur when working from a single tape of the interaction. For example, because there are minor variations in the speed at which each individual recorder records the interaction, the length of a pause on one tape can be slightly different from that on another tape. The reseacher must be consistent in dealing with this type of problem. In my transcription practice, for example, I time pauses by using the current speakers' tape as the definitive data source.

3.2. TRANSCRIBING DATA

In order to produce high quality transcripts, it is essential to use a good transcription machine. Transcription machines have heavy-duty mechanisms, which will not break down under the constant searching for particular passages of talk. Most good machines have foot-operated forward and reverse controls, which free up the transcriber's hands for data entry. They also allow voice pitch and tape speed to be manipulated, which can help transcribers understand otherwise unintelligible words or phrases, and may automatically reverse the tape a set distance after the stop button is pressed to facilitate multiple hearings of a difficult passage. In my experience, transcription machines are most effectively used in conjunction with high-quality external speakers rather than with headphones, as external speakers tend to have a better dynamic range than headphones.

Before discussing how CA workers set about preparing recorded data for analysis, I first briefly review how researchers working in the better-known quasi-experimental tradition of SLA studies typically view the job of transcription. Then I comment on the status that transcripts have qua data within a nomothetic epistemology. In this latter approach to doing ACD, it is fair to say that transcription is viewed as a tedious, mechanical task, which may be safely delegated to graduate students or junior collaborators. Furthermore, although producing a transcript is obviously a necessary first step, the resulting transcripts have low status as data. In an approach that privileges the quantification of observed phenomena, transcripts are raw data that must be quantified and statistically manipulated in order to yield valuable information. Indeed, it is the statistical tests and interpretations of why results did or did not reach predetermined levels of statistical significance, rather than the transcripts themselves, that are of primary interest to experimentalists.

In contrast to experimentalists, CA workers regard audio/video tapes and the resulting transcripts as their primary sources of data,[4] and thus almost always do their own transcription. This is because transcription is viewed as an essential part of the discipline of doing CA. The fine level of detail demanded by CA transcripts inevitably makes transcription a time-consuming business. For example, a dyadic conversation lasting one hour is relatively easy to transcribe in that there is little extraneous noise. However, even this kind of talk-in-interaction may take up to 20 hours to transcribe (van Lier, 1988). Clearly, the types of talk that occur during small group work are even more difficult to transcribe because analysts have to transcribe each group as a separate conversation. They must therefore exclude overheard talk from other groups, except, of course, when the participants themselves orient to what is going on in another group. Consequently, it may take up to 40 hours to transcribe one hour of recording for each group. Thus, when nine different groups or parties are formed during the course of a single one-hour lesson (see the background information provided in chapter 8), it may take some 360 hours to produce all nine transcripts of talk that occurs during this period of time. Even then, analysts may decide to go back to the recordings later to do further transcription work as issues that only emerge after a long acquaintance with the data emerge to the fore. In a real sense, therefore, a transcript is never finished; it is only a working hypothesis about how participants construct talk in real time.

Time-consuming and tedious though transcription may be, it is a necessary part of doing CA. From a practical standpoint, it is the close engagement with the data that enables analysts to know their data in intimate detail. Furthermore, from a more abstract, epistemological perspective, conversation analysts insist that transcripts are, in fact, important preliminary theoretical statements about what talk-in-interaction is (see Ochs, 1979; although Ochs works within a language-socialization perspective that is somewhat different from that of CA in some important respects, language-socialization specialists and CA workers are in complete agreement on this point). Of course, this is not to say that experimentalists therefore deny that transcripts reflect a particular theoretical orientation. After all, all transcripts are designed to represent in a convenient fashion the empirically observed phenomena that are of theoretical interest to the researcher. However, whereas transcripts are merely a means to a statistical end for experimentalists, the notion of transcripts-as-theoretical-statements achieves the status of a fundamental tenet of CA.

Given this essential difference in attitudes toward the relative status of transcripts qua data, it is not surprising that SLA transcripts such as the one exemplified in Excerpt 1.2 (reproduced here as Excerpt 3.1) rely on a relatively gross level of detail, which is largely limited to reproducing the words that participants spoke. For example, the only information included in this transcript about the quality of the talk produced by participants consists of the cut-offs at lines 4 and 10 and the pauses of unspecified length (represented by dashes) that occur at lines 3, 9, and 13,).[5]

Excerpt 3.1

Learner (NNS English)   **Interlocutor (NS English)**

1	and they have the chwach there	
2		the what
3	* the chwach ___ I know someone	
4	* that-	
5		what does it mean
6	like um like American people they	
7	always go there every Sunday	

```
8                                                          yes?
9        * you know___every morning
10       * that there pr- that- the American
11         pcoplc gct drcsscd up to go to um
12         chwach
13       *                                          oh to church____I see
           (Pica, 1987, p. 6).
```

This is not to say that experimental researchers who are interested, for example, in quantifying the occurrence of pauses as precursors of repair do not produce much more detailed transcripts that capture this particular phenomenon, it is just that CA transcripts do not predetermine what phenomenon is going to be studied. Instead, CA transcripts routinely provide extremely detailed information about what people say and how they say it. For example, as shown in Excerpt 2.4 (reproduced again here as Excerpt 3.2), CA transcripts provide detailed information about phenomena such as pauses and silences (lines 520–521; 524–525; 531–532; 534–535; 537–539) stress (lines 520, 541), lengthening of vowels (lines 528, 532, and 536) and cut-offs (line 520), overlaps (lines 526/527; 529/530; 532/533; 536/537, and 540/541), laughter tokens (line 537), in-drawn breaths or exhalations (line 526), and the affect that accompanies a particular utterance (line 541).

Excerpt 3.2

```
520 L11:  * ok (+) excuse me (+) uh: what what does it mean hab- (+) habi-
521       * (+)
522 T:      habitats
523 L11:    habitats
524 T:    * yeah (+) you had that word as well (+) what do you think it means
525       * (++)
526 L10:  * <hhh>//hh//
527 T:    *           //you// all spoke about habitats didn't it
528 L10:  * uh:m
529 T:    * the //m//ost important (1) habitat
530 L10:  *      //I//
531       * (++)
532 L10:  * I think (+) the habitats is the:[əm] (+) e//nvironment uh// and the
533 L9:   *                                     //environment//
534 L10:  * environment and uh (1) uhm
535       * (++)
536 L9:   * is it is //it the: nearest environment//
537 L10:  *          //for for (+) for the fish// you (mea be:) (hh)
538 T:    * <h> yeah what would be another word for a habitat then (+) it's like
539       * (1)
540 T:    * //it's hli-//
```

541 L11: * //I ha//ve <u>no</u> idea ((in an exasperated tone))
(NM: Class 1, Group 3)

The transcript in Excerpt 3.2 conveys much more information than what is commonly included in SLA transcripts. However, it is not particularly detailed by the latest transcription standards in CA. As shown by Excerpt 3.3, the advent of ever more powerful computer technology has made it possible to include stills from video clips to illustrate graphically what could otherwise only be conveyed by a verbal gloss (Goodwin, 1999).

Excerpt 3.3

1   Pam: Okay that should be, **we**t enough.

2   (1.5)

3   Pam: ° Hmph (0.7) *((holding trowel))*

4   Jeff: We're lookin at that right there?

5   (0.3)

6   Pam: Mmm,

7   (0.4)

8   Jeff: Much darker than tha:t.

9   Pam: Yeah. ⌐ I'm not-=

10 Jeff: └There

11 Pam: =I'm just tryin ta put it **in** the:re.=

12   =eh hih an(h)ywhere. °hih heh huh

Munsell Book

Note: Reprinted from the *Journal of Pragmatics*, Vol. 32, No. 9, 1999, C. Goodwin, "Action and embodiment within situated human interaction" © 1999, with permission from Elsevier Science.

An even more complex example of a transcript which integrates graphic information with more traditional textual information is illustrated in Excerpt 3.4. The activity that is being examined here is a game of hopscotch between three Spanish-speaking girls, during which one participant (Blue) accuses another (Yellow) of cheating (Goodwin, 1999). This transcript includes the usual CA information about what is said and how it is said. In addition, it integrates detailed graphic information about how and when the participants use hand gestures to indicate square numbers four and five, eye gaze information, the position of the left hand girl's feet as she

Excerpt 3.4

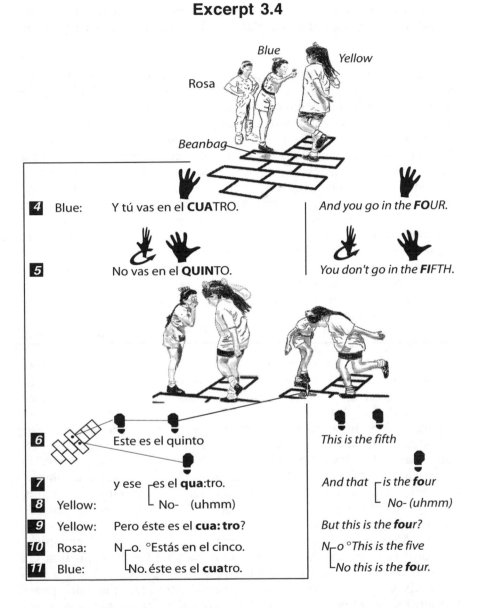

4	Blue:	Y tú vas en el **CUA**TRO.	And you go in the **FO**UR.
5		No vas en el **QUIN**TO.	You don't go in the **FI**FTH.
6		Este es el quinto	This is the fifth
7		y ese ⌐es el **qua**:tro.	And that ⌐is the **fo**ur
8	Yellow:	└ No- (uhmm)	└ No- (uhmm)
9	Yellow:	Pero éste es el **cua: tro**?	But this is the **fou**r?
10	Rosa:	N⌐o. °Estás en el cinco.	N⌐o °This is the five
11	Blue:	└No. éste es el **cua**tro.	└No this is the **fo**ur.

Note: Reprinted from the *Journal of Pragmatics*, Vol. 32, No. 9, 1999, C. Goodwin, "Action and embodiment within situated human interaction" © 1999, with permission from Elsevier Science.

says *no vas en el QUINTO*, and her performance of what Goodwin calls a *deictic stomp* (i.e., stamping her foot) to emphasize the square in which her interlocutor should have landed.

Obviously, these kinds of transcripts are pushing the limits of what information is technically possible to communicate to readers on paper. However, there is no doubt that WWW-based electronic transcripts are able to convey even more information, even more more elegantly than conventional paper transcripts can today. As seen Excerpts 3.3 and 3.4, electronic transcripts are still in their infancy. However, as electronic journals gain more acceptance in academia as a serious means of disseminating scholarship, the kind of information contained in Excerpts 3.3 and 3.4 will become both common-place and interactive. Not only will researchers be able to listen to the original data, and thus be able to evaluate the accuracy of the original researcher's transcription, but hot links from verbal glosses will call up streaming video files of how participants executed a particular hand gesture or deictic stomp. In classroom contexts, hot links will allow researchers to see what materials teachers and students are using, and read, hear, and see how learners interpret and perform the tasks set by the teacher or materials.

Of course, SLA researchers will need to critically evaluate whether displaying data in this way adds anything to a substantive understanding of fundamental issues in SLA studies or whether researchers are merely being seduced by the considerable attractions of a technological Brave New World. I believe that these very detailed descriptions of both conversational and gestural context are an important key to a better understanding of SLA processes. For example, if the talk that occurs in Excerpt 3.4 were between a NS (Blue) and a low level NNS of Spanish (Yellow), we would be able to document how the participants' use of gestures and language combined to provide Yellow with highly contextualized, and thereby presumably comprehensible, input about the number system in Spanish and the language of spatial relationships.

Also in need of discussion and development are clear ethical standards concerning what information is suitable for dissemination via the WWW and how this information is to be displayed. Whereas it is relatively easy to camouflage participants' true identities with paper transcripts, information that can be included in electronic transcripts makes the problem of protecting participants' identity much more complicated. In the end, however, whatever consensus emerges on these issues, it is safe to say that the trend toward greater complexity in CA transcripts will also affect how data are displayed in SLA transcripts, even if CA is not ultimately accepted as a viable methodology for SLA studies.

Finally, I address one aspect of CA transcripts that is somewhat controversial. In most of the excerpts that are reproduced in this book, standard English spelling, supplemented by the occasional use of phonetic script to capture non-standard pronunciations of words, is used to represent participants' talk (see, e.g., line 532 of Excerpt 3.2). However, the usual practice in most CA transcripts is to avoid using phonetic script, on the grounds that this is a tool of etic research. Consequently, as shown in Excerpt 3.5 from the *Two Girls* transcript, the characteristics of the participants' New York accents and various sandhi phenomena are represented through phonetic spellings (see lines 1, 2, and 5) invented by the transcriber.

Excerpt 3.5

```
1 Ava:    *  I'm so:: ti:yid.I j's played ba:ske'ball t'day since the
2         *  firs' time since I wz a freshm'n in hi:ghsch[ool.]
3 Bee:                                          [Ba::]sk(h)et=
4            b(h)a(h)ll? (h)[(°Whe(h)re.)
5 Ava:    *                [Yeah fuh like an hour enna ha:lf.
```

This has led a number of writers to criticize the use of "funny English" in CA transcripts on the grounds that it is demeaning to the participants (Preston, 1982, 1985) or an inconsistent means of representing participants' talk (Edwards, 1992). The issues surrounding how to transcribe participants' talk are in fact quite complex. (For a general overview of the technical issues involved in transcribing oral data, including critiques of CA transcription conventions, see Du Bois, 1991; Edwards & Lampert, 1993; Green, Franquiz, & Dixon, 1997; Ochs, 1979; Roberts, 1997). It is important for anyone working with L2 data to make a principled decision about how to transcribe non-standard pronunciations of English words. I find Preston's arguments in this regard to be compelling. My own preference when transcribing the talk of second language speakers of English, therefore, is to try to avoid any suggestion of ridiculing how participants talk by using standard English spelling, supplemented by phonetic script as appropriate.

3.3. ANALYZING DATA

The best way of understanding how CA researchers construct a conversation analysis is to follow an analysis as it is being constructed. I offer readers this opportunity in chapters 7 and 8. A few brief pointers that highlight the most characteristic ways in which arguments are constructed may be useful. As already noted in chapter 2, there are four defining characteristics of CA:

- It adopts a radically emic approach to research which, unlike ethnographic approaches to ACD, avoids the use of secondary data
- It generally avoids all but the most basic forms of quantification.
- It relies on analyzing prototypical examples of a particular phenomenon, using different kinds of text-internal, convergent evidence to establish the credibility of an analysis (this, to use ethographic terminology, amounts to what might be called text-internal triangulation of the data).
- It seeks to demonstrate that potential counterexamples have been anticipated and encourages other researchers to replicate initial findings with different sources of data.

In this section, I wish briefly to explain how CA researchers usually set about unpacking the structure of conversation.

3.3.1. Unpacking the Structure of Conversation

Generally speaking, CA unpacks the structure of conversation by analyzing either single cases or collections of talk-in-interaction. With single cases, the objective is to provide an in-depth analysis of a particular phenomenon that facilitates a deep understanding of how the phenomenon under study works. Analyses based on collections of similar data (e.g., particular types of repair) enable the analyst to see whether the practices to which participants are thought to orient are robust enough to account for a broad range of data gathered in different conversational contexts. Occasionally, as Schegloff (1968) demonstrated, these accounts have to be changed in order to account for one recalcitrant example that does not fit the pattern established for the overwhelming majority of other cases.

In a variation on this basic distinction between single-case and collection-based analyses of talk-in-interaction, I use in chapters 7 and 8 what may, at first glance, look like a conventional collection-based methodology. However, the collections I use as the databases for the analyses that are constructed in these two chapters are rather different from their traditional brethren and are also used to fulfill different analytical purposes. More specifically, these collections consist of thematically related sets of talk that occur during the course of two different lessons. The point of constructing these collections is not to collect similar conversational objects for the purpose of comparing how individual examples of a particular phenomenon demonstrate participants' orientations to common behavioral practices; rather, it is to document the longitudinal elaboration of members' understanding and learning behaviors over specific periods of time and to demonstrate how the same methodology is powerful enough to identify both successful and unsuccessful attempts to understand and learn new language.

3.4. CONCLUSION

In this short chapter, I have briefly outlined the techniques conversation analysts use to record, transcribe, and analyze CA data. I have also briefly touched on some ethical issues that need to be discussed as on-line publishing of conversational data on the WWW becomes more feasible and more common. Part II discusses how the construct of interactional competence is constituted in and through participants' talk.

NOTES

1. I am assuming here that the talk that is being recorded consists of face-to-face interaction in a conventional classroom. In electronic classrooms, however, students may be recorded by using each computer station's microphone. Furthermore, if the focus of the research is to analyze participants' turn-taking practices as they use synchronous conferencing software, the program's archiving facility provides a built-in way of generating transcripts of the interaction.

2. For example, in one class that I recorded, one of the participants, a Muslim woman, was wearing a veil, which frequently brushed against her lapel microphone when she moved her head. This produced a lot of white noise, which, in places, severely affected the intelligibility of the talk recorded on her tape. However, I was eventually able to transcribe most of her talk by listening to her partners' tapes, which also picked up her contributions to the conversation.

3. Of course, there is no guarantee that recordings that are made using the low tech Walkman solution in particular will not include talk from other groups, which can make transcribing such talk a nightmare. However, this low tech recording technique does have the advantage of giving the researcher a sense of where one group is in relation to

another because it picks up parts of other groups' conversations.

4. Occasionally, constructed examples or, alternatively, examples based on talk that the researcher overheard but was unable to record (sometimes identified as field notes; see, e.g., the discussion of the "What is death"? sequence in chapter 7, which is an example of how field notes are used by conversation analysts) are also used. There is no real substitute for attested talk, however, and the use of these other kinds of data is best avoided whenever possible.

5. If Ochs' (1979) argument is valid (i.e., that the left hand position in a transcript iconically represents the most important speaker in a conversation), then this transcript would identify the NNS as the most important member of this NNS–NS dyad. Compare this representation with how the speakers are represented in Excerpt 1.1. Here, the speech of T, the adult NS, is in the left-hand column, whereas that of H, the child NNS, is located in the right-hand column.

II: LOCATING INTERACTIONAL COMPETENCE

Chapter 4

Sequential Organization in Different Speech Exchange Systems

4.0. INTRODUCTION

This chapter first develops a general outline of the practices that constitute interactional competence, then shows how members' practices vary in terms of the sequential organization that characterizes three speech exchange systems that are of particular interest to SLA researchers: ordinary conversation, traditional classrooms, and non-traditional classrooms. Chapter 5 provides a similar account of how participants orient to different turn-taking procedures in these speech exchange systems, and chapter 6 shows how speakers do repair in the same three speech exchange systems.

4.1. INTERACTIONAL COMPETENCE

As Heritage (1987) pointed out, "[t]he central objective of conversation analysis is to uncover the social competences which underlie social interaction, that is, the procedures and expectations through which interaction is produced and understood" (p. 258). Thus, CA's concern with interactional competence converges with sociolinguistic notions of communicative competence (Bachman, 1990; Canale & Swain, 1980; Hymes, 1972). More specifically, under the most recent model of communicative competence proposed by Celce-Murcia, Dörnyei, & Thurrell (1995), the notion of interactional competence minimally subsumes the following parts of the model: the conversational structure component of discourse competence, the non-verbal communicative factors component of sociocultural competence, and all of the components of strategic competence (avoidance and reduction strategies, achievement and compensatory strategies, stalling and time-gaining strategies, self-monitoring strategies and interactional strategies). For purposes here, however, I argue that self-monitoring strategies and interactional strategies are particular instances of the conversational structure component of discourse competence.

At the same time, as I noted in chapter 2, although the principal interest of CA is to explicate the organization of talk-in-interaction in sequential terms, this does not mean that it dismisses the importance of sentence-level linguistic competence. Although CA is agnostic as to how linguistic knowledge is organized in the brain, it nonetheless emphasizes that members continuously use their knowledge of sentence-level grammar to analyze the status of an evolving turn in order to bid for the floor appropriately when current speaker reaches a possible completion point in his or her turn (Sacks et al., 1974). The conversation-analytic position on the role of sentence-level grammar in talk-in-interaction is therefore quite consistent with the Hymesian idea that communicative competence encompasses speakers' abstract knowledge of formal grammar — whatever form that knowledge takes. Furthermore, despite the insistence on the primacy of observable behaviors, this does not mean that CA is not interested in cognition. As Schegloff (1991a) argued, the knowledge to which members orient in order to repair conversational problems may in fact be analyzed as instances of socially shared cognition that are instantiated in members' conversational practices.

Also relevant to this discussion is Anderson and Lynch's (1988) notion that comprehension consists of an interaction between background schematic knowledge of the world and formal systemic knowledge about language. This interaction is mediated by contextual knowledge, or knowledge about a particular communicative situation and the co-text of talk. I have adapted this model of comprehension in Table 4.1.

More specifically, this model consists of four main components: schematic, interactional, systemic, and lexical knowledge. Whereas the schematic and systemic components are the same as in Anderson and Lynch's original model, I replace contextual knowledge with interactional knowledge to invoke CA's strict formulation of context (see the discussion of this issue in chapter 2) and I add the component of lexical knowledge because of the importance which adult L2 learners attach to learning new vocabulary (see Hatch, 1978).

Thus, when people talk, they orient to and display whatever schematic or background knowledge about the world (e.g., factual,

TABLE 4.1 A model of listening comprehension
Note: Adapted from A. Anderson & T. Lynch (1988, p. 13).
Reproduced by permission of Oxford University Press from
Language Teaching: Listening by Anne Anderson and Tony Lynch
© Oxford University Press 1988

Schematic Knowledge

Background knowledge about the world
- factual
- sociocultural
- personal

Interactional Knowledge

Knowledge of how language is used in talk-in-interaction
- sequential organization of talk-in-interaction
- turn-taking organization of talk-in-interaction
- organization of repair in talk-in-interaction

Knowledge of communicative strategies
- avoidance/reduction
- achievement/compensatory
- stalling/time-gaining

Knowledge of how verbal and non-verbal communicative factors interact
- gestures
- eye gaze

Systemic Knowledge

- syntactic
- semantic
- phonological
- morphological

Lexical Knowledge

- syntactic restrictions on vocabulary
- individual vocabulary items (including lexicalized verb forms)
- idiomatic phrases
- collocations
- proverbs
- metaphors and other forms of symbolic speech

sociocultural, personal information, etc.) that is relevant at particular moments in a particular conversation to achieve that conversation successfully. They also "do" or perform interactional knowledge by orienting to a sequential organization of talk, which is characterized by specifiable turn-taking and repair practices. These practices also organize the deployment of communicative strategies (e.g., the avoidance and reduction strategies, the achievement and compensatory strategies and the stalling and time-gaining strategies identified by Celce-Murcia et al., 1995). Verbal practices also interact with a variety of non-verbal communicative factors such as gestures and eye gaze (Goodwin, 1979).

In addition, members use their knowledge of syntax, semantics, phonology and morphology to parse current speaker's turn for an appropriate place to start speaking. Finally, they also invoke lexical knowledge. To a certain extent, there is some overlap here between systemic and lexical knowledge, as speaker-hearers must pay attention to whatever syntactic restrictions may operate on particular vocabulary items. Beyond this, a knowledge of lexis involves orienting to the appropriate use of individual vocabulary items (including lexicalized verb forms), idiomatic phrases, collocations, proverbs and metaphors, and other forms of symbolic speech. This final component of the model is potentially interesting in SLA terms, as the incidental acquisition of vocabulary through talk has historically been an under-researched area (Ellis, 1994, though see Wesche & Paribhakt, 1999, for recent developments in this area). As Hatch et al. (1990) also pointed out, next to no research has been done on the acquisition of symbolic lexical meanings.

In the remainder of this chapter, I discuss the interactional knowledge that participants deploy as they construct meaningful talk. More specifically, I review how sequences are organized in different speech exchange systems. I show how the organizational particulars of classroom talk differ (or at times do not differ) from those of ordinary conversation, so that researchers can avoid attributing institutional characteristics to classroom talk that may in fact also be typical of other speech exchange systems (see Lerner, 1995, for a discussion of this issue).

4.1.1. Sequential Organization in Equal Power Speech Exchange Systems

Before providing a technical specification of how members organize talk in terms of sequences, I first clarify what I mean by equal and unequal power speech exchange systems. As shown in more detail later on in this chapter and in chapter 5, speech exchange systems differ from one another in terms of whether members have equal rights to participate in talk or not. In ordinary conversation, for example, all participants are peers and therefore have equal rights to speak. Mundane conversation is thus an example of talk that is achieved as an equal power speech exchange system. Similarly, talk that occurs between student peers during small group work is typically much closer to the practices to which members orient during ordinary conversation.[1] Such talk is treated here, therefore, as an instance of a slightly modified equal power speech exchange system. In contrast, in teacher–student talk, teachers have privileged rights not only to speak but also to distribute turns to learners, whereas students have much more restricted participation rights. Teacher–student talk is therefore massively, though not exclusively,[2] achieved as an unequal power speech exchange system. This technical specification of teacher–student talk is equivalent to the lay characterization of a class as instantiating a "traditional" teacher-fronted style of pedagogy. Finally, talk between student peers is equivalent to the lay characterization of a class as instantiating a "non-traditional" student-centered style of pedagogy.[3] I now specify how members organize their talk into sequences in equal power discourse.

From a CA perspective, talk-in-interaction is organized in terms of *sequences*, of which the most basic example is the *adjacency pair* (Schegloff, 1972, 1979; Schegloff & Sacks, 1973). Adjacency pair sequences involve sequences that are (a) physically adjacent to each other (b) produced by two different speakers (3) constructed in terms of *first* and *second pair parts* (4) constructed such that Speaker 1's first pair part makes it *conditionally relevant* for Speaker 2 to respond with an appropriate second pair part.

The idea that Speaker 1's first pair part sets up an expected response by Speaker 2 in the second pair part slot is an example of a type of structure that is ubiquitous in talk-in-interaction, namely the *preference organization* of talk.[4] More specifically, in ordinary conversation, an invitation properly requires an acceptance or a refusal, a greeting properly requires another greeting in return, and a question or a summons properly require an answer. Note that adjacency pairs are a universal characteristic of the organization of all conversational interaction, irrespective of the particular language that is being spoken.[5] Consequently, from an SLA perspective, this kind of sequential structure may provide L2 learners with important resources for understanding what kinds of social acts fluent speakers of the target language are accomplishing as they talk, even if the learners do not initially understand the details of what is being said to them.

Question–answer adjacency pair sequences are particularly interesting conversational objects in that, as Excerpt 4.1 illustrates, they show rather clearly how participants achieve an equal power as opposed to an unequal power speech exchange system.[6]

Excerpt 4.1

```
135 L6:  Q1   what [ə]spur means? how do you how do you pronounce it s-p-u-r
136 T:   A1   spu:r
137 L6:        spur.=
138 T:         =//uh huh, <h>//
139 L6:  Q2   //what does this mean.//
140 T:   Q3   can I see the sentence?
141 L6:  A3   sure
142 T:   Q4   it depends on (1) uh::m (1) where was it again down here somewhere,
143            (+)
144 L6:  A4    it's supposed to be here (+) uh:m (++) <hhh>
145 L5:        (hhhhh) ((L5 laughs under his breath))
146 L6:  A4   uh:: oh, oh. (+) yeah its here
147            (+)
148 T:   A2   ok (3) to: in this case it's to encourage
149            ...
              (NM: Class 1, Group 1)
```

More specifically, in this excerpt, L6 asks two questions in his turn at line 135, the first relating to the meaning of the word *spur* and the second relating to the pronunciation of this word. At line 136, T (the teacher) answers the sequentially latest question and models the pronunciation of *spur*. Thus, L6 and T have constructed a prototypical question–answer adjacency pair (as shown by the Q1–A1 notation in the margin).

However, looking at the continuation of this excerpt, notice that T does not answer L6's next question (Q2) at line 139; note also that Q2 repeats the first part of the two-part question (Q1) that L6 asked at line 135. Instead of giving an answer as before, T asks a question of her own (Q3) at line 140 to clarify where the word *spur* occurs in L6's reading passage so that she can see its discoursal context before replying. Thus, the talk that occurs between lines 140 and 146 takes on the character of a necessary conversational detour, technically known as an insertion sequence (IS). This IS is itself organized into two sets of adjacency pairs (the first pair consisting of the Q3–A3 turns at lines 140–141, and the second of the Q4–A4 turns at lines 142, 144, and 146 respectively). In summary, the purpose of this IS is to obtain information that is conditionally relevant to T providing an answer (A2, at line 148) that appropriately responds to the first part of L6's initial question (Q1) at line 135 and to the repetition of this question (Q2) at line 139.

This is an important point: Although the turns at lines 135/139 and 148 are demonstrably physically separated from each other, this does not constitute an empirical counterexample to the theoretical notion that adjacency pairs constitute a fundamental resource for understanding the sequential structure of conversation. To the contrary, these data demonstrate that, even though conversationalists may need to do other, prior work in order to answer an initial question appropriately, they are still oriented to the necessity of providing an adequate answer to that first question. Indeed, if they do not answer this initial question appropriately, conversationalists may justifiably be held accountable for this omission in subsequent talk (Schegloff, 1972).

4.1.2. Sequential Organization in Unequal Power Speech Exchange Systems

As noted earlier, an important issue in CA is how the structure of institutional talk systematically differs from that of ordinary conversation. To the extent that talk in L2 classrooms is achieved as a variety of institutional talk, L2 classroom research can usefully be informed by a CA perspective. As I now demonstrate, CA is a methodology that can illuminate not just the structural differences between ordinary conversation and institutional talk, but, potentially, the ways in which naturalistic SLA differs from instructed SLA.

As I have already noted, ordinary conversation is a type of talk-in-interaction in which all conversationalists have equal rights to engage in a wide range of behaviors. Thus, any party to a conversation has the right to initiate a question–answer sequence. In contrast, research carried out in traditional (i.e., teacher-fronted) L1 secondary classrooms in Britain has shown that the prototypical mode of teacher–student interaction consists of recurring Initiation–Response–Feedback (IRF) sequences (Sinclair & Coulthard, 1975, 1992). The same three-part conversational object, which Mehan (1979) calls Initiation–Response–Evaluation (IRE) sequences and McHoul (1978) Question–Answer–Comment (QAC) sequences, has been observed in an elementary bilingual language arts classroom in the United States and an L1 high school geography classroom in Australia, respectively. Finally, the same organizational stucture has been found in American L2 classrooms (Fanselow, 1977). As shown in the data displayed in Excerpt 4.2, QAC sequences are a prototypical locus of talk that displays participants' orientation to a distinctively institutional variety of talk, in which members construct their differential status on a moment by moment basis.[7]

Excerpt 4.2

```
1 T: Q  Can you tell me why do you eat all that food?
2        Yes
3 P: A  To keep you strong.
4 T: C  To keep you strong. Yes. To keep you strong.
5     Q  Why do you want to be strong?
         (Sinclair & Coulthard, 1992, pp. 2-3)
```

More specifically, Excerpt 4.2 shows that teachers and learners implement a teacher-fronted pedagogical speech exchange system by orienting to an initial question–answer adjacency pair sequence, which is immediately followed by a second adjacency pair constituted by the answer and commenting turns (Mehan, 1979). That is, just as the initial question turn sequentially sets up the following answer turn, so the answer turn sequentially sets up the commenting turn.

Furthermore, there is a specific distribution of turn types among participants in this speech exchange system. Unlike ordinary conversation, this speech exchange system is characterized by unequal power relationships. Thus, teachers initiate pedagogical talk with Q turns (see line 1 of Excerpt 4.2), learners contingently respond with an A turn or turns (see line 3), and teachers close these QA sequences with an evaluative C turn (see line 4). These C turns provide learners with evaluative feedback concerning the adequacy of their responses in the preceding turn. Teachers then initiate the next QAC sequence with another Q turn (see line 5), and this process proceeds recursively for the duration of the lesson-as-speech-event.

To summarize the argument thus far, whereas ordinary conversation is an open-ended, locally managed speech exchange system, pedagogical talk in traditional classrooms is characterized by a considerable amount of pre-allocation of turns. Teachers maintain control over the moment-by-moment content and direction of classroom talk by reserving the right to ask questions. Students are thereby sequentially obligated to respond with answers. Furthermore, by reserving the right to do Q turns, teachers put themselves in a privileged sequential position that enables them to evaluate the quality of the student's answer in the third position C turn. This third turn can either close the sequence or can serve as the launch pad for requests by teachers that learners do further elaborative work. Teachers and learners jointly accomplish these elaborations through the vehicle of further QAC sequences.

In SLA terms, both speech exchange systems potentially provide for extensive scaffolding and modeling of target language structure, lexis, and phonology by teachers. However, the two speech exchange systems differ considerably in terms of learners' opportunities to initiate and restructure talk through the use of repairs such as clarification requests, comprehension checks, and confirmation checks. Furthermore, they differ not only in terms of the numbers of questions that learners initiate but also the kinds of questions that teachers typically ask.

Learners typically ask few questions in teacher-fronted lessons (see Carlsen, 1991; Dillon, 1981, 1988, for quantitative analyses of the numbers of questions asked by teachers and learners in L1 classrooms and a similar analysis of ESL teacher and learner questioning behaviors by White & Lightbown, 1984).[8] Teachers ask far more display (known information) questions than referential (new information) questions (Long & Sato, 1983; Pica & Long, 1986. See Koshik, 1999, and, to a lesser extent, Banbrook & Skehan, 1990; Markee, 1995, for a critique of this distinction between display and referential questions). This teacher behavior has an important effect on students' responses because referential questions seem to promote more syntactically complex and connected student answers than do display questions (Brock, 1986). For these reasons, Pica (1987) claimed that the unequal power relationships that typify traditional

Option 1: Sequential trajectory for a teacher using an A strategy

Ownership of the turn: (L)   (T)   (L)
Sequential structure: Q   A   C

Option 2: Sequential trajectory for a teacher using a CQ(R) strategy

Ownership of the turn: (L)   (T)   (L/T)   (T) (L)
Sequential structure: Q1   CQ(R)   A/CQ(R)   A1 C

Q   Question turn
A   Answer turn
C   Commenting turn
CQ   Counter Question turn
CQ(R)   Counter Question turn done as a referential question

FIG. 4.1   Two alternative trajectories for teachers' answering students' questions.

classroom discourse may hamper the process of SLA by limiting learners' opportunities to modify their interactions with teachers.

This conclusion obviously suggests that non-traditional instruction (e.g., small group-oriented, task-based language teaching) might provide a better environment for language learning. Whereas such a claim cannot yet be made, the difficulty of implementing small group-oriented, task-based language teaching in non-traditional ways can be documented. For example, student–student interaction during task-based, small group work should look different from teacher–student talk because teachers can exercise much less direct control over what learners say and how they talk during group work. However, the fact that learner–learner patterns of interaction are qualitatively different does not mean that the quality of teacher–student interaction during small group-mediated tasks also changes (Markee, 1995). In fact, teachers tend to revert to a traditional form of unequal power discourse, even when students are ostensibly supposed to be "in charge" of the talk. To illustrate this point, I show how three different teachers and their respective students reconstructed QAC sequences when students did not know a word that they had encountered in a reading passage.

When students ask teachers a question, teachers have to decide how to respond. The decision(s) teachers make at this juncture in talk can have a surprisingly wide variety of sequential consequences. As already shown in Excerpt 4.1, teachers can either answer a student's question directly or ask for clarifying information before answering the student's question. Following Markee (1995), the first option is called an A strategy. To complexify the analysis of Excerpt 4.1, the second is called a Counter-Question (CQ) strategy that employs a Referential (R) question format. The sequential trajectories of these two options are shown in Fig. 4.1.

Option 1 shows that, on the surface, the basic QAC structure of classroom talk is preserved when a teacher uses an A strategy to respond to student questions. However, closer examination reveals that it is now Learner X who, by owning the initial Q turn, is in topical control of the talk. In addition, it is also Learner X who is in sequential control of the talk, as he or she now owns both the Q and C turns in the sequence.[9] The result, as shown in Excerpt 4.3 (which is the full version of the talk partially shown in Excerpt 4.1) is that L6 controls the moment-by-moment content and direction of classroom talk over 5 main sequences: Main sequence 1 (MS1) at lines 135–138, MS2 at lines 139 and 148–151, MS3 at lines 152–158 and 160, MS4 at lines 159 and 161–169, and MS5 at lines 170–172 (note that IS1 at lines 140–146 has already been discussed in relation to Excerpt 4.1).

Excerpt 4.3

135 L6:   MS1   what [ə]spur means? how do you how do you pronounce it s-p-u-r
136 T: MS1   spu:r
137 L6:   MS1   spur=
138 T: MS1   =//uh huh, <h>//
139 L6:   MS2   //what does this mean.//
140 T: IS1   can I see the sentence?
141 L6:   IS1   sure
142 T: IS1   it depends on (1) uh::m (1) where was it again down here somewhere,
143   (+)
144 L6:   IS1   it's supposed to be here (+) uh:m (++) <hhh>
145 L5:   (hhhhh) ((L5 laughs under his breath))
146 L6:   IS1   uh:: oh, oh. (+) yeah its here
147   (+)
148 T: MS2   ok (3) to: in this case it's to encourage
149   (+)
150 L6:   MS2   to en//courage//
151 T: MS2   //to ((unintelligible)) (into)// courage <hh>
152 L6:   MS3   does it have another meaning too
153 T: MS3   yeah you know uh on a ho:rse (+) uhm (+) when you're riding (+) you
154   MS3   have on you::r (hh) (+) on your shoe a sp//ur//
155 L6:   MS3   //yeah//
156 T: MS3   and you use that to:
157 L6:   MS3   ok //I understand//
158 T: MS3   //make the horse// go faster <hhh>it comes from //there it's//
159 L6:   MS4   //excuse me//
160 T: MS3   called a spu:r (+) and so the verb (1) here to spur would be to encourage
161 L6:   MS4   so is it //a: verb//
162 L5:   MS4   //<hhh>//
163 L6:   MS4   and noun too yeah=
164 T: MS4   =yeah a spur (+) //is//
165 L6:   MS4   //sp//ur=
166 T: MS4   on your shoe=
167 L6:   MS4   =is a noun
168   (+)
169 T: MS4   and to spur- it could be to spur or to spur on is to encourage
170 L6:   MS5   so you pronounce it [ə]spur
171 T: MS5   spur (+) uh //huh//
172 L6:   MS5   //ok//
173   (1)
          (NM: Class 1, Group 1)

What is remarkable about Option 1 in Fig. 4.1 and its exemplars in Excerpt 4.3 is that the "pedagogical" talk done by L6 and T has been naturalized, that is, made similar to ordinary conversation, to such an extent that the teacher is no longer in control of the interaction.[10] Thus, on the basis of the evidence reviewed so far, it might be understood that the structure of teacher–student interaction during task-based, small group-based instruction approximates the open-ended, locally managed organization of ordinary conversation. If sustainable, such a conclusion would obviously be exciting, both for SLA specialists and for researchers interested in developing an empirically based theory of teaching because it would imply that teachers and learners were constructing the kind of equal power discourse that is thought to be conducive to SLA (Pica, 1987). However, reaching such a conclusion is unfortunately premature (Markee, 1995).

Teachers in fact rarely select Option 1 as a response strategy. Indeed, the data displayed in Excerpt 4.3 represent the overwhelming majority of cases in which an A strategy is used by any of the teachers in my database of four completely transcribed classes. What prototypically happens instead is that teachers (including the one whose talk is reproduced in Excerpts 4.1/4.3) respond with a CQ turn that employs a Display (D) question format. The resulting trajectory for this type of sequence is displayed in Option 3 of Fig. 4.2.

Option 3: Sequential trajectory for a teacher using a CQ(D) strategy

Ownership of the turn:	(L)	(T)	(L)	(T)
Sequential structure:	Q	CQ(D)	A	C

Q   Question turn
A   Answer turn
C   Commenting turn
CQ   Counter Question turn
CQ(D) Counter Question turn done as a display question

FIG. 4.2 The effect of CQ(D) turns on the sequential structure of QAC sequences.

More specifically, CQ(D) turns are a resource that all three teachers in the database use to regain topical and sequential control of classroom talk. As illustrated in Excerpts 4.4, 4.5, and 4.6, teachers insert CQ(D) turns (at lines 242 and 245–246 of Excerpt 4.4, at lines 337 and 341 of Excerpt 4.5, and at line 77 of Excerpt 4.6)[11] immediately after learners' initial Q turns (at lines 237 and 240 of Excerpt 4.4, at lines 338 and 340 of Excerpt 4.5, and at line 77 of Excerpt 4.6). According to the preference rules that organize this speech exchange system, this puts learners in the position of having to do A turns in response (at lines 247–248 of Excerpt 4.4; at lines

339–341 and lines 351 and 353–354 of Excerpt 4.5; and at lines 78–81 of Excerpt 4.6). At the same time, the use of a CQ(D) turn also puts these teachers back in sequential position to do C turns (at line 249 of Excerpt 4.4, at lines 342 and 356–357 of Excerpt 4.5, and at line 82 of Excerpt 4.6).

Excerpt 4.4

237 L13:	Q	... what's that mean (1) coastal vulnerability
238		(1)
239 L14:		fulnerability is:
240 L13:	Q	coastal vulnera- vulnerability
241 T:		((T overhears L13 and L14 as she approaches the dyad))
242	CQ(D)	what d'youthink it means
243		(1.3)
244 L14:		uh?
245 T:	CQ(D)	what what d'you think a- where are areas of coastal
246	CQ(D)	vulnerability (++) <h> if you think about uh:m
247 L14:	A	it's not safe[t] (+) areas which are not safe[t] (1) right?
248 L13:	A	It's it's very easy to be:: (+) damage
249 T:	C	yea:h (+) especially by (+) water, (+) by flooding,
		(NM: Class 1, Group 4)

Excerpt 4.5

331 L6:		there is a problem here she //doesn't// underst(h) and
332 L15:		//(huh h)//
333 L7:		(huh)
334 L6:	Q	and we don't understand what <h> //what means exactly this//
335 L15:		//why we can't get auswit[ʃ]// (+) oh
336 L6:	Q	we cannot get by ausch[v]itz
337 T:	CQ(D)	ok (+) what d'you think it might mean
338 L15:		(uh huh) (+) (uh huh //h)//
339 L6:	A	//it// might [b]ean (+) probably u::h we::: (+)
340	A	cannot have another Ausch[v]itz again if uh germany unites o:r
341	A	maybe <hh>
342 T:	C/CQ(D)	does it mean that?
		((9 lines of transcript omitted))
351 L14:	A	does it mean that u:hm <hh>
		((1 line of transcript omitted))
353 L14:	A	that if the uni- if (+) the germany unite again <h> the ausch[v]it
354	A	might exist, <hhh>
355		(+)
356 T:	C	yeah. that's ba- we can't- when you can't get by something that's
357	C	<hh> you can never forget.
		(NM: Class 2, Phase 2, Group 2)

Excerpt 4.6

75 L7:	Q	I don't understand stake //what does it// mean
76 T:		//stake//

```
77        CQ(D)   who can define stake
78  L8:   A       stake is something that uh what's at stake wha- what are you going
79        A       to give up //or//
80  L12   A                    //what's// the point
81  L8:   A       how are you going to get something
82  T:    C       (what's th-) uh huh right or what is the purpose
                  (NM: Class 3, Phase 1, Group 2)
```

4.2. SUMMARY

To summarize the revised argument to date, at the decision point under consideration, the use of an A response by teachers to learner's Q turns (see Option 1 and Excerpts 4.1/4.3) is conversationally dispreferred, in the technical sense of being marked instructional language behavior that results in a loss of topical and sequential control by the teacher. Preferred teacher behavior consists of doing a CQ(D) turn immediately after a learner's Q turn.[12] In so doing, teachers are able to regain the conversational initiative and thus control how the rest of the lesson unfolds on a moment-by-moment basis. This analysis shows that, during teacher–student interaction that occurs in the context of task-based, small group instruction, teachers and students prototypically orient to a speech exchange organization that is specifiably different from that of ordinary conversation and technically indistinguishable from that of traditional, teacher-fronted instruction. That is, teachers retain — indeed, forcefully re-assert — the right to ask questions and evaluate learners, while students can, as in traditional classroom talk, only properly provide answers to teachers' questions.[13]

4.3. CONCLUSION

What are the implications of these results from an SLA perspective? It is easy to find at least two kinds of supporting evidence in the database from which the excerpts analyzed are extracted for Pica's (1987) claim that unequal power discourse is acquisitionally restrictive for students. For example, with one or two exceptions, learners had in fact already done considerable amounts of unsuccessful definition work in their small groups prior to asking for the teachers' help. Thus, the teachers' use of a CQ(D) strategy effectively forced these students to try to solve problems that, unbeknownst to the teachers, they had already failed to resolve. Furthermore, the use of a CQ(D) strategy also required learners to solve these problems by orienting to a speech exchange system that inhibits conversational restructuring and is therefore acquisitionally less useful than the more open-ended speech exchange system to which they had been orienting in the teachers' absence.

Despite the fact that conversational restructuring seems to be a necessary factor in the acquisition of some types of language structure, very little is known about the processes through which new linguistic knowledge emerges from conversation and becomes incorporated into learners' evolving interlanguage systems. Thus, it may be that the way in which a teacher constructs a CQ(D) turn can trigger sequences that, in conjunction with other sequences in which participants are orienting to a more locally managed turn taking system, contain material that is acquisitionally useful. This is the position that I argue in chapter 7. However, before I develop this idea further, I discuss in greater detail how turn-taking and repair work in different speech exchange systems.

NOTES

1. Of course, there are times when students' orientation to an equal power speech exchange system during small group work changes. For example, if a group secretary is appointed, either by the teacher or by the learners themselves, the group secretary may function as a kind of proxy teacher who arrogates to himself or herself the teacher's delegated rights to privileged access to the floor. But such modifications to an equal power speech exchange system must, in all cases, be achieved and validated as accountable acts by all participants.

2. See Excerpt 4.1 and note 6.

3. The distinction between lay and technical specifications of "traditional" and "nontraditional" classrooms is important because it problematizes the understanding of everyday behaviors, whose complexity, because they are so familiar, might otherwise be overlooked.

4. In linguistic terminology, the conditional relevance that binds first and second pair parts of adjacency pairs together can be considered as a form of coherence (Schegloff, 1990). However, the domain of preference rules is not limited to issues of coherence. In invitation sequences, for example, there is evidence that the preferred response to an invitation is an acceptance, the dispreferred response a refusal (Davidson, 1984; Schegloff, 1980). In this sense, preferred and dispreferred responses are similar to the linguistic notions of unmarked and marked responses, respectively (Levinson, 1983).

5. Of course, I do not mean to claim that all speech acts are accomplished in exactly the same way in different languages. For example, whereas greeting sequences are typically short and simple in English, they tend to be long and elaborate in Arabic. Nonetheless, the basic adjacency pair organization of one greeting requiring another greeting in return obtains in both languages.

6. Although this datum is an example of teacher–student talk, the adjacency pair organization of this excerpt does not reflect an orientation by L6 to the norms of unequal power discourse. This example illustrates the principle that a particular instance of talk cannot be characterized a priori as "traditional" or "non-traditional" just because of the biographies of the participants. Teacher–student roles are achieved on a moment-by-moment basis in and through the talk of participants. In this particular example, the teacher is not able to assert her role as teacher, and the talk therefore "comes off" as an instance of relatively equal power discourse (see also note 9). For another example of this phenomenon, see the well-known transcript of Igor's talk in Allwright (1980).

7. For an alternative account of QAC sequences and their relationship to ordinary conversation, see Tsui (1989, 1994).

8. Obviously, this observation does not mean that learners never ask any questions; however, when they do ask questions, this behavior is typically previously invited by the teacher.

9. The final C turn is shared by both the teacher and the learner in Excerpt 4.1. More specifically, L6's commenting turn at line 137 is a repetition of T's pronunciation modeling turn at line 136. Furthermore, L6 pronounces the word "spur" with a decisive downward intonation, indicating that he is ready to move on to his next question. With exquisite timing, T latches her response at line 138 (=//uh huh, <h>//) in a bid to assert her right to provide evaluative commentary. However, L6 retains control over the trajectory of the conversation by overlapping T's turn with his next Q turn (//what does this mean.//) at line 139. In other words, T is orienting to doing pedagogical talk, whereas L6 (who eventually "wins" this competition) is orienting to doing a kind of talk in which power is distributed more equally than in pedagogical talk.

10. There is nothing distinctively pedagogical about the achievement of CQ(R) sequences located in positions 2 and 3 of Option 2 in Fig. 4.1

(see also the IS at lines 140–146 of Excerpt 4.3), as this type of object is endemic not only in ordinary conversation (Schegloff, 1972) but also in service encounters (Merritt, 1976).

11. The CQ(D) turn at line 244 of Excerpt 4.4 is an elaborated repeat of T's first CQ(D) turn at line 241, and the CQ(D) turn at line 341 of Excerpt 4.5 functions both as a commenting turn that indicates that L6's answer is unsatisfactory and as a Q turn that simultaneously asks for another, more satisfactory answer.

12. A CQ(R) sequence may also be used to set up a subsequent CQ(D) sequence (Markee, 1995). The trajectories of such sequences are shown in Option 4 of Fig. 4.3.

Option 4: Trajectory of a (CQ(R) + CQ(D) turn sequence

Ownership of the turn:	(L)	(T)	(T)	(L)	(T)
Sequential structure:	Q	CQ(R)	CQ(D)	A	C
		(+ IS)			

Q	Question turn
A	Answer turn
C	Commenting turn
CQ	Counter Question turn
CQ(D)	Counter Question turn done as a display question
CQ(R)	Counter Question turn done as a referential question
IS	Insertion sequence

FIG. 4.3 An alternative trajectory for a CQ(R) sequence.

Except 4A further illustrates how CQ(R)-->CQ(D) sequences are achieved. L10 does a Q turn at line 187 to which T responds with a CQ(R) turn at line 189. This marks the beginning of a short CQ(R)1-->A1 insertion sequence at lines 189–191. However, instead of responding to L10's initial question with an A turn (as in Option 1 of Fig. 4.1 and Excerpt 4.1/4.3), T does a CQ(D) turn at line 193, which skews the rest of the talk in the usual way.

Excerpt 4A

```
187 L10: Q      excuse me what is c-o-r-a-l
188             (+)
189 T:     CQ(R)1 can I: (+) open //(h)// <h> (++) get an idea (+) see where's that <h>
190 L10:                        //(h)//
191 L10: A1     I don't know whether the-
```

```
192                (+)
193 T:    CQ(D) corals (+) does anyone know? (+) where you find corals?
                  (NM: Class 1, Group 3)
```

13. This analysis implies that learners do not have the right to ask teachers questions that might be interpreted as CQ(D) turns. As shown in Excerpt 4B, this is, in fact, correct.

Excerpt 4B

```
198 L9:           ((formally)) ((T's name))?
199 T:            uh huh?
200 L9:           your input plea//(h huh //huh// huh)//
201 T:                                //huh//
202 L11:                          //(h huh //huh// huh// huh) <huh>
203 L9:   Q       there is this e::h (+) some sort of an idiom you pretend to pay us
204       Q       and we pretend to work
205 T:    CQ(D)1  ok. what do you think that could be: (+) do you have any idea?
206 L11: CQ(D)2   do you know what the word pretend means
207               (++)
208 T:    CQ(D)3  do I know what the word pretend means
209 L11:  A       yeah (+) I- I [dawt] (+) I don't know that see
210 T:    CQ(D)4  oh ok who- do- does anybody know what the word pretend means.
211               ...
                  (NM: Class 2, Phase 1, Group 3)
```

Things proceed normally as far as line 205: L9 does a Q turn at lines 203–204 and T does a CQ(D)1 turn in response at line 205. L6 then does a turn at line 206 which T interprets as a CQ(D)2 turn. T reacts very negatively to this turn, treating it as a challenge to her authority as a native speaker and teacher (see line 208); she achieves this by doing another CQ(D)3 turn of her own. T's turn triggers the A turn at line 209 (this A turn is the second pair part of an IS, in which L6 attends to repairing the talk at line 206 that he now understands T to have interpreted as a challenge to her authority). Having accepted L6's explanation that he did not know the problem item in the first part of her next turn, T then proceeds to do another CQ(D)4 turn at line 210 and the rest of the sequence (not reproduced here) runs off smoothly. See also note 6 in chapter 7.

Chapter 5

Turn-Taking
in
Different Speech Exchange
Systems

5.0. INTRODUCTION

The previous chapter demonstrated that the sequential organization of talk differs in equal and unequal power speech exchange systems and that L2 learners use this ubiquitous organizational structure as a means of understanding the kinds of social acts that more fluent interlocutors perform, even if they do not understand the details of what is being said. In this chapter, I analyze the structure of talk-in-interaction at a more micro-level of organization, namely, the turn. From a CA perspective, this level of analysis clarifies how speakers routinely implement the collaborative and orderly achievement of talk. From an SLA perspective, this level of analysis illuminates how and why learners may be able to learn new language by doing talk.

I begin by defining key terms (the *turn* and its constituent elements, *turn constructional units*) within a CA framework, as a conversation-analytic definition of turns differs in important respects from those current in the SLA literature. This preliminary review sets the stage for a discussion of how turn-taking practices may function as a resource for doing both conversation and language learning. Finally, I close with a technical description of how members' turn-taking practices differ in equal and unequal power speech exchange systems.

5.1. TOWARD A CONVERSATION ANALYTIC DEFINITION OF TURNS

Crookes (1990) provided what he called a "common" definition of a turn as "one or more streams of speech bounded by speech of another,

usually an interlocutor" (p. 185). To illustrate this definition, he
provided the following constructed example, in which A is said to have
two turns and B one.

Excerpt 5.1

1 A: Are you going home
2 B: Sure, I'll be leaving in ten minutes
3 A: Great.
        (p. 185)

Crookes' definition of this construct has the virtue of being
simple to understand and, from an experimental perspective, easy to
quantify. However, it is not clear how this definition accounts for the
kind of empirically observed interaction illustrated in Excerpt 5.2,
which contains substantial amounts of overlapping talk.

Excerpt 5.2

332 T: hh gunter grass (+) where is gunter grass from
333 L11:   huh?
334 T: gunter gra- (h) I can't pronounce it (+) gun//ter//
335 L15:   //g//unter? (+) grass

         ...
356 T: you think //it's east? (+) //I// think he is//
357 L5:   //he's//
358 L11:   //from which magazine is that,//
             (NM: Class 2, Phase 2, Group 1)

Using Crookes' definition, T's turn at line 334 ends after the
first syllable of "gunter" because the second syllable of this word is
overlapped at line 335 by the /g/ of "gunter" in L15's utterance.
Things become more complicated when more than two people are
implicated in overlapped talk, as at lines 356–358. If only T and L5's
talk at lines 356 and 357 are considered for the moment, T's talk is
bounded after the short pause by L5 saying "he's," so that T's turn is
analyzed as "you think it's east? (+)." However, L11 is also involved
in this talk, and his utterance at line 358 "from which magazine is
that" starts overlapping T's turn after "you think." These competing
analyses regarding the length of T's turns at lines 334 and 356 are
logically and empirically mutually incompatible: T's turns are much
more convincingly analyzed as the complete utterances instantiated at
lines 334 and 356. A more sophisticated definition of turns is needed
to handle data such as these in a more elegant fashion.

The key issue in this discussion is the notion of the
projectability of talk (Sacks et al. 1974). As Crookes correctly noted,
turns are a superordinate analytical category. Thus, in CA

terminology, turns are constructed out of smaller turn constructional units (TCUs), which may consist of sentential, clausal, phrasal, or lexical objects (Sacks et al. 1974). As I noted in chapters 2 and 4, speaker-hearers use their knowledge of sentence-level syntax to project when a turn might roughly be coming to a possible completion point and use these hypotheses to determine when they can appropriately start or continue with their own talk.

As Excerpt 5.2 empirically demonstrates, however, the fact that a potential next speaker analyzes current speaker's talk as having reached a possible completion point does not therefore mean that current speaker has indeed finished producing his or her on-going turn. For this reason, the occurrence of overlaps in talk-in-interaction is not only routine but massive. These overlaps happen for a wide variety of reasons, ranging from collaborative offers of help (as at line 335, where L10's overlap models the pronunciation of the German name "gunter" for T) to competitive interruptions (not illustrated here). Thus, the talk produced by T at line 334 may be analyzed as consisting of a single turn constructed out of two TCUs, separated by the small pause between the words "it" and "gunter." Similarly, the talk produced by T at line 356 also consists of one turn constructed out of two TCUs, separated by the small pause between the words "east" and "I." Both of these turns are overlapped by other speakers. As I have already indicated, such overlaps do not necessarily define the boundaries of current speaker's turn, unless he or she stops talking (which T does not do). This discussion therefore yields the following definition: A *turn* is defined as a spate of talk that is collaboratively constructed by speakers out of one or more TCUs, whose projectability allows possible next and current speakers to identify when current speaker's turn might hearably be coming to an end.

5.2. TURN TAKING: A RESOURCE FOR SLA

What does such a definition provide us in SLA terms? First, TCUs are indistinguishable from Bygate's (1988) construct of *satellite units* (SUs),[1] examples of which are given here in the italicized clauses:

Noun group
Excerpt 5.3

S3:   and on the stairs there is a lit ther is a little erm . little .. bear and a toy
S1:   * *a little toy*
S3:   aha
S1:   * *bear* is it a bear

Prepositional phrase
Excerpt 5.4

S12:   * a *at the door*
S11:   * yes *in the same door* I think
S12:   * *besides the man who is leaving*
S11:   * *behind him*

Adjective group
Excerpt 5.5

S8:   aha they're very polite
S7:   * *polite really polite* that's er one of their characteristics

Excerpt 5.6

S20:   it's big your country
S18:   * *big. .* no it's not big

Adverb group
Excerpt 5.7

S10:   is it a big country
S8:   * *more or less* . Not as big as Brazil

Verb group
Excerpt 5.8

S3:   and the point is that we can start
S2:   * *compare*
S3:   yes

Excerpt 5.9

S12:   he has his hands in his back
S11:   * *looking down*
S12:   his feel his hair his head is down

Pronoun
Excerpt 5.10

S1:   some of the girls . No one girl
S2/3:   * *one*

Subordinate clause
Excerpt 5.11

S11:   well that man I think he is a robber . A thief
S12:   he might be
S11:   * *because he is running with a handbag*
S12:   yeah

Excerpt 5.12

S10:   Brazil
S8:   * no *because it doesn't limit with the Pacific Ocean*
        (p. 68)

What is interesting from a psycholinguistic perspective is that, according to Bygate (1988), participants use SUs, or what I prefer to call TCUs, not only as a means of constructing turns but as vehicles for constructing progressively more complex syntax-for-conversation.

> ... it is clear that satellite units do occur as turns, or as parts of turns. Not only can we say that turns do not need to be made up of independent finite clauses, but also that even when communication does require the use of such clauses, they may well be accompanied by satellite units. Taken together, these facts can be interpreted as evidence of the flexibility with which a speaker may draw on different kinds of units in order to maintain communication.
>   We would suggest that the advantage of this feature of discourse is that it can enable learners to produce dependent units appropriately in the context of discourse, without imposing the additional processing load implied by the requirements of having to produce "complete sentences." So, for instance, a learner may be able to produce dependent adverbial or conditional clauses without also having to monitor himself for the satisfactory production of the main clause. This is a consequence of the fact that oral interaction involves the joint elaboration of discourse. ... In this sense, there are grounds for thinking that, apart from the particular semantic challenge provided by any given task, the management of interaction itself (including the management of the production of speech) contributes to the learning of language. (pp. 74–75)

Clearly, this position implies that, apart from a relatively small subset of core syntactic structures, syntax-for-conversation (see Goodwin, 1979; Lerner, 1991; Schegloff, 1996, for CA perspectives on this notion) is essentially a discoursally mediated resource for communication (Celce-Murcia, 1990a, 1990b). Furthermore, it is consistent with the notion that syntax grows out of conversation (Hatch, 1978). What is not clear from this position, however, is precisely how participants successfully manage to achieve changes in speakership. In order to understand how participants allocate turns to each other and, further, how L2 learners may learn new language by doing talk-in-interaction in naturalistic and instructed contexts, a technical understanding of how members' turn-taking practices differ in equal and unequal power speech exchange systems must be developed. It is these issues that I now address.

5.3. SPEECH EXCHANGE SYSTEMS: AN OVERVIEW

Different speech exchange systems (e.g., ordinary conversation, interview, business meeting, news conference, courtroom, therapy, classroom, debate or ceremonial talk) lie on a continuum with respect to how turns are allocated to different speakers (Sacks et al. 1974).

> The linear array is one in which one polar type (exemplified by conversation) involves "one-turn-at-a-time," allocation, i.e. the use of local allocational means; the other pole (exemplified by debate [or ceremony]) involves pre-allocation of all turns; and medial types (exemplified by meetings [or classrooms]) involve various mixes of pre-allocational and local-allocational means (p. 729).

The more locally managed a speech exchange system is, the more likely it is that many participants will be treated as potentially licit next speakers. However, such a turn-taking system (e.g., conversation) is not designed to ensure an equal distribution of turns among potential speakers. On the one hand, this kind of system tends to reduce the amount of talk that each individual participant can include within a single turn; on the other, it allows for increasing syntactic complexity in a turn's TCUs. In contrast, the more pre-allocated a speech exchange system is (e.g., a debate), the more likely it is that comparatively few participants will be treated as potentially licit next speakers. Those speakers who have the right to speak will do so in a fixed order and for a fixed period of time, thus producing extended, multi-TCU turns. Sacks et al. concluded that:

> we should not be understood as proposing the independent or equal status of conversation and ceremony as polar types. It appears that conversation should be considered the basic form of speech exchange system, with other systems on the array representing a variety of transformations of conversation's turn-taking system, to achieve other types of turn-taking systems. (p. 730)

On the basis of these observations, I highlight the following logical conclusions. In order to understand in discoursal terms how the processes of SLA work, ordinary conversational data should be treated as a theoretical and empirical base line, against which other data (e.g., classroom data) must be explicitly compared. Furthermore, particular attention should be paid to the observation that the closer the structural organization of a speech exchange system is to that of ordinary conversation, the more syntactically rich it is.[2]   Ordinary conversation is also a self-regulating system that enables participants to repair breakdowns in communication and thus allows them to gain access to this syntactic richness.   This implies that ordinary conversation represents a vital resource for L2 learning.   As shown, this is precisely the position originally articulated by Long (1980) and further developed by Bygate (1988), Pica (1987), and others.

5.4.   TURN-TAKING PRACTICES IN EQUAL POWER SPEECH EXCHANGE SYSTEMS

What are the grossly observable facts of an equal power speech exchange system such as ordinary conversation for which a constitutive model of turn-taking must adequately account?   Sacks et al. proposed a list of 14 points.

1.   Speaker-change recurs, or at least occurs.
2.   Overwhelmingly, one party talks at a time.
3.   Occurrences of more than one speaker at a time are common, but brief.
4.   Transitions (from one turn to a next) with no gap and no overlap are common.   Together with transitions characterized by slight gap or slight overlap, they make up the vast majority of transitions.
5.   Turn order is not fixed, but varies.
6.   Turn size is not fixed, but varies.
7.   Length of conversation is not specified in advance.
8.   What parties say is not specified in advance.
9.   Relative distribution of turns is not specified in advance.
10.   Number of parties can vary.
11.   Talk can be continuous or discontinuous.
12.   Turn allocation techniques are obviously used.   A current speaker may select a next speaker (as when he addresses a question to another party); or parties may self-select in starting to talk.
13.   Various "turn constructional units" are employed; e.g., turns can be projectedly "one word long," or they can be sentential in length.
14.   Repair mechanisms exist for dealing with turn-taking errors and violations; e.g., if two parties find themselves talking at the same time, one of them will stop prematurely, thus repairing the trouble (pp. 700–701).

The model that Sacks et al. proposed to deal with these facts differentiates between two types of turn allocation techniques. The first involves current speaker selecting next speaker, and the second involves self-selection. This turn-allocational component is formalized into a finite set of conversational rules or "practices."

1.   For any turn, at the initial transition-relevance place of an initial turn-constructional unit:

   a. If the turn-so-far is so constructed as to involve the use of a "current-speaker-selects-next" technique, then the party so selected has the right and is obliged to take next turn to speak; no others have such rights or obligations, and transfer occurs at that place.
   b. If the turn-so-far is so constructed as not to involve the use of a "current-speaker-selects-next" technique, then self-selection for next speakership may, but need not, be instituted; first starter acquires rights to a turn, and transfer occurs at that place.
   c. If the turn-so-far is so constructed as not to involve the use of a "current-speaker-selects-next" technique, then current speaker may, but need not, continue, unless another self-selects.

2.   If, at the initial transition-relevance place of an initial turn-constructional unit, neither 1a nor 1b has operated, and, following the provision of 1c, current speaker has continued, then the rule-set a-c re-applies at the next transition-relevance place, and recursively at each next transition-relevance place, until transfer is effected. (p. 704)

These rules were originally formulated to describe the turn-taking practices of fully competent L1 speakers. However, Excerpt 5.13 demonstrates that they also account for the turn-taking behaviors of functionally competent L2 speakers of English, in this instance a Dane (H) and an Indian (G) (native language unknown), who are negotiating an international sale of dairy products.[3]

Excerpt 5.13

```
11                ...
12 G: 1a     hallo?
13 H: 1a     hello mister gupta (.) how are you?
14 G: 1a     fi:ne (.) how're you:
15 H: 1c     fine than' you (.) you know now the summer time had-
16           t-come to d'nmark as well (.) ((laugh)) hh:uh=
17 G: 1b     =((laughing)) huh hheh:eh heh heh heh :.hh
18 H: 1b/a   so for:: the:- us here in denmark it's hot
```

```
19              (.) it's uh twenty five degree, (.) but for y//ou// it will be-
20 G:                                                    //yah,//
21 H: 1a       it would be cold (.) I think
22 G: 1b       no, here in this pwu:h forty- forty two
23 H: 1b       yes?
24             (1.0)
25 H: 1b       //Well//
26 G: 1b       //yes//
27             (1.0)
28 H: 1b       well I prefer twendy five. (.) it's better to me
29             (0.9)
30 G: 1b       yeah
31             (1.1)
32 H: 1b       GOOD ...
               (Firth, 1995, pp. 190–91 & 193)
```

More specifically, G and H use "current-speaker-selects-next" techniques to accomplish the identification and greeting adjacency pair sequences at lines 12–14. At line 15, H uses a "current-speaker-continues" technique when he says "you know now the summer time had-" after the first transition relevance point that occurs at the immediately preceding micro-pause. His laughter tokens at line 16 invite (but do not oblige) G to take next turn. Thus, G's reciprocating laughter tokens at line 17 are an example of a "first-starter-begins-talking" selection technique. At line 18, H also constructs the first part of his turn "so for:: the:-" as a "first-starter-begins-talking" selection technique. However, he then sets up a contrast between "us" at line 18 and "you" at line 19, which constructs the rest of his turn as a "current-speaker-selects-next" technique. At line 20, G acknowledges that he is being explicitly selected to speak next by doing an anticipatory overlap of the word "you" in H's turn with with his own "yah" which he follows up with his own turn at line 22. Finally, the last seven turns displayed in this excerpt show both speakers using a "first-starter-begins-talking" selection technique at lines 22–3, 25–6 and 28, 30, and 32. These turns preface the closing down of the social talk in which the parties have been engaging. Indeed, in the rest of G's turn at line 32 (not reproduced), they then move on to discuss the substantive business of the call.

In summary, based on the data displayed in Excerpt 5.13, it is to these empirically grounded practices that speakers demonstrably orient as they talk. More specifically, these practices are the mechanisms that enable speakers to collaboratively construct and exchange talk that ranges in size from individual turns, through sequences of various kinds, to lengthy multi-turn and multi-sequence conversations-as-speech-events. Excerpt 5.13 also demonstrates that, to the extent that L2 users' lingua francas and L2 learners' interlanguages are real (though evolving) languages, L2 users of language X orient to the same kinds of turn-taking rules as NSs of target language X.

Because little, if anything, has been written on how members constitute non-traditional (language) instruction through their turn-taking practices (though see Lerner, 1995), the observations that can be made on this subject are preliminary. As should be clear from the analyses of data offered in chapter 4, (language) classrooms are non-traditional to the extent that members orient for at least part of the time to a speech exchange system that approximates that of ordinary conversation. Thus, whether a classroom is traditional or non-traditional has nothing to do with the a priori concept of so-called pedagogical methods. Whatever claims the proponents of pedagogies such as Total Physical Response, etc., may make that their ideas represent significant breaks with mainstream teaching practice, this method is quite traditional from a turn-taking perspective: Participants still orient to unequal power speech exchange systems that pre-allocate different kinds of turns to teachers and learners. Therefore, SLA research should be restricted to discovering and analyzing what teachers and learners actually do in classrooms (Long, 1989), particularly those that are mediated by small group work.

As shown in the earlier discussion of the sequential function of teachers' CQ turns in chapter 4, members rarely orient to a locally managed speech exchange system when teachers participate in small group work. However, as demonstrated in Excerpt 5.14, when teachers are not group members, the "default" setting for student–student interaction during small group work is a locally managed, equal power speech exchange system.

Excerpt 5.14

```
74  L10: * shall we write it?
75          (++)
76  L10:    that on //the line//
77  L9:  *           //do you// have uh the information to write
78  L10:    <hhh>
79  L9:     ok
80          (2)
81  L9:  * (I don't write you go right ahead)
82  L?     ((cough))
83          (+)
84  L11: * uh:m you- how about you read
85  L?:    uh
86  L11:    these two
87          (+)
88  L9:     yeah
89  L11: * you- you read //these two//
90  L10:                 //these two//
91  L9:     ((cough))
```

```
92  L11:    pa//ragraph//
93  L9:          //paragraph//
94  L10:    ok
95  L11!  *  and (+) I read (+) these (+) uh- I read (++) you've already finished?=
96  L10:    =yeah yeah
97  L9:     yeah
            (NM: Class 1, group 3)
```

Although the talk displayed in this excerpt is not isomorphous with ordinary conversation (the content of the talk has been pre-specified by the teacher, as has the possible length of the conversation), the turn-taking system to which L9, L10, and L11 orient is clearly locally-managed. For example, all three learners freely initiate turns to suggest how the task of reading an article might be fairly divided (thus, L10 initiates talk at lines 74; similarly, L9 initiates talk at lines 77 and 81, as does L11 at lines 84, 89, and 95). Furthermore, L9 and L10 specifically agree to the work-load proposed by L11 (see lines 88, 94, 96, and 97).

5.5. TURN-TAKING PRACTICES IN UNEQUAL POWER SPEECH EXCHANGE SYSTEMS

I now show how the turn-taking practices just discussed are modified to implement an unequal power speech exchange system such as the one that obtains in traditional, teacher-fronted (language) classrooms. McHoul's (1978) work on the turn-taking practices that constitute traditional content classrooms provides an important point of departure for understanding the turn-taking practices of traditional (language) classrooms. As might be expected, McHoul's turn-taking model is an adaptation of the turn-taking practices worked out by Sacks et al. (1974) for ordinary conversation.

I.   For any teacher's turn, at the initial transition-relevance place of an initial turn-constructional unit:

   A) If the teacher's turn-so-far is so constructed as to involve the use of a "current-speaker-selects-next" technique, then the right and obligation to speak is given to a single student; no others have such a right or obligation and transfer occurs at that transition-relevance place.
   B) If the teacher's turn-so-far is so constructed as not to involve the use of a "current-speaker-selects-next" technique, then current speaker (the teacher) must continue.

II. If I(A) is effected, for any student-so-selected's turn, at the initial transition-relevance place of an initial turn-constructional unit:

A) If the student-so-selected's turn-so-far is so constructed as to involve the use of a "current-speaker-selects-next" technique, then the right and obligation to speak is given to the teacher; no others have such a right or obligation and transfer occurs at that transition-relevance place.

B) If the student-so-selected's turn-so-far is so constructed as not to involve the use of a "current-speaker-selects-next" technique, then self-selection for next speaker may, but need not, be instituted with the teacher as first starter and transfer occurs at that transition-relevance place.

C) If the student-so-selected's turn-so-far is so constructed as not to involve the use of a "current-speaker-selects-next" technique, then current speaker (the student) may, but need not, continue unless the teacher self-selects.

III. For any teacher's turn, if, at the initial transition-relevance place of an initial turn-constructional unit either I(A) has not operated or I(B) has operated and the teacher has continued, the rule set I(A)-I(B) re-applies at the next transition-relevance place and recursively at each transition-relevance place until transfer to the student is effected.

IV. For any student's turn, if, at the initial transition-relevance place of an initial turn-constructional unit neither II(A) nor II(B) has operated, and, following the provision of II(C), current speaker (the student) has continued, then the rule set II(A)-II(C) re-applies at the next transition-relevance place and recursively at each transition-relevance place until transfer to the teacher is effected. (McHoul, 1978, p. 188)

Of course, content classrooms differ from language classrooms in two significant respects. First, the content of the lesson that provides the empirical database for McHoul's work is the geography of Australia. In contrast, most language education typically has no content beyond language learning itself. Second, teachers in content classrooms such as the one studied by McHoul do not use choral drills, as many teachers in English as a Second Language (ESL) classrooms still do. This is graphically illustrated by Excerpt 5.15, in which it is shown how the simultaneous use of an L2 as both medium and object of instruction results in a highly distinctive embedding of what Ulichny (1996) called *conversational*, *corrective* and *instructional* talk (in this case, substitution drills). It is this multilayered embedding of different kinds of talk that distinctively constitutes traditional language lessons-as-speech-events

Although the transcript is not as detailed as it might be[4] (see, e.g., the inexact transcription of overlaps at lines 61–63), enough details are given to evaluate whether the turn-taking structure of the

Excerpt 5.15

		Conversation	Correction/conversational replay	Instruction
28	T:	you were delivering mail to the		
29		patients?//		
30	K:	yah//		
31	T:	how many times did you go//=		
32	K:	=no no// the I should go but I		
33		didn't go//		
34	T:		I was SUPPOSED to go//	that's a good one//. I was
35				SUPPOSED to go [taps table
36				rythmically while repeating]//
37				everyone//
38				I was SUPPOSED to go// .
39	A:			again//
40	T:			I was SUPPOSED to go// .
41	C+:			but I couldn't// . but I couldn'=
42	T:			=but I couldn't//
43C-				(ev-?) again//
44	T:			but I couldn't//
45	A:			I was supposed to go but I
46	T:			couldn't// again
47				I was supposed to go but I
48	C+:			couldn't//
49	T:			I was supposed to go but I DIDN'T//
50	T:			you can also say but I DIDN'T/
51			uh-huh [rising intonation]//because the	
52			baby's sick//	
53				
54		aah// is the baby still very		
55		sick?// what's the matter		

```
56  K:     (he?) don't know//
57  T:     [expressive breath intake
58         indicating possibly surprise,
59         sympathy] oh// (that's a
60         problem then?)//
61  S:  *  does she have high
62         temperature
63  K:  *  no
64  ...
```

Participants

K: Katherine
T: Ms. Towers
S: Suki

A: Members of the class and Ms. Towers
C+: Members of the class participating chorally
C-: A few members of the class, not functioning in unison

Transcription conventions

//   End of an idea unit, not necessarily a pause
.   At the end of a word, a short pause of one conversational beat
*   Inserted in words, elongated enunciation
    overlapped speech
,   rising intonation mid-utterance (e.g., in listing)

?   Rising terminal intonation indicating a question
(..?)   unintelligible utterance with candidate hearings
[ ]   comments about delivery
CAPS   emphasized tonic movement
=   latched contributions, no beat between exchange of speakers

(pp. 747–748, 751)

talk displayed in this excerpt can also be accounted for in terms of McHoul's modified set of practices for doing pedagogical talk-in-interaction. A preliminary analysis suggests that the entire excerpt is organized in terms of the IA-IIB adjacency pairs shown here:

T:	lines 28-29	IA		T:	line 44	IA
K:	line 30	IIB		A:	line 45	IIB*
T:	line 31	IA		T:	lines 46-47	IA
K:	lines 32-33	IIB		C+:	lines 48-49	IIB
T:	lines 34-38	IA		T:	lines 50-55	IA
A:	line 39	IIB*		K:	line 56	IIB
T:	line 40	IA		T:	lines 57-60	IA
C+:	line 41	IIB		S:	lines 61-62	IIB (overlap)
T:	line 42	IA		K:	line 63	IIB (overlap)
C-:	line 43	IIB*				

However, a closer analysis shows that the asterisked turns by A at lines 39 and 45 do not quite fit into the set of practices proposed by McHoul. More specifically, according to practice IA, if a teacher selects a particular party as next speaker (in this case, this party is constituted by all the students in the class), then only that party has the right and obligation to speak. In the case of the talk by A, the whole class does a choral response, as expected, but T simultaneously models the phrase "I was SUPPOSED to go" in the IIB second pair part of this adjacency pair, thus also selecting herself as a licit member of the students-as-other-party-to-the-talk category. In contrast, T does not select herself as a member of this category in the responses done by C+ at lines 41 and 48–49. It therefore seems as if the following rider should be added to rule IA:

I.   For any teacher's turn, at the initial transition-relevance place of an initial turn-constructional unit:
    A. If the teacher's turn-so-far is so constructed as to involve the use of a "current-speaker-selects-next" technique, then the right and obligation to speak is given to a single student or group of individual students (and, optionally, also to the teacher); transfer occurs at that transition-relevance place.

Notice that the additional rider "or group of individual students" is motivated by the talk by C- at line 43, which poses an interesting problem for any analysis of classroom talk that treats students as a multi-party, but nonetheless monolithic, respondent to teacher talk (McHoul, 1978). Such an analysis assumes that all learners behave in the same way. Yet, as line 43 demonstrates, not all students produce a response during this turn, even though no other interlocutor(s) have been nominated by T since she identified "everyone" at line 38 as selected next speaker. In chapter 6, the same problem arises when the phenomenon of repair is addressed.

5.6. CONCLUSION

In summary, the turn-taking practices that characterize equal and unequal power speech exchange system can be specified in terms of a finite set of turn-taking rules to which members orient as they co-construct talk-in-interaction. Ordinary conversational data constitute the theoretical and empirical base line against which other data must be compared. Thus, although classroom talk can vary subtantially in the extent to which members orient to turn-taking practices that instantiate equal or unequal power speech exchange systems, it nonetheless represents a more or less important modification of the rules of ordinary, mundane conversation. In classrooms where teachers (e.g., the one in Ulichny's data) explicitly assert their differential status as a resource for controlling the classroom agenda, there are at least seven modifications of the grossly observable facts about ordinary conversation mentioned by Sacks et al. (1974) that describe how members do traditional classroom talk. More specifically, whereas ordinary conversation:

- is characterized by the local management of turns, traditional (language) education involves a substantial pre-allocation of different kinds of turns to teachers and learners. This fundamental modification of members' turn-taking rights and obligations yields the distinctive Q-A-C sequential structure of classroom talk discussed in Chapter 4;

- favors the production of talk by one party at a time, traditional (language) classroom talk provides for the frequent production by learners of A turns that are done in a choral repetition mode;

- favors the production of short turns, traditional (language) classroom talk enables the teacher to produce long, multi-TCU turns. Note that the length of learners' turns is entirely determined by the teacher. Typically, learners' turns are short. However, learners may also, with the teacher's permission, produce multi-TCU turns, as when they report on an assignment;

- often favors the production of turns made up of clausal, phrasal, or lexical objects, traditional (language) classroom talk often requires learners to produce elaborated, sentence-length turns (as when teachers require learners to display their knowledge of sentence-level grammar by speaking in full sentences);

- varies considerably in terms of how long a given speech event lasts, the length of lessons-as-speech events is fixed well in advance by institutional factors such as time-tabling;
- does not specify in advance the content of what is to be said, traditional (language) classroom talk often conforms to a (more or less) explicitly stated curriculum or lesson plan, which predetermines what learners will talk about during class time.

NOTES

1. SUs may be defined as:

> moodless utterances ... which lack a finite verb group ... [and also] all other instances of syntactically dependent units, finite or non-finite, which have been uttered in a turn which (A) does not include a main finite clause to which the unit in question may be attached, or (B) does include a related main finite clause, for which the dependent unit is however syntactically superfluous. All units that can be classified in either of these ways we will refer to as "satellite units." (Bygate, 1988, p. 64)

2. This position ties in with Brock's (1986) finding that the use of referential questions by teachers resulted in learner replies that were syntactically more complex than those that followed display questions.

3. Although the sequential structure of this telephone conversation is somewhat different in a number of important ways from that originally described by Schegloff (1979) for telephone talk in North America, this does not affect the way turns are deployed by the participants.

4. See Ulichny's transcription conventions given at the end of the transcript, which differ in several respects from those given in appendix A.

Repair in Different Speech Exchange Systems

6.0. INTRODUCTION

As demonstrated in chapter 1, conversational repairs are conventionally broken down in the SLA literature into functional categories such as comprehension checks, clarification requests, confirmation checks, verifications of meaning, definition requests, and expressions of lexical uncertainty (Porter, 1986). The acquisitional function of these conversational adjustments is to make complex language accessible to learners. Repair is thus seen as the engine that drives interlanguage development forward (Pica, 1987). Although I agree that repair can fulfill this acquisitional function (see the analyses offered in Part III), I argue that the use of a functional approach to analyzing repair is problematic.

As Pica (1987) pointed out, the question of whether learners incorporate new language they get from repair work into their evolving interlanguage is still an empirical matter. Now, if SLA researchers are to demonstrate that learners do indeed learn new language as a result of the repair work in which they engage, it seems to me that a sequential, rather than a functional, analysis of repair is better suited to address this issue. More specifically, a sequential analysis such as the one proposed by Jefferson (1974), Schegloff et al. (1977) or Varonis and Gass (1985) can potentially demonstrate whether and how members exploit repair on a moment-by-moment basis as a resource for learning new language. A functional analysis, on the other hand, merely labels in researcher-relevant terms what participants are doing, without providing any participant-relevant explanation of how their interlanguage becomes destabilized.

For these reasons, I devote the rest of this chapter to reviewing how repair in different speech exchange systems is analyzed from a sequential perspective. I begin with a brief review of a social psychological model of repair. I then discuss repair from a conversation-analytic perspective, beginning with the organization of repair in equal power speech exchange systems and ending with how repair is done in unequal power speech exchange systems.

6.1. THE ORGANIZATION OF REPAIR: A SOCIAL PSYCHOLOGICAL MODEL

Before I review the work on repair that has been done within a CA framework, I briefly discuss an SLA-oriented model of repair derived from social psychology. This model was developed by Varonis and Gass (1985) to account primarily for the negotiation of meaning in NNS–NNS talk. However, to the extent that this model is also held to account for the negotiation work done by NS who do not share linguistic or cultural backgrounds and values, I present its main outlines here rather than in the subsection that discusses the organization of repair in L2 talk-in-interaction. This procedure highlights some of the main differences between CA and non-CA-oriented ways of analyzing repair.

Varonis and Gass (1985) begin by noting that:

> When the interlocutors share a common background and language, the turn-taking sequence is likely to proceed smoothly, reflecting what Jones and Gerard (1967) call a "symmetric contingency", each speaker responding to the utterance of the previous speaker, while maintaining her own sense of direction in the discourse. However, in discourse where there is not shared background, or in which there is some acknowledged "incompetence", the conversational flow is marred by numerous interruptions. These may be seen as vertical sequences in a horizontal progression. (pp. 72–3).

Varonis and Gass' model posits that trouble-free conversation proceeds "horizontally," and that when trouble occurs, talk is "pushed down vertically" to deal with these troubles before "popping" back to its horizontal flow. The model also provides for the possibility that multiple levels of embedded vertical sequences may occur before talk returns to its horizontal flow. Vertical sequences consist of a so-called trigger, which contains a problematic item. Triggers sequentially lead to a resolution phase, composed of an indicator (I), a response (R), and a reaction (RR). Note, incidentally, the similarity of the I-R-RR parts of this sequence to the QAC sequences discussed in chapter 4, a point to which I return in this chapter.

As I see it, the major contributions of this model to SLA theory are that it (a) identifies embedded vertical sequences as a locus where learners can get negative evidence (for a recent exhaustive review of the necessity or otherwise of negative evidence for SLA, see Long, 1996); and (b) provides a sequential account of repair.

However, I do not agree with the model's theoretical assumptions that vertical push down sequences (or repair sequences in CA terminology) "mar the flow" of a conversation (see also Firth & Wagner, 1997, for a similar critique of this interpretation and, 1998, for a response to these arguments). From a CA perspective, repair is the principal resource that conversationalists have at their disposal to maintain intersubjectivity, that is, to construct shared meanings (Schegloff, 1992b). Thus, far from marring the flow of talk-in-interaction, repair is what ultimately enables speakers to maintain their social relationships; but the accomplishment of this intersubjectivity is a supremely delicate matter, which may have complicated consequences for language learning.

Furthermore, there is a methodological problem with the way this model is formulated. As I pointed out, there is an important similarity between the I-R-RR parts of this sequence and QAC sequences that are typical of institutional talk. This is no accident because the examples that Varonis and Gass (1985) used to illustrate how their model works come from institutional varieties of talk gathered in non-naturalistic settings, including NS–NNS talk in which NSs constitute themselves as interviewers and NNSs as interviewees, teacher–student talk, and psychotherapist–patient talk. This lack of differentiation between different speech exchange systems is problematic because the issue of how these institutional varieties of talk might vary from ordinary conversation is not addressed. Thus, from a CA perspective, the fact that these repairs occur as I-R-RR conversational objects strongly suggests that the account of repair offered by Varonis and Gass may not be relevant to members orienting to the repair practices of an equal power speech exchange system.

6.2. THE ORGANIZATION OF REPAIR IN EQUAL POWER SPEECH EXCHANGE SYSTEMS: A CONVERSATION ANALYTIC MODEL

I now review how CA accounts for the phenomenon of repair and show what insights SLA theory might obtain from incorporating such accounts into its theoretical domain. I begin this section with an account of repair in L1 talk and follow this up with a review of how repair has been analyzed in L2 talk. Finally, I discuss how repair functions in non-traditional language classrooms.

6.2.1. Repair in L1 Talk

From a CA perspective, all repairs are likely to be signaled by various markers of incipient repair (pauses, silences, sound stretches, cut-offs, and phrases such as "you know" and "I mean"). Repair is also dependent on members orienting to the turn-taking procedures that constitute a given speech exchange system. However, repair is also an independent form of conversational organization, whose accomplishment is analyzable in terms of highly distinctive sequential trajectories. More specifically, the organization of repair can be anlayzed in terms of (a) its position in relation to an initial trouble source; (b) who initiates repair — either "self" (i.e., current speaker) or "other" (i.e., interlocutor) — and who completes it (again analyzed in terms of "self" or "other" speaker roles); (c) whether a repair effort is successful or unsuccessful (Schegloff et al., 1977).

Such an analysis yields four sequential positions in which repairs may occur. First and third position repairs involve work that is initiated by self following the occurrence of a trouble source (or, in Varonis & Gass' terms, the occurrence of a trigger). Second and fourth position repairs, on the other hand, are other-initiated. Repairs initated from all these positions are typically also completed by self, although other-completed repairs are also found (self- and other-completion being the CA equivalents of the resolution phase of Varonis & Gass' model). Note also that, as already suggested by Varonis and Gass' discussion of push-down sequences, because any talk is potentially repairable, including repair work that is currently underway, repair sequences often contain inserted repairs of repairs. For the sake of simplicity, I now outline how canonical versions of first, second, third, and fourth position repairs sequentially unfold.

First position repairs are placed within the same turn as the trouble source; that is, self both initiates and completes the repair. A minor variant of this type of repair occurs when the repair is placed within the transition space of the turn that contains the trouble source. Again, self both initates and completes the repair. Thus, same turn and transition space repairs have no sequential consequences because self does all of the repair work.

Second position repairs occur in the turn that immediately follows a trouble source and are initiated by other through objects called *next turn repair initiators* (NTRIs). These objects are often constructed as wh- questions. NTRIs not only initiate a repair sequence but also "withhold" a potential completion of the repair by other in second turn; this facilitates the resolution of this kind of repair by self in the following (third) turn. Although this is the trajectory of most second position repairs, more repair work that extends over several further turns may occur and may result in either self- or other-completion. Alternatively, and more rarely, repair is accomplished immediately by other in the second turn, without giving self the opportunity to complete the repair.

Third position repairs occur in the third turn of a repair sequence, under the following circumstances: Speaker A produces a seemingly adequate first turn (T1), which Speaker B therefore treats as such and to which she or he responds in T2 in a sequentially appropriate way (e.g., by answering a question in T1 with an answer in T2). However, in T3, Speaker A displays to Speaker B that Speaker B's understanding of T1 was erroneous by undertaking work that repairs this erroneous understanding.[1]

Fourth position repairs are the least numerous type of repair. Not only are they rare, they are also analytically the least robust type of repair and should therefore be treated with caution (Schegloff, 1992b). These repairs involve a T1, say, a question (Q1) done by Speaker A; it is this turn that ultimately turns out to be the source of trouble. T2 consists of Speaker B's sequentially appropriate response to T1, in this case, an answer (A1) to Q1. T3 consists of Speaker A's next turn, say another question (Q2) that follows up on Q1 in some way. This Q2 turn then displays to Speaker B that his or her initial understanding of Speaker A's Q1 in T1 was faulty, at which point he or she proceeds to initiate a fourth position repair of the content of T1 in T4.

These different repair types are not mutually interchangeable. First, the sooner trouble is dealt with, the shorter repair work is going to be. Thus, as already noted, first position repairs entail no sequential consequences, whereas second, third, and fourth position repairs require speakers to do progressively more, and indeed more complex, amounts of work to repair a trouble source. Second, there is a preference for self- over other-correction of conversational trouble (Schegloff et al., 1977). Furthermore, to the extent that repair potentially involves a loss of "face" (Goffman, 1974), there may be a preference for participants not to engage in doing any repair work at all or to mitigate the doing of repair by disguising it as something else, such as a list of alternatives (Lerner, 1994).

6.2.2. Repair in L2 talk

One of the questions this discussion of repair raises for SLA researchers is whether the preference for self-initiated, self-completed over other-initiated, other-completed repair found in ordinary L1 conversations also obtains in mundane L2 talk. Schegloff et al. (1977) noted:

The exception [to the preference for self-initiated, self-completed repair] is most apparent in the domain of adult–child interaction, in particular parent–child interaction, but may well be more generally relevant to the not-yet-competent in some domain without respect to age (p. 381).

L2 learners potentially fall into a "not-yet-competent without respect to age" category.[2] Although they do not address the issue of self-completion, Varonis and Gass (1985) concluded that the preference for self-initiation does not hold.

We have established that negotiations of meaning occur with greater frequency in NNS–NNS dyads than in dyads that include native speakers. Among NNS–NNS pairs, this need for negotiation is probably due to the lack of shared background between non-native speakers. This is true even for native speakers of the same ethnic background, because the medium of communication — English — is foreign to both. Among NS–NNS pairs, there is also a lack of shared background that would presumably lead to an amount of negotiation of meaning which is greater than or equal to what is found in NNS–NNS pairs. However, we suggest that the inequality in the status of the participants (with regard to the language medium) actually discourages negotiation, because it amplifies rather than masks the differences between them. As a result, there is a greater tendency for conversation to proceed without negotiation. Among NS–NS speakers, shared background is maximized, and, as a result, there is little need for linguistic negotiation. (p. 86)

In contrast, two CA-inspired studies (Gaskill, 1980, who focused on NS–NNS talk, and Schwartz, 1980 who focused on NNS–NNS talk) both concluded that the preference for self-completed (though not necessarily self-initiated) repair found in L1 talk also held for L2 talk. Despite these findings, there is still plenty of room for research in this area as no follow-up studies using the same methodological framework have been carried out on this topic since 1980. Furthermore, the study by Gaskill contained at least four methodological inadequacies.

1.   The data were gathered using a sampling strategy, so that the entire speech event was not transcribed. Gaskill thus failed to provide an exhaustive account of the data potentially available for analysis.

2.   The settings from which the data were gathered included talk-
        in-interaction that constituted quite different speech exchange
        systems, thereby potentially affecting the preferences to which
        speakers oriented as they repaired their own and each others'
        talk.
3.   Some of the NNSs were teachers, while others were not, which
        may have affected the "ordinary" character of the talk that
        was recorded).
4.   As pointed out by Kasper (1985), neither study attempted to
        explain the preference organization discovered in the data in
        terms of participants' needs to maintain face (Goffman,
        1967).

6.2.3. Repair in Nontraditional Language Classrooms

The most principled way of conceptualizing how participants do repair
in such classrooms is to say that teachers and learners accomplish
some tasks (e.g., reporting back to the whole class what a group has
previously found out about a topic during task-based activity) by
orienting on a moment-by-moment basis to a range of more or less
pre-allocated turn-taking systems and associated repair preferences.
By the same token, they also accomplish other tasks (particularly
those that involve information gaps that are solved in small group
work that does not include the teacher as a participant) by orienting to
more locally managed turn-taking systems. It is the organization of
the repair preferences to which participants orient as they do these
more locally managed tasks that I now describe.
        In the data I present here, students talk about information
(usually related to current affairs) that they have read about in articles
from newpapers and magazines. In Extract 6.1, for example, the
theme is German reunification. After discussing the information, they
write academic position papers organized according to various
rhetorical styles such as comparison and contrast, process, argumentation, etc. The tasks they have to accomplish are set out in written
form in pedagogical materials that are prepared in-house, often by the
teacher teaching the lesson.

Extract 6.1

Lesson Plan

Part I. Select a partner and read your article. You have ten minutes to
read your article and five to answer the questions that accompany your
article.

Part II. Separate from your partner. Form a group of 4 or 5 and select a secretary. Read the following:

In the articles you have read in the last few days, you have seen that there are many concerns and problems associated with the unification of Germany. As a group, list those concerns. Each group member will be expected to add to the list any information gleaned from the article he or she has read today. As a group look at your list and decide which issues or concerns are the most important. Select three issues in order of importance and be ready to explain why they will be important.
On Monday you will be synthesizing this information and using it for an in-class essay entitled, "Problems Facing a Unified Germany."
[...]

Article: Jane Mayer: East German Circus Faces New Music

1.   What is happening to subsidized enterprises in East Germany?
2.   What does it mean that circus people will have to profit or perish?
3.   What does "you pretend to pay us and we'll pretend to work" mean?
4.   What kinds of problems will German unification pose for the work force?

Thus, these instructions specify that learners have to accomplish two tasks, which are achieved as different parts of the lesson. During the first phase, they have to read an article, such as the one titled "East German Circus Faces New Music." Having read it, they then have to discuss it with other learners in their group to make sure they have reached a common understanding of the issues highlighted by the comprehension/discussion questions. The four questions listed in Extract 6.1 are typical of the kinds of questions teachers ask through their materials. In the second phase, learners have to reconfigure their groups so that every group member has read a different article. This change sets up a multiparty information gap, whose resolution enables learners to write an argumentation essay entitled "Problems Facing a Unified Germany."
As these instructions show, participants end up orienting to as many as four different texts: the source readings, which contain the information they have to discuss; the pedagogical materials, which describe the tasks that are to be completed; the participants' own talk; and later, the essays that are the final products of all this pedagogical activity. Here, I consider only how information drawn from the source texts and the comprehension/discussion questions asked by the

pedagogical materials constrain the repair preferences to which participants orient as they talk.

The fact that three texts are simultaneously in play poses an interesting analytical problem. Technically, the trouble source is in one text (the source reading). However, the initiation of repair occurs in another text (the comprehension/discussion questions in the pedagogical materials). Finally, the accomplishment of repair is done in yet another text (the learners' talk) in which the teacher often does not participate at all.

The best way to deal with this problem is to see how the participants deal with it. As shown in Excerpt 6.1, L11 specifically orients at lines 48 and 54 to the comprehension/discussion questions as the initiators of repair and at lines 54–57 to the source texts as the locus of potentially repairable information respectively. However, L11 also instantiates, and thereby appropriates as his own, both the locus of potential trouble and the repair initiation in his own talk. More specifically, L11 first locates the trouble source by reading directly from the source text (see lines 55–57) and then offers a candidate completion of the repair (see lines 56–57) in same turn, which L9 accepts at lines 58 and 60. According to this analysis, therefore, L11 has accomplished this repair as a self-initiated, self-completed repair.

Excerpt 6.1 (simplified)

```
44 L11:    °did you read that,° ((whisper))
45 L9:     °uh?° ((whisper))
46 L11:    are you ready?
47 L9:     I'm thinking go ahead
48 L11:  * the questions are here so
49          (++)
50 L9:     <hh>
51 L11:    uhm:
52 L9:     ((L9 reads in an unintelligible mutter which trails off into silence))
53         (11)
54 L11:  * that means that (+) the first question (+) you can read it here (+) the
55       * companies' subsidies and the ((unintelligible)) are losing their key of
56       * the state treasury ((reading)) (+) that means, (+) they will not get any
57       * money more. <hh>
58 L9:   * uh u:h. ((yawning)) it's losing this key to
59 L11:    yeah
60 L9:    * the state treasury
           (NM: Class 2, Phase 1, Group 3)
```

An inspection of learners' talk during small group work in which the teacher does not participate in this and two other classes that are organized along the same lines reveals that, when they can, learners accomplish repairs by orienting to a preference for self-initiation and completion. Given the turn-taking organization to which learners are orienting at this time, this is not surprising; with minor variations, this speech exchange system approximates the practices of ordinary conversation, which tend toward minimalization (Sacks et al., 1974). There are also instances of talk in which learners are not able to resolve problems so easily, typically when they do not understand a lexical item or phrase. Under such circumstances, extremely lengthy sequences may be constructed, during which learners try to resolve comprehension problems by doing self-initiated, other-completed repairs. Within this sequential context, repairs of repairs frequently occur, and these are usually done as self-completed second position repairs.

I now examine how L9 and L11 construct the beginning of such a lengthy sequence in the talk that is reproduced in Excerpt 6.2. This sequence represents these two learners' attempts to answer Question 3 (What does "you pretend to pay us and we'll pretend to work" mean?) in Extract 6.1:

Excerpt 6.2

```
109 L9:   * ºwhat does your pretended pay uh you mean pretend to workingº
110          ((whisper; L9 is talking to himself, working out the answer to Question 3
111          in the pedagogical materials))
112          (++)
113 L11:  * ºwhat means pretend?º ((whisper; L11 seems to be picking up on the fact
114          that L9 may know the answer to Question 3))
115 L9:   * uh, (+) pretend? (+) to pay a: cent you know pre//tend// to //help//
116 L11:  *                                                 //yeah//    //uh// what
117       * means pretend?
118       * (+)
119 L9:   * to: (+) if you are not (+) you are actua-  you are not (+) doing actually (+)
120       * the actual thing that <hh> you are doing somethi:ng (+) you are
121       * pretendi- like if I am hurt with you
122 L11:    yeah,
123 L9:   * <hhh> I might pretend that I am not and s- (+) continue laughing and
124       * pretend I am laughing and pretending to be happy but while I am not
125       * <hhh>
126 L11:  * ah it means [ja] [ja]
             (NM: Class 2, Phase 1, Group 3)
```

More specifically, L9 begins by doing a self-initiated, self-completed repair under his breath, during which he seems to be working out what the answer to the question might be (see line 109). This talk therefore conforms to the standard repair practices of knowledgeable

learners. L11 overhears this talk and initiates a separate repair of his
own on the same problem which, however, invites L9 to provide
assistance (see line 113). L9 consequently does an other-completion
of L11's repair initiation in next turn (see line 115). However, his
answer is not helpful to L11, who immediately does an NTRI in his
next turn (see lines 116–117). L9 thereupon tries again by engaging in
further definition work, which he first constructs as an explanation
(see lines 119–121). Presumably because he is dissatisfied with the
clarity of his explanation, he reconstructs his explanation in mid-turn
as an example. To do this, he begins to do a self-initiated, self-
completed repair of his own talk (see line 121). L11 invites L9 to
continue with this seemingly more promising way of helping him out,
and L9 thereupon completes his example (see lines 123–125). The
first pass at doing this repair work ends when L11 does a preliminary
claim of understanding in his next turn (see line 126).

    In summary, when students know the answer to a comprehen-
sion question contained in pedagogical materials, they answer it
immediately, with minimal discussion with their partners. The little
repair work that they do is accomplished by orienting to a preference
for self-initiated, self-completed repair. When they do not know the
answer to a question, particularly vocabulary-oriented questions, very
lengthy sequences ensue. For example, Excerpt 6.2 consists of the
first 18 lines of definition work which L9 and L11 (and at times also
the teacher and other students) carry out on the phrase "you pretend
to pay us and we'll pretend to work." This extended sequence lasts for
a total of 186 lines of transcribed talk. In such extended sequences,
the first attempt at repair may be constructed as a self-initiated, other-
completed repair. As the sequence unfolds, however, all other repair
types are theoretically available to participants. In practice, however,
only second position repairs (usually self-completed) are attested with
any regularity; other repair types are either extremely rare or non-
existent. I have only found one example of a third position repair in
all my tape recordings and have never encountered any instances of
fourth position repairs. It therefore seems that learners' preferences
for two distinct types of repair (self-initiated, self-completed repair
versus self-initiated, other-completed repair) reflect their relative
states of knowledge at particular moments in the talk-in-interaction.

6.3. THE ORGANIZATION OF REPAIR IN UNEQUAL POWER SPEECH EXCHANGE SYSTEMS

In his study of the organization of repair in a traditional content
classroom, McHoul (1990) concluded that the preference for self-

completion found in ordinary conversation holds for instructed talk-in-interaction, but not the preference for self-initiation. This result is corroborated (subject to the methodological caveats already expressed) by the research on NS–NNS and NNS-NNS talk by Gaskill (1980) and Schwartz (1980) respectively.[3] More specifically, McHoul found that second position repairs were the most frequent category of repair, followed by first position repairs. Second position repairs were preferentially completed by self, although some other-completions were sometimes found in specific sequential environments. That is, other-completions occurred when redirections, reformulated questions, or clues had failed to elicit a self-completion, or when recipients' answers to the teacher's question were procedurally, though not substantively, inadequate, as when students answered out of turn.[4]

Regarding the organization of repair in traditional language-oriented classrooms, Kasper (1985) studied the repair patterns that occurred in an English as a foreign language classroom at a Danish gymnasium and distinguished between two types of language teaching or learning activity: language-centered and content-centered phases respectively. The language-centered phase consists of a translation task, during which the participants focus on grammatical correctness, whereas the content-centered phase involves learners being able to understand and express their attitudes toward the ideas contained in the literary text also used during the translation task. In other words, Kasper claimed that the organization of repair in classroom talk is contingent on members' conversational accomplishment of structurally different phases during a lesson.

6.3.1. Repair During the Language-Centered Phase

Kasper argued that, during the language-centered phase, the organization of repair is rather different from that found in ordinary conversation. For example, self-initiated repair is rare. When it occurs, learners do not complete repairs but instead appeal for help from the teacher. More generally, repair sequences are prototypically organized as four turn objects, whose trajectories unfold as follows: Trouble sources occur in learners' turns. Teachers are responsible for other-initiating repairs on these trouble sources in next turn, and learners are made sequentially responsible for completing repairs in third turn. Finally, the sequence is closed in fourth turn by teachers' confirmations of the repair done in previous turn.

Unlike many researchers who, for turn-taking purposes, treat teachers as one party to a conversation and students as the other, collective, party to the talk (see, e.g., Lerner, 1993; McHoul, 1978;

Mehan, 1979,1982; Payne & Hustler, 1980; Schegloff, 1987), Kasper
distinguished between individual learners' contributions to repair
sequences. Thus, as shown in Table 6.1, which identifies eight logically
possible repair trajectories according to whether teachers or students
are potential selves or others, Kasper distinguished between the learner
(L) who produces a trouble source and other learners (Lo) who may
complete the repair for L.

TABLE 6.1
Types of repair in classroom discourse

	Trouble Source	Repair Inititiation	Repair Completion	Confirmation
T self-self (1)	T	T	T	-
T other-self (2)	T	L	T	-
T self-other (3)	T	T	L	T
T other-other (4)	T	L	L/Lo	T
L self-self (5)	L	L	L	T
L other-self (6)	L	T/Lo	L	T
L self-other (7)	L	L	T/Lo	(T)
L other-other (8)	L	T/Lo	T/Lo	(T)

(T = teacher, L = learner producing trouble source, Lo = other learner)

Note.   From G. Kasper (1985, p. 203).   Reprinted with the permission
of Cambridge University Press.

On the basis of this distinction, Kasper concluded that there is
a preference for what she called *delegated repair* (i.e., other-
completed repairs done by Los) over self-completed repairs done by
Ls.   Thus, according to this analysis, the preference for delegated
repair during the language-centered phase (which is analyzed as a
product of the organizational structure of translation tasks, which
distributes turns-at-talk to as many participants as possible), constitutes a marked departure from the preference organization of repair
found in L1 and L2 ordinary conversation and traditional content
classrooms.

6.3.2. Repair During the Content-Centered Phase

During this phase, Kasper found that participants oriented to different, and indeed more complex, patterns of repair. Kasper distinguished between four types.

1. As in ordinary conversation, teachers and learners both prefer self-initiated, self-completed repairs. These kinds of repairs are typically found in the sequential context of elicitations and vocabulary teaching.
2. As in the language-centered phase and in ordinary L2 conversation between NS and low-level NNS (Faerch & Kasper, 1982), but unlike in ordinary L1 conversation, other-initiated, other-completed repairs are also frequently done by teachers, who typically do not delegate repair to learners during this phase.
3. As in ordinary, mundane L2 talk, but unlike during the language-centered phase, participants avoid interrupting content-oriented talk when linguistic trouble sources are repaired.
4. As in the language-centered phase, Ls appealed for help from the teacher rather than complete a repair.

6.4. CONCLUSION

Kasper's (1985) paper made two important contributions to the SLA and CA literatures. First, Kasper suggested that first position repairs may not be particularly useful for acquisitional purposes because they do not engender enough restructuring work by participants. Second, although the distinction between L and Lo completion of repair departs from common analytical practice in CA[5] — a departure which has important analytical consequences in terms of how the organization of repair in pedagogical talk-in-interaction is understood — this unorthoxy is fully justified. More specifically, as chapter 8 demonstrates, learners construct their individual identities in and through repaired talk and therefore have a stake in maintaining face vis-a-vis the teacher and their peers. This fact is best captured by recognizing the independent existence of Lo-completed repair as an organizational resource of pedagogical talk.

   As already shown, the two variants of first position repairs identified by Schegloff et al. (1977) do not engage learners in elaborate restructuring of conversational input and output because same turn and transition space repairs have no sequential consequences. At the other end of the repair continuum, fourth position repairs seem to be rare in L1 talk and have yet to be attested in L2 talk. Their presumed rarity in L2 talk suggests that this type of repair is unlikely to be of much acquisitional use to learners. This therefore leaves second and perhaps third position repairs as the best candidates for conversational modifications that engage learners in getting conversationally modified input that may be acquisitionally useful in a qualitative sense and that naturally occurs frequently enough in talk-in-interaction to function as a resource for destabilizing learners' interlanguages.

Finally, I speculate about the necessity of repair as a resource for SLA. There is evidence that repair is a necessary but not sufficient resource for SLA. It has also been suggested that the different amounts of repair that occur in NNS–NNS, NS–NNS and NS–NS dyads respectively are attributable to the different linguistic competences and statuses of NS and NNS participants (Varonis & Gass, 1985).

To these insights, I add the following hypothesis: Repair (particularly other-repair) is a necessary but nonetheless an essentially dispreferred conversational activity. That is, at particularly delicate moments in a conversation, the construction and maintenance of intersubjectivity may be just as, if not more, socially important to conversationalists than learning new language, even when, as in formal language instruction, language learning is the avowed purpose of engaging in talk-in-interaction. Thus, an important reason why talk-in-interaction cannot be a sufficient locus for naturalistic L2 learning is that, whereas repair (rather like cod-liver oil) may be acquisitionally good for you, it is nonetheless potentially face-threatening. It would therefore be interesting to recast the rather vague notion of a so-called *affective* filter potentially hindering acquisition when it is "up" (Krashen, 1980) in terms of face-saving issues, to see if there is any conversational evidence that face considerations inhibit successful SLA. This is an issue I take up in chapter 8.

NOTES

1. Note that third position repair is organizationally different from third turn repair (Schegloff, 1992b). Third turn repair occurs when self produces a seemingly adequate T1, which other therefore does not treat as repairable in T2. However, in T3, self then goes back to repair an object in T1 without calling into question other's understanding of what was meant in T1. In other words, third turn repairs are sequentially very similar to first position repairs, in that the act of repair is both initated and completed by self within what is essentially the "same" turn as the trouble source. Even though this may initially

seem an unimportant distinction, it is relevant to the organization of repair in unequal power speech exchange systems (see note 4).

2. However, see Firth and Wagner's (1997) critique of this position.

3. While Gaskill and Schwartz discussed their results in terms of the preferences that govern repair in ordinary conversation, the fact that they both gathered their data in a laboratory setting means that their results are best understood as instantiating the repair preferences that are relevant to an institutional variety of talk, specifically interviews (Liddicoat, 1997).

4. No third or fourth position repairs were found, although McHoul notes that the QAC organization of pedagogical sequences regularly provides a slot for teachers to initate repair in the third commenting turn of such sequences. However, as noted in the discussion of repair in ordinary conversation (see note 1), there is a sequentially motivated distinction between third turn and third position repairs in ordinary conversation. Similarly, there is an important sequential difference between repairs initated in C turns of QAC sequences and third position repairs.
Recall that third position repairs are self-initiated and completed objects that correct trouble located in an apparently trouble-free first turn produced by self. The troublesome nature of this first turn emerges for self when other's talk in second turn is designed in a sequentially appropriate manner but demonstrates to self that the content of the message in first turn was ambiguous. At this point, self then corrects this misinterpretation through a third position repair.
However, repairs done in the commenting slot of QAC sequences are prototypically second position repairs. That is, as the second pair part of an AC adjacency pair (Mehan, 1979), the organizational function of C turns is to enable teachers to initiate repair work on the preceding A turn, which is done by students, not on the first Q turn, which is done by teachers. This being said, there is no structural reason why, for example, teachers cannot repair badly phrased questions done in first turn with third position repairs during instructed talk-in-interaction. However, such conversational work does not specifically orient to the tripartite organization of pedagogical QAC sequences.

5. See also the related discussion of this issue in chapter 5.

III: DEMONSTRATING CONVERSATION ANALYSIS

"Coral":
A Case of Comprehended Input
that Leads to Understanding
and Learning

7.0. INTRODUCTION

As chapter 1 demonstrated, a substantial body of research has emerged which attempts to validate hypotheses concerning the theoretical importance of comprehensible — or, in Gass' (1997) terminology, *comprehended* — input as a necessary catalyst for SLA. This approach to SLA studies has been significantly influenced by Long's (1985a) research program, which involves three steps:

1. Show that linguistic or conversational adjustments promote comprehensible input.
2. Show that comprehensible input promotes acquisition.
3. Deduce that linguistic or conversational adjustments promote acquisition.

While Long's (1985a) research program has motivated a great number of valuable insights into the processes of SLA, it is not without its critics. As Ellis (1990) remarked, most SLA studies inspired by this program have concentrated on Step 1: that is, showing that interactional adjustments promote comprehensible input. However, due to the methodological difficulties involved in experimentally testing Krashen's (1981) i+1 hypothesis (see Gregg, 1984; White, 1987), no studies have (at least, until recently) demonstrated that comprehensible input actually promotes acquisition. Ellis (1990) therefore concluded that "Long's proposal for an indirect approach to studying the relationship between meaning-focused interaction and acquisition is of doubtful value because of the difficulty of accomplishing Step 2" (p. 62).

It seems to me that it would be premature to accept Ellis' conclusion, and yet, if further insights are to be gained into the relationship between meaning-focused interaction and acquisition, an approach to analyzing conversational data will need to be developed that is able to show whether, when, and how L2 learners first understand and subsequently learn a new piece of language in real time. However, if this direction is pursued, the ways in which such questions are addressed will have to undergo a number of important modifications.

First, if Step 2 is truly the Achilles heel in Long's research program, then I believe that qualitative research may in fact be the only means available to us to demonstrate the learning consequences of meaning-focused talk. As I argued in chapter 2, this means that qualitative research will take on an unorthodox hypothesis-confirming function in this revised research program, instead of being limited to its more usual hypothesis-generating function. But given the relative dearth of qualitative research in SLA studies, this is a development that is neither to be avoided nor deplored.

Second, it seems that adult learners, at least, may find conversation more useful for learning vocabulary than for learning syntax (Hatch, 1978; Sato, 1986; however, see also Wagner-Gough & Hatch, 1975 on the function of conversation as a resource for getting syntax, and Gass & Varonis, 1989; Mackey, 1999; Swain & Lapkin, 1998 on the acquisition of morphosyntax). Thus, as Ellis (1990) also suggested, it may be that the types of data that allow direct access to Step 2-related issues are primarily lexical rather than morphosyntactic. As the analyses in this and the next chapter demonstrate, the incidental acquisition of vocabulary from meaning-focused interaction does, indeed, lend itself well to qualitative research. However, these analyses also demonstrate that vocabulary is embedded in specific conversational contexts. Consequently, learners necessarily also have to orient to, and deploy, substantial syntactic and other resources in the course of learning new lexis. It is therefore to be expected that learning new vocabulary also entails learning new syntax or, at the very least, how to deploy previously known syntax in more fluent, complex, or accurate ways.

What might such a qualitative methodology look like? I believe that one (though not necessarily the only) candidate would be an ethnomethodologically based approach to CA. More specifically, as I argued in chapter 2, this methodology should be:

- based on empirically motivated, emic accounts of members' interactional competence in different speech exchange systems;
- based on collections of relevant data that are themselves excerpted from complete transcriptions of communicative events;
- capable of exploiting the analytical potential of fine-grained transcripts;
- capable of identifying both successful and unsuccessful learning behaviors, at least in the short term;
- capable of showing how meaning is constructed as a socially distributed phenomenon, thereby critiquing and recasting cognitive notions of comprehension and learning.

In the remainder of this chapter, I illustrate how this methodology can be used to reconstruct whether, when, and how an ESL learner (L10) and her interlocutors (T, L9, and L11) orient to the structure of talk-in-interaction as a resource for understanding and acquiring the word *coral*. More specifically, I discuss the empirical database that is available for analysis, outline the data collection procedures used to gather the data, describe the tasks which learners had to accomplish, provide a definition of spoken definitions, and describe the procedures used to identify and verify the conversational structure of spoken definitions. I then provide a detailed conversation analysis of successful language learning behavior. Finally, I make some further connections between CA and broader issues in SLA studies.

7.1. THE DATABASE

The complete database for this project consists of 14 lower to upper intermediate ESL classes at a university located in the mid-western United States. These classes were video- and audiotaped during spring semester, 1990. Each class lasted 50 minutes. Currently, the conversations of four teachers and 45 learners (10 in Class 1, 13 in Class 2, 11 in Class 3, and 11 in Class 4) interacting in ordinary classrooms[1] have been fully transcribed, using the transcription conventions shown in appendix A.

The collection of excerpts reproduced in appendix B come from Class 1 and constitutes the majority of the data used in this chapter. For ease of reference, I number the excerpts from this collection that are reproduced in this chapter according to their sequential position in the original transcript, not according to the order in which I discuss them. Thus, for example, Excerpt 7.5 refers to Excerpt 5 in appendix B. This is done so that readers may easily recognize whether a given excerpt occurs before or after another excerpt in the original transcript. When I refer generically to an excerpt (e.g., Excerpt 3), readers should consult the collection of excerpts in appendix B. Excerpts that do not come from the collection in appendix B are labeled Excerpt 7A, 7B, etc.

7.2.   DATA COLLECTION PROCEDURES

Two video cameras were used to film the participants, who were visually identified by a number pinned to their clothing (i.e., L1, L2, L3, etc.); the video signals were fed into an electronic switcher operated by an assistant. Camera 1 (the main camera) recorded learners interacting in groups or whole class activities, while Camera 2 filmed teacher-fronted activities and/or presentations by students using

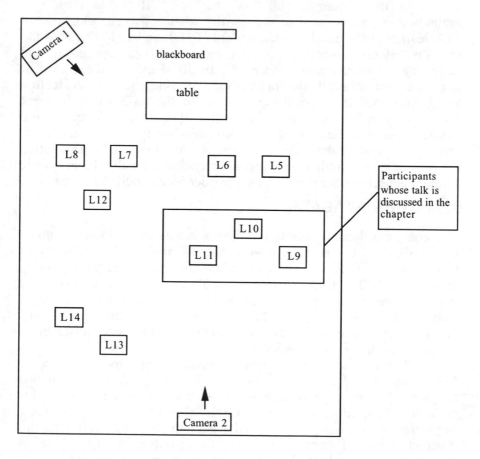

FIG. 7.1 Layout of Class 1

the blackboard or overhead projector. These video recordings were primarily used to visually check who was speaking to whom when this information could not be determined from the audio data (see Fig. 7.1 for a graphic representation of the layout of the class, the position of the two cameras, and the composition of the groups in Class 1).

The audio recordings are the primary sources of data. Each participant was issued a numbered Walkman-sized stereo cassette recorder and a lapel microphone, as described in chapter 3. The number on each recorder (and on each cassette) corresponded to the number pinned to the participants' clothing. This set-up allowed the analyst to identify participants visually on the videotape and aurally on their audiotapes. Transcripts for each group and teacher in every class were produced on the basis of these multiple recordings; in the case of Class 1, this yielded a total of six transcripts for the lesson (four parallel transcripts for the four groups; one teacher's transcript and one transcript consisting of collections of definitions excerpted from the class interaction).

7.3. THE TASKS

The tasks learners had to complete in Class 1 involved an open-ended four-way exchange of information. Students first read and discussed one of four thematically related magazine articles on the greenhouse effect in four small groups. A representative or representatives from each group then presented the information contained in each reading with an overhead projector in an oral, whole class activity. The end product was some written work, which was done in a later class that was not recorded. Approximately 30 minutes (which include 5 to 10 minutes of silent reading, depending on the group) were allocated to small group discussion and about 20 minutes were given over to three oral presentations. The first seven excerpts in appendix B were collaboratively produced by group 3 during the group work phase; Excerpt 8 was produced by L10 (a member of group 3) during the oral reporting phase to the whole class.

7.4. A DEFINITION OF SPOKEN DEFINITIONS

For the purposes of the analysis of the larger corpus from which these data were taken, the defining characteristics of spoken definitions[2] were not determined on the basis of a priori categories but, as is usual in this kind of research, on the basis of an analysis of the interaction in all four fully transcribed classes. Thus, spoken definitions are not defined here as linguistic products (see Watson, 1985, for an analysis

of the linguistic structure of definitions) or as logical forms (see
Flowerdew, 1991; 1992 for an analysis of definitions inspired by
speech act theory). Rather, they are defined as any turn(s)-at-talk that
are hearable by participants as explanations of lexical items or phrases
whose meaning is actually or potentially unclear.[3] More specifically,
participants achieve definitions by simultaneously orienting to the
resources of turn-taking and repair available to them as conversationalists and by using a range of "vocabulary elaboration" strategies
(Chaudron, 1982) to resolve problems. These strategies (which may
be used singly or in combination with each other) include the use of
iconic, non-verbal means of defining, such as pointing, acting, drawing,
and showing pictures. They also include the use of explicit verbal
strategies such as simplification, synonymy, antonymy, classification,
approximation, exemplification, comparison, and translation. Finally,
these explicit strategies are complemented by such implicit verbal
elaboration strategies as apposition, parallelism, and paraphrase.

7.5. PROCEDURES USED TO IDENTIFY THE CONVERSATIONAL STRUCTURE OF SPOKEN DEFINITIONS

The data were first examined to establish the prototypical conversational structure of definitions. In student–student talk, definitions are
prototypically achieved as sequences. These sequences consist of a
question and answer adjacency pair (Schegloff & Sacks, 1973) followed
by an evaluation turn (itself the second pair part of an answer and
comment adjacency pair; Mehan, 1979) in which participants indicate
whether they have understood the definition. As shown by the talk
reproduced in Excerpt 7A, this basic three-part object may be repaired,
typically immediately after the A turn of the first adjacency pair
sequence (see the asterisked turn at line 190). As also demonstrated by
L13's repair at line 190, learners prefer (in the technical sense of this
term) to self-complete repairs, if at all possible.

Excerpt 7A

```
187 L13: Q    what is inundate
188           (+)
189 L14: A    inundate is (+) e://:h flood// yeah
190 L13:  *                 //under the water?//
191 L13: C    under the water. (+) u:::h ((creaky voice))
              (NM: Class 1, Group 4)
```

In the question turn(s) of the adjacency pair, participants
predominantly use wh- questions such as "what does X mean", "what's

the meaning of X", "what is X," (or interlingual variations thereof) to initiate definitions; however, a number of other forms (such as Yes/No questions or declarative statements with rising intonation) are also found. In the answering turn(s), participants define problematic terms using the kinds of elaboration strategies identified by Chaudron (1982). And in the third and final commenting turn(s), participants typically use change-of-state tokens like "oh (ok)," which assert understanding and which may close the sequence down (Heritage, 1984).[4]

As I previously noted (Markee, 1995), a striking characteristic of definitions produced during student–student talk is that they are typically achieved as local solutions to local problems (even if they are initiated by the teacher/materials designer through comprehension questions, as in Excerpt 7B).[5] That is, learners prototypically do not treat definition sequences as opportunities for pedagogically oriented explorations of new vocabulary nor do they spend much time doing definitions. They usually move on to do other work as soon as they have enough information to get a general sense of what a word means (see also Hatch, 1978). Thus, as shown in Excerpt 7B, definitions that are constructed as a result of student–student interaction are anything but dictionary-like; rather, they tend to be approximate in terms of their semantic accuracy (see the asterisked turn at lines 564–566).

Excerpt 7B

```
562 L6:    five (+) number five is hydroelectric (+) power
563 L5:    it means water (+) right,
564 L6:*   yeah (+) getting energy from the water (+) yeah you know (+) falling water
565    *   (1) electric water a:nd (2.5) I think it's the  (+) idea (+) it's the main idea
566    *   that's it  (+) it's enough
567 L5:    ok <h> is there any-
           (NM: Class 1, Group 1)
```

In contrast, during teacher–student talk, teachers tend to turn students' questions about unknown words or phrases into explicitly pedagogical sequences that are designed to get the learners to work out what a word means. As already noted in chapter 4, teachers may use a variety of strategies to do this. However, the most important is the use of a CQ(D) strategy (see also Markee, 1995). A prototypical example of such a pedagogical definition sequence is shown in Excerpt 7C (already cited as Excerpt 4.4 in chapter 4; see also Excerpts 4.5 and 4.6). The teachers' CQ(D) turns in Excerpt 7C occur at lines 241 and 245–246.

Excerpt 7C

```
237 L13:      ... what's that mean (1) coastal vulnerability
238           (1)
239 L14:      [f]ulnerability is:
240 L13:      coastal vulnera- vulnerability
241 T: CQ(D)  ((T overhears L13 and L14 as she approaches the dyad)) what d'you
242              think it means
243           (1.3)
244 L14:      uh?
245 T: CQ(D)  what what d'you think a- where are areas of coastal vulnerability (++)
246    CQ(D)  <h> if you think about uh:m
247 L14:      it's not safe[t] (+) areas which are not safe[t] (1) right?
248 L13:      it's very easy to be:: (+) damage
249 T:            yea:h (+) especially by (+) water, (+) by flooding,
              (NM: Class 1, Group 4)
```

Interestingly, as this excerpt also demonstrates, the quality of learners' definitions produced during small group work in which the teacher is a participant is not noticeably more formal than that of definitions constructed during student–student talk. Furthermore, the use of a CQ(D) strategy normally takes away next turn from the learner who asks the preceding Q turn.[6] This therefore sets up a preference for what Kasper (1985) called *delegated Lo repair* (see chapter 6) at this particular decision point in the talk.

The explanation for this preference is that teachers treat learners who do such Q turns as non-knowers and other group members as potential knowers, who can therefore display the requisite knowledge to the student who does the Q turn that initiates these sequences. However, unknown to teachers, students who solicit the teacher's help normally do so because their groups as a whole have already exhausted their own resources for understanding unknown words or phrases. Students who initiate Q turns are therefore acting as spokespersons for their peers, who all have the same status of non-knowers. However, in Excerpt 7C, L13 and L14 have not had the opportunity to discuss the meaning of the phrase "coastal vulnerability" because the teacher takes over the talk at lines 241–242 before they have an opportunity to discuss the meaning of this phrase. L14 is therefore not constrained from answering at line 247, even though he is treated by T as a non-knower at lines 241 and 245–246.

What guarantees are there that participants do not achieve definitions in other ways? More specifically, is there any possibility that the prototypical structure described for these sequences is not a product of inadvertent analyst bias? I checked for such a bias by investigating whether participants (a) achieved definitions in ways that did not conform to these prototypical patterns, and (b) oriented to sequences that superficially conformed to these prototypical patterns as bona fide definitions.

In order to understand how these precautions were implemented, consider Excerpts 7B and 7D, which constitute a two-excerpt collection on the meaning of the phrase "hydroelectric power."

Excerpt 7B
(Group work phase)

562 L6: five (+) number five is hydroelectric (+) power
563 L5: it means water (+) right,
564 L6: yeah (+) getting energy from the water (+) yeah you know (+) falling water
565   (1) electric water a:nd (2.5) I think it's the (+) idea (+) it's the main idea
566   that's it (+) it's enough
567 L5: ok <h> is there any-
         (NM: Class 1, Group 1)

Excerpt 7D
(Whole class oral discussion phase)

745 L5:   ... the
746   number five (+) hydroelectric hh or uh: water (+) uh energy power <h>
         (NM: Class 1, Whole Class)

The talk at line 746 in Excerpt 7D, which occurs during the whole class oral discussion phase that follows the small group work done earlier by L5 and L6 in Excerpt 7B, is constructed by L5 as a definition. This analysis is motivated by the fact that L5 identifies his talk at line 746 as an answer to comprehension question number 5 (see note 5), thus explicitly linking Excerpt 7D with L5 and L6's earlier definition talk at lines 562-566 of Excerpt 7B. Consequently, the gloss of "hydroelectric power" as "or uh: water (+) uh energy power" is not just a casual first position repair but designed to function as a definition for a specific set of recipients, namely, L5's peers in the rest of the class. Data such as these, therefore, demonstrate that definitions can also be constructed as first position repairs.[7]

In regard to the second dimension of inadvertent analyst bias, field notes from a fifth class (not yet fully transcribed) indicate that sequences beginning with a "What is X" turn, followed by the prototypical answering and commenting turns, are not necessarily constructed by participants to function as definitions of unknown terms. For example, a learner in this fifth class (which was discussing euthanasia) rhetorically asked "What is death?" His interlocutor initially oriented to this question as a request to define this word and began to provide a definition in his answering turn. But it immediately becomes clear when the first student interrupts this definition in progress with his own answering turn that he had asked this question so that he could develop his own views on euthanasia, not because he did not know the meaning of "death." The final commenting turn done by the second student confirms the rhetorical nature of this "definition," as he indicates that he has understood that the first learner was not in fact asking for help in understanding the meaning of "death".[8]

On the basis of these procedures, a total of 97 attempted and/or completed spoken definitions[9] have been identified in the four classes that constitute the current database in the larger corpus. The eight definitions reproduced in appendix B are representative of the range of definition types used in the database as a whole.

7.6. CONVERSATION ANALYSIS

What conversational practices do the participants orient to as potential resources for learning in this collection? Note that (with the exception of Excerpt 3) all of these excerpts consist of definition requests. Now, as I argued in chapter 1, definition requests constitute one of the functionally-defined categories of conversational repairs that are thought to promote SLA. However, as I also argued in chapters 2 and 6, what is of particular interest here is the sequential organization of repair. And from this perspective, all of the definition talk in Excerpts 1–8 is itself heavily repaired.

Of course, there is nothing unusual from a conversation-analytic perspective about these repairs. All talk is potentially repairable, including repairs (Schegloff et al. 1977). However, counting the numbers of conversational adjustments that occur in a given corpus with a view to establishing whether the number of occurrences of these phenomena is statistically significant is of little interest (Aston, 1986; Schegloff, 1993). What needs to be shown is that the participants are orienting to repair sequences and using them as resources for learning new language. But how can it be demonstrated that repaired conversations are used as a resource for language learning? More specifically, what evidence can be used to show that L10 orients to sequentially organized repair as a resource for not only understanding but also learning what *coral* means, at least in the short term?

The most important evidence that speaks to this issue occurs in the talk that occurs between lines 394 and 416 of Excerpt 7.5:

Excerpt 7.5

394 L10: * ok uh:m also is a food for is a food for fish uh and uh
395   * (+)

```
396 L9:  *  food?
397      *  (+)
398 L10: *  foo-
399 L9:  *  no it is not a food it is like a stone you know?
400 L10: *  oh I see I see I see I see I see I know I know (+) I see (+)
401      *  a whi- (+) a kind of a (+) white stone <h> //very beautiful//
402 L9:  *                                    //yeah yeah// very big yeah
403      *  //sometimes very beautiful and// sometimes when the ship moves
404 L10: *  //I see I see I ok//
405 L9:     //ship tries ((unintelligible)) I think it was the ((unintelligible; the final
406      *  part of this turn is overlapped by L10's next turn))
407 L10: *  //oh I see (+) I see the chinese is uh (+)// sanku
408         (++)
409 L11: *  unh?
410 L10: *  sanku
411         (+)
412 L9:  *  what
413 L10: *  c//orals//
414 L11: *     //corals//
415 L9:     corals oh okay
416 L10:    yeah
            (NM: Class 1, Group 3)
```

More specifically, at line 394, L10 asserts that coral is food for fish. Following a short trouble-relevant pause at line 395, L9 initiates a second position repair at line 396 by repeating the word "food" with a high rising intonation. Another short trouble-relevant pause follows at line 397 indicating that L10 has picked up on L9's previous indication of potential trouble. L10 therefore repeats the word "food" at line 398, presumably to restate her claim that coral is food for fish. However, L9 cuts her off at line 399 with another, more direct (i.e., other-completed) second position repair, and adds in the last part of her turn the information that coral is like a stone.

This overt negative evidence, which, as I have just argued, L9 and L10 crucially co-construct as a repair sequence, seems to trigger a breakthrough in understanding for L10. More specifically, L10 starts by vehemently asserting at line 400 that she has understood (which minimally indicates that L10 is rather confident that she has indeed understood this word and is willing to expose herself to a potential loss of face if she turns out to be wrong). She then continues at line 401 to independently provide the extra information that coral is white and very beautiful,[10] which L9 corroborates as true at line 402. At lines 403, 405, and 406, L9 provides more descriptive information about coral, which L10 overlaps with further insistent assertions that she has understood at lines 404 and 407. In addition, in the last part of her turn at line 407, and also at line 410, L10 again goes further by providing a translation of this word into Chinese. Because L9 is not a

Chinese speaker, she does not understand these translations (see lines
409 and 412); consequently, L10 translates the Chinese term back into
English by saying "corals" at line 413. The correctness of this
translation is corroborated by L11 (who is also a Chinese speaker and
who has arguably herself only understood what "coral" means at line
409).[11] More specifically, L11 overlaps L10 at line 414 by also saying
"coral," thereby incidentally asserting that she in fact knew all along
what "coral" meant. It may therefore be concluded with some
confidence that (a) L10 has indeed understood what the word "coral"
means by the end of Excerpt 7.5, and (b) L9, L10, and L11 were
demonstrably orienting to the sequential resource of repair at the
precise moments that L10 achieved her breakthroughs in understanding (specifically, by deploying second position repairs at lines 396,
399, 409, and 412 of Excerpt 7.5).

Before I consider the empirical evidence that demonstrates
that L10 not only understands the word *coral* in its immediate local
context but also learns it (at least in the short term), I make a
preliminary point that relates to the acquisitional usefulness of the
range of conversational resources to which L10 orients in order to
understand the word *coral*. Note that in Excerpts 1, 4, 5, and 6, during
which the learners engage in student–student talk, the participants are
orienting to an equal power turn-taking system, which approximates
the turn-taking practices of ordinary conversation (see chapter 6 for
details). Since Excerpt 5 is the locus of the acquisitionally most
important talk in the collection, it might be tempting, following Pica
(1987), to posit a link between the micro-moments of understanding
that L10 co-constructs with her peers and the participants' orientation
to a locally managed, equal power speech exchange system.

However, it should also be noted that T participates in
Excerpts 2, 3, and 7. In these three excerpts, the participants orient
to an unequal power speech exchange system, as demonstrated by the
fact that T does CQ(D) turns at lines 193 and 538 of Excerpts 7.2 and
7.7 respectively and, as shown above, instructs the learners what to do
during a later phase of the lesson in Excerpt 7.3.

Excerpt 7.2
(Group work phase)

187 L10:   excuse me what is c-o-r-a-l
             ...
193 T: CQ(D) corals (+) does anyone know? (+) where you find corals? ...
             (NM: Class 1, Group 3)

Excerpt 7.7 (simplified)
(Group work phase)

520 L11:   ok (+) excuse me (+) uh: what what does it mean hab- (+) habi-
                 ...
538 T: CQ(D) <h> yeah what would be another word for a habitat then (+) it's like ...
                 (NM: Class 1, Group 3)

L10 in fact uses language that was constructed during both student–student and teacher–student interaction as a resource not only for doing understanding but also for doing learning (at least in the short term). This latter behavior therefore goes beyond her merely understanding the word *coral* in its immediate local context in the interaction. As I hinted in the conclusion to chapter 4, therefore, this finding suggests that Pica's (1987) position that teacher-fronted talk necessarily inhibits SLA is perhaps premature.[12]

As noted in chapter 1, finding evidence for behavior that demonstrates learning in data that are transcribed from a single lesson is difficult because learning is not necessarily always public and usually occurs over extended periods of time. Furthermore, as Hatch (1978) pointed out, it is possible that adult learners only elicit new vocabulary in order to be able to participate on a moment-by-moment basis in a conversation, and not explicitly to learn new words. Fortunately, however, the oral report that L10 produces for the rest of the class some 10 minutes after the end of the small group work phase of the lesson provides the kind of empirical evidence needed. More specifically, L10 gives her peers a definition of the word *coral* by borrowing the highlighted words in Excerpts 7.2, 7.3, 7.5, 7.6, and 7.7 and recombining these elements to produce her own original definition of *coral* in Excerpt 7.8, also highlighted in bold text.

Excerpt 7.2
(Group work phase)

204 L10: **at the bottom of the of the s- (+) sea?**
                 ...
208L9:   **at the bottom**
                 (NM: Class 1, Group 3)

Excerpt 7.3
(Group work phase)

330 L10:   oh okay, okay **coral reefs**
                 (NM: Class 1, Group 3)

Excerpt 7.5
(Group work phase)

389 L10: //the corals,// is means uh: (+) s somethings at **bottom of**
390 L9:   //((unintelligible))//
391 L10: //the// **sea**
392 L9:   //yeah,//
393 L9:   **at the bottom of the sea,**
          (NM: Class 1, Group 3)

Excerpt 7.6 (simplified)
(Group work phase)

419 L10: **fissel** (++) **fissel** ((whisper)) (+) <h> **I think** (+) **the coral is also is a fis**
420   (("fis" is whispered)) **is a fi-** f:: ((unintelligible whisper))
421 L9:   fi-shing?
422 L10: if- (1) how to s-   how to spell <hhh>
423   (1)
424 L10: //**fis-**//
425 L9:   //**foss**//il (+) f//ossil//
426 L10:   //**fossil?**// how to F U ? ((L9 and L10 spell the word "fossil"
427   together))
428 L9:   f- F-O
429 L10: F-o
430   (+)
431 L9:   //f-o-S-S-I-L//
432 L10: //f-o-S-S-//I-L
433   (+)
434 L9:   **fossil is a**
435 L10: I-
436 L9:   //**fossil** is uhm//
437 L10: //**I also think**// **of the- coral** (+) **is a is a kind of fossil**
438   ...
          (NM: Class 1, Group 3)

Excerpt 7.8
(Whole class oral discussion phase)

923 L10: ... <h> in my section I think the main point is the: <hh> raising of
924   the sea (+) sea level <hh> we are accompanied uh global
925   tempera increasing <hh> (+) so these (+) put he co[l]al (+) at
926   [l]isk. <h> **I think the co[l]al is the kind of fossil** (+) <h>
927   **fossil at the: botto of the sea.** <hh> **the: co[l]al reef**
928   you are one of the imp- very important, <hh> **habitats** (+)
929   fo:r fish that support th[´]:m more than (+) <h> one (+) more
930   than one third of topic- topical species. <hh> the **habitats**
931   is the: **home** (+) is the **home** for animal living <hh> so this is
932   very important (+) very important <hhh> so: now, the
933   conversationalist uh want to find some [v]ay: (+) to save

934   these uh (+) to: (+) solve this problem.
         (NM: Class 1, Whole Class)

Note also that, by using the same kinds of methodological cross-checking that was used to analyze the relationship between Excerpts 7B and 7D, it is certain that the highlighted parts of Excerpt 7.8 are intended by L10 to be understood as a definition because T had earlier requested L10's group to give a definition of *coral* at lines 318-329 of Excerpt 7.3.

Excerpt 7.3
(Group work phase)

318 T: yeah give a definition of //uh of corals//
319 L10:   //oh okay what// is corals maybe uh
320   (+)
321 L10:   or say-
322 T: or give an example say //for// instance in //austra://lia (+) around
323 L9:   //((unintelligible whisper))//
324 L10:   //oh yeah,//
325 T: australia you get lots of barrier reefs
326 L9:   (barrier reefs)
327 T: //o//therwise people might not kno:w (+) might not be
328 L10: //oh//
329 T: familiar with that word
         (NM: Class 1, group 3)

On the basis of these data, it can therefore be claimed that L10 has learned what the word *coral* means, at least in the short term. To be sure, at first sight, the definition given in Excerpt 7.8 looks rather different from what might be found in a dictionary (though see the analysis that follows of the structure of this definition). Furthermore, the association of *coral* with the word *fossil* is not strictly correct, as corals are not fossils. Nonetheless, to the extent that the word *fossil* evokes associations with a hard, stone-like material, L10 is clearly in the right "semantic ball-park," even if the translation evidence from Excerpt 7.5, showing that she knows what *coral* means in Chinese, were not available.

L10's attempt to incorporate the word *fossil* into her definition of the word *coral* in Excerpt 7.8 raises other interesting issues. I argue that whereas the talk in Excerpt 7.5 illustrates how L10 gets conversationally modified comprehended input from her interlocutors, the talk in Excerpt 7.8 shows how L10 constructs comprehended output that is syntactically more complex than the original input.

Although the strategy of recombining lexical elements from previous excerpts seems to border on the formulaic, the talk that L10 produces in Excerpt 7.8 nonetheless begins to achieve the structure of a logical definition. That is, L10's talk contains the prototypical elements of logical definitions, which are often constructed as three-part statements (Abelson, 1967) like the following: An A is a B, which does C. More specifically, coral constitutes the A part of this statement. The information classifying coral as a type of fossil found at the bottom of the sea fits the B part of the statement. Finally, the information about coral being an important habitat or home for fish rounds out the C part of the statement.

The fact that L10 constructs her definition in this way is surely no accident. First, as Crookes (1989), Foster and Skehan (1996), and Skehan (1998) argued, learners who have the opportunity to plan their speech tend to produce language that may be more fluent or syntactically more complex or accurate. Thus, whereas L10's talk in Excerpt 7.8 is not more fluent or accurate than what she produces in previous excerpts, it is certainly more complex. Second, the formal quality of the definition that L10 produces in Excerpt 7.8 is not accidental either. Indeed, I argue that by constructing her definition in Excerpt 7.8 as a formal, logical object, L10 is specifically orienting to the kind of abstract knowledge that is valued in institutional contexts. Compare the quality of this definition with the one which L10 originally develops in Excerpt 5 or with the asterisked definition that L11 initially offers in Excerpt 7.1 at line 165:

Excerpt 7.1
(Group work phase)

```
163 L10:    <hh> hhhh what is th- what is the (+) coral (+) what's ((whisper)) (+) I
164         don't know (h)
165 L11:  * just- look at it (+) as a (+) an m- material that's all (+)
166 L9?:    uhm don't worry about it
167         (+)
            (NM: Class 1, Group 3)
```

L11's definition in this excerpt is clearly constructed as a local solution to a local problem and therefore has the same approximate, informal quality that was observed in the definitions reproduced as Excerpts 7A–7D. This is because this definition is produced during student–student talk, when members are orienting to a speech exchange system that approximates that of ordinary conversation. L10's definition in Excerpt 5, although more elaborated than the one in Excerpt 7.1, is nonetheless locally constructed and focuses on the immediately observable qualities of

coral as a beautiful colored stone. However, the definition in Excerpt
7.8 is no longer constructed as a local solution to a local problem, nor
does it refer to any of the immediately observable qualities of coral.
Instead, L10 transforms her definition into the observably more
abstract and complex form shown in Excerpt 7.8 and thereby socially
constructs herself as a student displaying her knowledge for the
benefit of the the teacher and her fellow students.

7.7. CONNECTING CA WITH BROADER ISSUES
IN SLA STUDIES

In the course of developing the conversation analysis set out in the
previous section, I have implicitly invoked the constitutent elements
of the model of listening comprehension outlined in Table 4.1 of
chapter 4 to explain the behaviors of L10 and her interlocutors. For
example, it is clear that when L10 starts to delimit the semantic
boundaries of the word *coral* by asserting in Excerpt 7.5 that it is food
for fish, that it is a beautiful colored stone, and that the Chinese
translation is *sanku*, she is drawing on her schematic knowledge of the
world, or what Gass and Varonis in their various papers called
familiarity.
　　　　What is also interesting about the data in this collection is
that the distinction between systemic and lexical knowledge in the
model is blurred. L10 and her co-members conceptualize the problem
to be resolved as a lexical problem. In working out what *coral* means,
L10 not only has to parse her interlocutors' unfolding turns to decide
when to take her own turns, she also has to reassemble, complexify,
and transform the raw material that she obtains in the first seven
excerpts into an academically valued logical definition in Excerpt 7.8.
In so doing, it is possible that L10 is trying to fit this raw material
into the kind of partly lexicalized, partly syntacticized structure
identified as a lexicalized sentence stem in chapter 1 (Pawley & Syder,
1983, cited by Skehan, 1998).[13]
　　　　L10 and her co-participants orient to their knowledge of how
to do interaction in the context of different speech exchange systems
(McHoul, 1978, 1990; Sacks et al. 1974; Schegloff et al. 1977). In
particular, repair sequences initiated by next turn repair initiators are
crucially implicated in L10's scaffolded breakthroughs in understanding (Hatch, 1978; Long, 1980,1981, 1983a, 1983b, 1985a) in the
student–student talk reproduced in Excerpt 7.5. These repairs also
contribute to L11 getting what *coral* means when L10 translates this
word into Chinese. Furthermore, L10 constructs her final definition
in Excerpt 7.8 from material recycled from previous student–student
and teacher–student talk. The product of all these efforts, namely,

the definition that L10 constructs in Excerpt 7.8, is thus clearly the result of a concerted group effort. It is in this sense that the language learning that occurs in the collection that constitutes appendix B can be considered as an instance of socially distributed, not just individual, cognition (Schegloff, 1991a).

It is also clear that in getting comprehended input in Excerpt 7.5 and in producing comprehended output in Excerpt 7.8, L10 has to deploy considerable syntactic, semantic, phonological, and morphological resources in order to develop her understanding of the word *coral*. I have already dealt at length with the kind of syntactic and semantic knowledge that L10 deploys; here, I briefly consider the kinds of phonological and morphological resources that L10 orients to as she struggles to understand the word *coral*. I begin with an analysis of the kind of morphological information to which L10 orients in Excerpt 7.3.

Excerpt 7.3
(Group work phase)

```
312 T:        ok when you're explaining that to the: uh to the
313 L9:       uh
314 T:        class or (+) whoever is <h> probably //you'll// have to say (+) what
315 L9:                             //((unintelligible  whisper))//
316 T:    *   corals (+) are //=because//
317 L10:*              //what is// corals
318 T:    *   yeah give a definition of //uh of corals//
319 L10:*                     //oh okay what// is corals maybe uh
320           (+)
321 L10:      or say-
322 T:        or give an example say //for// instance in //austra://lia (+) around
323 L9:                     //((unintelligible  whisper))//
324 L10:                             //oh yeah,//
325 T:    *   australia you get lots of barrier reefs
326 L9:  *   (barrier reefs)
327 T:        //o//therwise people might not kno:w (+) might not be
328 L10:      /oh//
329 T:        f//amiliar with that word//
330 L10:*    //oh okay, okay coral reefs//
331           (1)
              (NM: Class 1, Group 3)
```

At lines 316–319, T and L10 talk about "coral<u>s</u>." At line 325 and possibly at line 326, however, T and L9 respectively switch to talking about "barrier reefs." Whether she is conscious of what she is doing or not, L10 then uses this model to produce the noun phrase (NP) "coral reefs" at line 330, thus omitting the plural -s morpheme and transforming the word *coral* from a noun into an adjective.

Although this NP is the form that is recycled into the logical definition in Excerpt 7.8, there is some interesting evidence of both morphological and phonological backsliding in this excerpt. For example, L10 talks about "the: co[l]al reef you are one of the imp-very important, <hh> habitats (+) fo:r fish." Thus, she omits the plural -s morpheme on the noun *reef*. Furthermore, whereas in all of the previous excerpts she has correctly pronounced the /r/ sound in *coral*, she now pronounces this sound as /l/ in Excerpt 7.8. This seems to indicate that L10 is in the process of incorporating different dimensions of the new knowledge that she has recently acquired into her interlanguage and that this process is accompanied by the characteristic destabilization of previously correct forms.

Finally, I briefly address the question whether Gass' (1997) longitudinal model of L2 learning (see chapter 1) can also be used with cross-sectional data to account for learning on a moment-by-moment basis. More specifically, I ask whether there is any evidence that the stages of apperceived input, comprehended input, intake, integration, and output are observable in the data that constitute appendix B.

As shown in chapter 1, the apperception of input involves learners realizing that there is a gap between their present state of knowledge and the knowledge that they need in order to understand a piece of language that is new to them. In the data analyzed in this chapter, there are repeated instances of L10 explicitly noticing — in the sense of making public — that she does not know what the word *coral* means. More specifically, she initiates definition sequences in Excerpts 1, 2, 4, and 5. In Excerpt 3, L10 receives directions from the teacher that she should define this word for the rest of the class, and in Excerpt 8, she publicly makes this word a potentially noticeable item for her peers by defining the word for them.

As shown in the previous section, the way that L10 obtains input that allows her to comprehend in a preliminary fashion what *coral* means is through intensive conversational negotiation and modification of her interlocutors' talk. The conversational resources to which she orients include the collaborative construction of repair sequences mediated through equal and unequal power speech exchange systems. By orienting to these resources, L10 is able to put together a general semantic picture of *coral* as a kind of material (Excerpt 1) that is on the bottom of the sea (Excerpt 2 and the first part of Excerpt 5). In the second part of Excerpt 5, she then starts getting and developing the much more precise information that coral is a beautifully colored stony material, whose translation equivalent in Chinese is *sanku*.

When she uses these communication strategies, L10 is clearly integrating the word *coral* into her pre-existing schematic knowledge of the world. These conversational behaviors give observable discursive form to the psycholinguistic constructs of intake and integration, although it is probably impossible to distinguish between these two phases on the basis of the data analyzed in this chapter.[14] Finally, in Excerpt 8, L10 produces the complex, institutionally relevant definition of coral as comprehended output.

It therefore seems that Gass' model of L2 learning is indeed relevant for cross-sectional, moment-by-moment descriptions of understanding and learning as well as for longitudinal descriptions of SLA. However, the CA methodology that has been used to develop a preliminary validation of this model (and indeed other theoretical issues in SLA, such as Long's (1985a) research program to demonstrate the role of comprehensible input in SLA) also problematizes traditional psycholinguistic constructs such as cognition, understanding, and learning by describing these notions in terms of performed, socially distributed behaviors. As I claimed in chapter 2, the advantage of looking at these constructs in such an empirically driven way is that this allows analysts to document the specific, direct consequences of particular conversational behaviors for SLA. Despite the apparent smallness of the learning acts performed by L10, therefore, the learning behaviors described hold considerable theoretical interest for the SLA field.

7.8. CONCLUSION

I have shown in this chapter how a CA-based methodology can be used to pinpoint whether, when, and how L10 and her interlocutors oriented to the structure of conversation as a resource that enabled L10 to understand and acquire the word *coral*, at least in the short term. More specifically, I have argued that this methodology has five dimensions.

First, it is based on empirically motivated, emic accounts of members' interactional competence in different speech exchange systems. So, for example, I have shown that the differences in the sequential structure of definition sequences in student–student and teacher–student talk are artifacts of the speech exchange systems to which members orient as they construct these definitions.

Second, it is based on collections of relevant data that are excerpted from complete transcriptions of communicative events. Notice in this context that the use of collections allows analysts to check whether participants have actually comprehended input that they get during the course of talk-in-interaction. That is, thematically related collections of excerpts allow analysts to check whether members' assertions of understanding (which Hawkins, 1985, operationalizes as appropriate answers to questions; see also Firth, 1996) can be trusted, without having to rely on ethnographic techniques such as retrospective think aloud protocols.

Third, it is capable of exploiting the analytical potential of fine-grained transcripts. For example, the analysis of how members do repair in the different speech exchange systems exemplified in the excerpts discussed in this chapter is contingent on highly detailed transcriptions of participants' talk.

Fourth, as demonstrated by the conversation analysis set out in this chapter, it is capable of identifying successful attempts to learn, at least in the short term.

And finally, CA is capable of showing how meaning is constructed as a socially distributed phenomenon, thereby critiquing and recasting cognitive notions of comprehension and learning.

However, more empirical studies along the same lines are needed in order to further test the potential utility of this methodology for SLA studies. One interesting avenue of research would be to see whether the same methodology could be used to show how and why a learner fails to understand an unknown word or phrase under similar conditions. If the same methodology could successfully be used to examine this other side of the SLA coin, this would suggest that SLA researchers are indeed on the (or, at least, a) right track in attempts to understand the role of comprehended input in SLA. It is to this issue that I turn in chapter 8.

NOTES

1. That is, the teachers could teach what they wanted, how they wanted. This contrasts with the more experimental nature of much classroom research, in which the kinds of activities teachers use are pre-specified by the researcher and variables such as the composition of groups (in terms of gender and proficiency level, etc.) are also carefully controlled by the investigator.

2. Field notes indicate that although definitions are not unknown in ordinary conversations between fully competent native speakers, they may routinely never be instantiated. For example, an analysis of three transcripts of NS ordinary conversation, *Two Girls*, *SN-4* and *Auto discussion*, showed that no definitions occurred in these conversations and yet the data presented here indicate that they can be frequent in

L2 classrooms. Definitions may therefore be understood as a typically pedagogical form of talk.

3. For a stretch of talk to count as a definition, analysts cannot rely on their subjective impressions regarding participants' possible psychological motivations for doing a definition. They must be able to show on the basis of empirical data from the transcript that the participants are demonstrating to each other (and thus to the analyst) that a term is actually or potentially problematic and that it therefore needs to be explained.

4. In Excerpt 7A, the commenting turn at line 191 is achieved by L13 repeating her candidate gloss "under the water" with a low fall declarative intonation, which contrasts with her previous high rise questioning intonation at line 190.

5. When L6 refers to "five (+) number five" at line 562, he is referring to the fifth question in a list of comprehension questions prepared by the teacher.

6. See, for example, note 13 in chapter 4 and the use of the word "anybody" at line 207 of Excerpt 4B or at line 193 of Excerpt 2 in appendix B. This usage is clearly to be understood as "anybody except previous speaker."

7. However, the reverse is not true: There is no empirical evidence to suggest that all first position repairs are designed as definitions.

8. This is the sole example of a third position repair that I referred to in my discussion of repair in chapter 5.

9. Preliminary counts of the number of attempted and/or completed spoken definitions instantiated in the data indicated a total of 95 definitions had been produced in the four classes, of which 94 were ascertained to target words or phrases that occurred in the original source readings. Thus, only one definition focused on a word or phrase that had been locally occasioned by the talk itself. This occurred in Class 2 during a short period of time when the composition of the groups was being reconstituted and two students briefly engaged in light-hearted banter, which included a word that one of the participants did not understand. Due to the massive preponderance of definitions done on words or phrases from the source readings across the three classes, a number of passes were subsequently made through the data to

make sure that this figure was accurate. These passes identified two more definitions of words that were locally occasioned by the talk itself in Class 2, but which defined material offered as a paraphrase of a phrase from one of the source readings. This lop-sided distribution is probably caused by the way in which the tasks were set up by the teachers, who focused the learners' attention on the importance of understanding the source readings and thereby unconsciously directed the learners to organize their talk around these readings.

10. What L10 does at line 401 is to produce a short list of coral's attributes. As Lerner (1994) argued, the production of lists in the immediate environment of a repair may be used by conversationalists as a means of downgrading the directness of a prior repair. This demonstrates that, even when learners are confident that they have guessed the meaning of a word correctly, issues of face remain important.

11. As I pointed out in my discussion of this excerpt in chapter 2 (see Excerpt 2.1), it is legitimate in this instance to appeal to the linguistic biographies of the participants to make the argument that L10 has understood the word *coral*, since they themselves orient to whether they are speakers of Chinese or not.

12. Of course, this conclusion should not be taken as an empirically based justification for a reliance on traditional teacher-fronted instruction. Rather, it speaks to the infinite complexity of SLA, which is ultimately grounded in the practices of individuals constructing a specific conversational context.

13. Caution must be used against pushing this connection too far. The construct of lexicalized sentence stems is predicated on the need to explain the fluency of natural speech, despite the fact that speakers are acting under severe individual cognitive-processing constraints (Skehan, 1998). Yet, if fluent talk-in-interaction is analyzed from a CA perspective, members' consistent and massively pervasive ability to take turns and repair their own and others' talk with exquisite timing must be recognized. In other words, the conclusions drawn from cognitive and sociolinguistic approaches to SLA are difficult to reconcile at this point. Perhaps this situation is just another example of the inherent messiness of current SLA theory. Alternatively, perhaps these two positions are fundamentally irreconcilable. Only time will tell which is the correct conclusion.

14. These two phases are, in any case, closely intertwined in Gass'
model.

"We Cannot Get by Auschwitz": A Case of "Comprehended" Input That Does not Lead to Understanding and Learning

8.0. INTRODUCTION

In the previous chapter, I demonstrated how a conversation-analytic methodology can be used to document whether, when, and how learners could successfully co-construct learning, at least in the short term. In this chapter, I use exactly the same emic, collection-based methodology to investigate the conversational behaviors of a different group of students. These learners, who were enrolled at the same university, engaged in similar classroom tasks to those described in chapter 7 and also produced thematically related definition sequences that are similar to those produced by L10 and her interlocutors. In other words, the data in this chapter replicate rather closely the data described in the previous chapter.

However, in this instance, the problem item that is to be resolved is more complex. It consists of an idiomatic phrase, "We cannot get by Auschwitz," which, in the context of a debate on German reunification in 1990, is heavily laden with metaphorical meaning. More specifically, in the context of an article written by the left-wing German writer Günter Grass, this phrase means that Germany's Nazi past is an insuperable impediment to German reunification.

These data are particularly interesting from an SLA perspective for two reasons. First, as Hatch et al. (1990) pointed out, there is currently no theory of SLA that has attempted to account for the acquisition of either vocabulary or metaphorical language.[1] These data therefore speak rather directly to an underresearched area of SLA studies. Second, although the learner in question, L15, was able eventually to understand the meanings of the constituent elements of this phrase, she never worked out why Grass believed that Auschwitz was a barrier to German reunification. In other words, she never comprehended its larger symbolic meaning. As the CA that is provided in this chapter demonstrates, L15's inability to understand what Auschwitz means is not so much a linguistic problem as a lack of appropriate schematic knowledge of the world.

We are therefore faced with an interesting problem. L15 and her interlocutors used the same kinds of conversational resources and strategies that L10 and her peers used to get comprehended input. Yet she was not nearly as successful as L10 was. The obvious question to ask, of course, is: why? Furthermore, the data contained in the collection reproduced in appendix C speak to other important issues in SLA, such as why comprehended input is necessary but not sufficient for language learning to occur. Most importantly, these data ultimately lead to a problematization of the notions of comprehended input and output.

In the remainder of this chapter, I briefly lay out some background information about the participants, the tasks, and the data base. I then provide a detailed CA of the data reproduced in full in appendix C, in which I analyze how the participants conceptualize the problem that they have to solve. Next, I explain why the input L15 got from her interlocutors was not sufficient for her to comprehend the metaphorical meaning of the problem item. Finally, I discuss the ways in which the construct of comprehended input must be complexified in order to account for data such as those discussed in this chapter.

8.1. THE PARTICIPANTS AND THE TASKS

The data analyzed in this chapter come from an intermediate-level ESL class for undergraduates that was taught at a midwestern US university during spring semester, 1990. The class lasted 50 minutes and was taught by an experienced teacher through a task-based, small group methodology, using pedagogical materials that the teacher had developed for this class. The task that was recorded and transcribed for research purposes required students to read and discuss thematically related readings on what was at the time the potential reunification of Germany. The task was accomplished during two distinct phases of group work. During the first phase, students were divided into five groups (see Fig. 8.1).

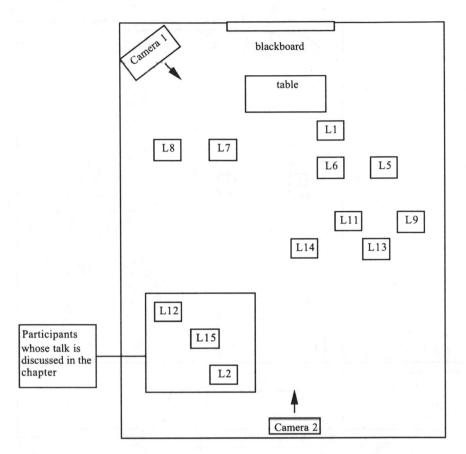

FIG. 8.1 Layout of Class 2, Phase 1.

Each group read one of five articles. Group members then discussed their source reading to ensure that they all understood the position that the author of their article took on the question of whether German reunification was desirable or not. In the second phase, the five groups were dissolved and three larger groups were formed (see Fig. 8.2).

Thus, these newly formed groups were composed of learners who had read different articles. This jigsaw task design (Johnson, 1982) set up a five-way information exchange in which each individual learner had to give and also get information from their peers so that they could later write an essay on the pros and cons of German reunification.

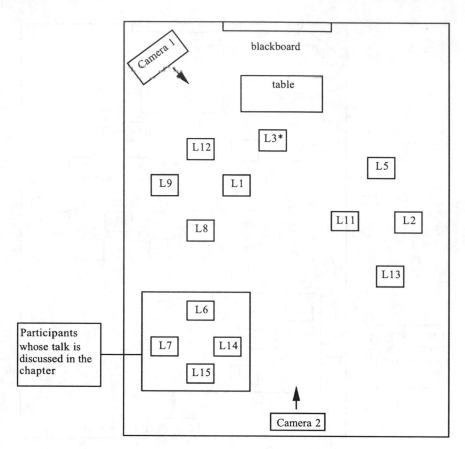

* L3 arrived late and did not participate in Phase 1

FIG. 8.2 Layout of Class 2, Phase 2.

8.2. THE DATA

The recorded talk was transcribed using the techniques described in
chapter 3 and yielded a total of 10 transcripts (8 group transcripts, 1
transcript of the teacher's talk, plus a summary transcript of all the
definition talk that occurred in this class).   The data consist of a
collection of seven thematically related oral definitions (Excerpts 1–4
and 6–8), plus one other excerpt (Excerpt 5) in which participants
comment on their understanding of the work they have done during
previous oral definitions (see appendix C for the complete collection).
These data have been excerpted from the full transcripts of the class.
The definitions focus on the larger meaning of the word "Auschwitz"

and/or the phrase "We cannot get by Auschwitz." This item is problematic for one learner in particular, who is identified here as L15. This learner is a member of group 4 during phase 1 and then joins group 2 during phase 2.

The first four instances of these oral definitions, plus the excerpt containing the participants' commentary on their understanding of what they have done so far, occur during the first phase of small group work, whereas the remaining three definitions occur during the second phase. The teacher participates in three of the seven definitions and is also an indirect protagonist in the excerpt containing the learner commentary on what they have achieved. However, the teacher does not display any evidence of hearing this learner commentary, as her participation in the talk in this excerpt is limited to making a public announcement to the class as a whole.

Two of the definitions in which the teacher participates occur within minutes of each other at the beginning of the first phase; the third occurs toward the end of the second phase some 15 minutes later. Thus, the teacher does not have access to any of the student–student talk that occurs in five out of the eight excerpts that constitute the database. As in chapter 7, I number the excerpts reproduced in this chapter according to their sequential position in the original transcript, not according to the order in which I discuss them here. Finally, in order to make the data more accessible to readers, I have broken up some of the larger excerpts (which run to over 100 lines of text) into smaller, self-contained chunks of data.

8.3. CONVERSATION ANALYSIS

The true nature of the problem the learners wish to solve is highly ambiguous because the learners' analyses of what is problematic are not stable. Consequently, the information they provide to each other, and also to the teacher, is inconsistent from one excerpt to the next.

As shown in Excerpt 8.1, L12 begins at line 83 by identifying the proper noun "Auschwitz" as an unknown lexical item. At lines 84–85, L15 attempts to address this question but indicates at lines 88–89 that she can't help L12. Consequently, L12 calls the teacher over at line 91 to obtain help. At line 94, the teacher turns this question over to other learners in other groups, momentarily transforming a small group task into a whole class activity.

Excerpt 8.1

82   ...
83 L12:   uh (1.3) could you tell me what is ausch (+) //ausch[v]it//

```
84 L15:   *                                          //that- don't// have it-
85        *     you kno(h)w (+) <hh> (hhh)
86 L12:         ausch[v]it
87              (ı)
88 L15:   *     I can't get that ausch[v]ltz (++) they don't want to know  (1) maybe (2)
89        *     maybe that's german way (2) they didn't ((unintelligible whisper))
90              (1)
91 L12:   *     <h> ((T's name))
92 T:           yeah
93 L12:         what's the meaning of (+) ausch[v]itz?
94 T:     *     d- uhm does anybody here know what auschwitz was?
               (NM: Class 2, Phase 1, Group 4)
```

At lines 103–105, L6, who is a member of another group, then provides the public explanation that Auschwitz was a Nazi concentration camp during WWII.

Excerpt 8.1 (continued)

```
103 L6:   *     uh its a concentration camp, and (+) uh they would send some uh (+) jews
104       *     there, to (++) to gas them to kill them (++) uh during the world war two
105       *     (+) in germany (1) //I don:'t kno:w I'm// not (+) quite sure
106 L12:                          //for (+) jews,//
               (NM: Class 2, Phase 1,Group 4)
```

At line 114, which occurs immediately after the conclusion of some further public talk (not reproduced here) between L6 and another learner, L12 checks privately whether L15 has understood L6's definition of Auschwitz. When it transpires at line 116 that L15 has not understood this word, L12 provides her own definition at lines 117–119 and 122, explaining that "Auschwitz" was a building where Hitler gathered Jews. However, as is clear from lines 128, 130 and 132, this second definition does not help L15 understand what Auschwitz means. Thus, the problem remains unresolved for L15.

Excerpt 8.1 (continued)

```
114 L12:  *     you understand, (+) ausch[v]itz,
115             (1)
116 L15:  *     n://o//
117 L12:  *     //au//sch[v]itz it's (2) probably during world war two: <hhh> that hh
118       *     (++) ah I can't draw (1) straw. (1) hit- gathered the jewish (+)
119       *     in (+) one place?
120 L15:        yeah,
121 †T:         write your answers on the //paper because you'll be separating// ...
122 L12:  *                                //that's a building? and that means//
123             ausch[v]itz?
124 L15:        oh the building?
125 L12:        yeah
```

```
126 L15:    oh
127 L12:    do you think so? did you remember that?
128 L15:  * no I don't kno(h)w
129 L12:    oh h
130 L15:  * I don't remem//ber//
131 L12:                    //I// think so
132 L15:  * can you give me
133 L12:    I don't know (+) <hh>
            (NM: Class 2, Phase 1, Group 4)
```

Excerpt 8.2 reveals that the nature of the problem that confronts L12 and L15 is more complex than understanding a single lexical item. The problem consists of understanding why Grass claims that Auschwitz poses a moral impediment to the unification of Germany. At lines 211–212, 214, 216, 218, and 220 of Excerpt 8.2, L12 asks why Grass is afraid of a strong united Germany. At lines 223–225, L15 identifies the passage in the reading which explains why Grass believes that Germany can't be trusted. L12 then comments on this information at lines 230–232 and 234–237. As shown by the surprised way in which she does saying "<hu:::> (1) go:d," at lines 236–237, L12 seems to have a revelation of some kind here about what she is reading; however, due to the fact that much of the talk at lines 235–236 is unintelligible, it is unclear precisely what L12 has understood. Given that L15 has focused the discussion on the part of the passage that explains the link between Auschwitz and Grass' anti-reunification stance, it would be analytically consistent to claim that it is at this point in the lesson that L12 potentially understands the nature of Grass' argument.

Excerpt 8.2

```
211 L12:  * did he solve (+) af- (+) this also solve (+) like uh (+) afraid of (++)
212       * strong germany? (+) in europe?
213 L15:    where,
214 L12:  * did he <h> afraid of (1) f- ok (+) why
215 L15:    he- (+) yeah- he h (+) //he//
216 L12:  *                    //why// he against
217 L15:    he is against a united germany for (+) why oh
218 L12:  * //why
219 L15:    becau:se,
220 L12:  * why //
221 †T:     //we have to tape it (+) put it this to you here? (++) and that goes like that
222         h ok.//
223 L15:  * I think you see we have a reason <hh> (1) we cannot get hh (+) we
224       * shouldn't even trust (au[ʃəʃiʃ]) ((L15 is reading from the article from"we
225       * cannot get" onward))
226 L12:    <h> the:n (+) she:
227         (+)
```

```
228 L15:    I think
229          (+)
230 L12:  * she: (1) she will no- (+) he's a- (+) he is afraid of that uh <hhh> u:::h (++)
231       * <hh> is a stron:g germany in:: (++) d- (+) during second world war but
232       * before second world war (+) this is uh
233 L15:    (world //war,)//
234 L12:  *            //like-// so <hh> h uh we cannot get by ausch[v]i (+)
235       * ausch[v]it ((reading)) <hhh> ((unintelligible)) we try: (++) (reading)) I
236       * think we already ((unintelligible)) because ausch[v]itz belong (++)
237       * <hu:::> (1) go:d ((high pitch on the in-drawn breath; L12 sounds very
238         surprised))
239         (1) (bad) (1.3) we finally are ourselves
240         (+)
241 L15:    ((unintelligible muttered reading)) we can't get by au[s]witz
            (NM: Class 2. Phase 1,Group 4)
```

It is interesting that there is no independent corroborating evidence in Excerpt 8.2 that L15 has understood why Auschwitz might be viewed as an obstacle to German unification, even though it is L15 who has correctly identified the part of the article where Grass explains his position on this issue. This is confirmed by evidence contained in the following excerpt.

At line 272 of Excerpt 8.3, L12 again checks whether L15 has understood the significance of Auschwitz. L15's negative response at lines 273–275 indicates to L12 that L15 has not, in fact, understood why Auschwitz poses a problem for German reunification. After presumably thinking about this during the 10-second silence at line 277, L12 then calls on the teacher for help.

Excerpt 8.3

```
272 L12:  * so hh ((whisper)) (1) do you know (++) //that means//
273 L15:  *                                //I can't understand// why? (+) he
274       * (+) <h> (+) why he doesn't want (+) united germany (+) I mean (1.3) we
275         can't get (1) hhh
276         (1)
277 L12:  * we can't get (10) <hh> hh (+) ((T's name))
            (NM: Class 2, Phase 1, Group 4)
```

The way in which L12 asks for help is rather misleading. At line 279, L12 uses the word "still," implying that the problem about which she is seeking help is the same problem as the one identified in Excerpt 8.1, namely, the word "Auschwitz." The teacher again redistributes the question to another student, L2, whom she asks to join L12 and L15 at lines 281, 283, 286, and 291–292.

Excerpt 8.3 (continued)

```
277 L12:    we can't get  (10) <hh> hh (+) ((T's name))
278 T:       yeah?
279 L12:  *  I still
280            (+)
281 T:     *  I have uhm (+) ((L2's name)) reading your article.
282 L12:    uh huh,
283 T:     *  ((L2's name)) have you finished?
284            (1)
285 L2:      yeah just (1) I'm in the last sentence
286 T:     *  o//k.// (+) could you move here with,
287 L12:    //ok//
288            (+)
289 L12:    yeah
290            (+)
291 T:     *  'cause they're having trouble with the article and I think you may be able
292        *  to clear something up h
293 L2:      ok
             (NM: Class 2, Phase 1,Group 4)
```

At line 294, L12 confirms the focus on the word "Auschwitz" by asking the teacher whether "Auschwitz" is a building — a gloss which derives from the follow-up L12 initiated at lines 114–128 of Excerpt 8.1 after L6's first definition at lines 103–105 in the same excerpt. The teacher then directs L2 to explain what "Auschwitz" means (see Excerpt 8.3, lines 296 and 299). In the private talk that follows between L2, L12, and L15, the information which L2 provides therefore initially focuses on explaining what "Auschwitz" was. More specifically, Auschwitz is identified as a death camp (lines 301 and 306) during the second world war (lines 305), where Hitler killed six million Jews (lines 309 and 311). Finally, it is glossed as the most important concentration/death camp at lines 311-314.

Excerpt 8.3 (continued)

```
294 L12:  *  yeah ausch- ausch[v]itz is a building?
295 L2:      <h> auschwitz ((whisper))
296 T:     *  no its a- uhm ((L2's name)), (++) you know  what's auschwitz is
297            don't you.
298 L2:      yeah
299 T:     *  ok could ////you// explain it//// to ((L12's name))
300 L12:              //ok//
301 L2:   *          //the death camps//
302 L12:    (uhh) (1) I think <h> is where[z ə] they keep (huh)
303 L15:    yeah (h)
304 L12:    (keep why there) this //article//
305 L2:   *                  //remem//ber (+)  when there is second world war I
306        *  (+)  there is the death camps,
```

```
307          (+)
308 L15:     //what,//
309 L2:    * //that// hitler killed like <h> six million uh
310 L12:     uh huh yeah
311 L2:    * jews so (+) they were taken to the: (+) the most important uh
313        * concentration uh death camp <h> when (+) where he killed all those
314        * people (+) was ausch- auschwit- au- //whatever I'm saying//
             (NM: Class 2, Phase 1, Group 4)
```

At line 315, L15 asks whether Auschwitz is a place name, which L2 confirms at line 316. At line 318, L2 again confirms that this understanding is correct but also repeats the previous information that Auschwitz was a death camp. At this juncture, L12 also repeats the information that Auschwitz is a place at line 319 and then proceeds to make the larger connection at lines 321–325, 327–328, 330 and 332 between Auschwitz as a symbol of the Nazi era in Germany and the problems that the history of Nazism presents for the reunification of East and West Germany.

Excerpt 8.3 (continued)

```
315 L15:   * //is that the name of the// place,
316 L2:    * yeah
317 L15:     ok
318 L2:    * yeah (+) that was the (+) the name of the death camp
319 L12:   * place, (+) oh and //uh//
320 L2:                     //au//schwitz
321 L12:   * <hh> and uh (+) he draw a (+) german has a very strong idea <hh> we
322        * are very (++) goo:d nation in the world (+) like a (+) strong german and
323        * we wi- (+) we will be ((unintelligible)) we are very s- (+) intelligen:t (+)
324        * goo:d <h> (1) people in the world (+) they believe (+) then, <hhh> they
325        * killed jewish
326 L15:     uh
327 L12:   * during second world wa:r <h> then <h> I think< (+) he <h> he (+) he
328        * was afraid of that <hh> too much a strong germany (+) do you think so?
329 L2:      <hh>
330 L12:   * why (+) why he
331 L15:     we- well he
332 L12:   * against a united <h> yeah (+) germany
             (NM: Class 2, Phase 1, Group 4)
```

However, as demonstrated by the evidence in lines 335 and 336–338, neither L2 nor L15 understands the larger connection that L12 is making here (the question to which L2 refers at line 335 is a comprehension question in the students' materials, which asks them to define what the phrase "We cannot get by Auschwitz" means). As a result, at lines 339–341, 343, 346, 348, 350–351, 353–355, 357, 360, 362–365, 367, 370 and 372, L12 engages in a further explanation of why countries like Poland and France might be opposed to German reunification. But, as shown by L15's response at line 373 to this information, L15 focuses instead on economic reasons why a reunified Germany might not be in the best interest of other countries. This suggests either that L15 has understood the article differently from L12 or that she does not understand L12's historical analysis.

Excerpt 8.3 (continued)

```
332 L12:     against ////a// united// <h> yeah (+) germany
333 L15:          //so//
334 L2:          //a united germany//
335 L2:    * I don't (+) I don't (1) h I don't get the an//swer to that question//
336 L15:   *                                  //yeah (+) I// can't get any-
337        * why  (+) he (+) strongly against it (+) I mean
338        * //<hh> you can't get-// (+) sh //hhh// ((sigh))
339 L12:   * //<hh> you know//          //hhh// ((sigh)) (1) yeah it's uh (++) you
340        * know (+) I had a chance to talk with (+) polish <hhh> she was so (+) she
341        * don't like (+) deutsch (+) deut- (+) deutsche? (+) german people?
342 L2:      uh huh
343 L12:   * <hh> yeah? (+) because uh (++) because (+) ausch[v]itz wa- (+) by hitler?
344 L2:      uh //huh//
345 L15:          //uh// huh
346 L12:   * <hhh> polish was (++) uh h (+) controlled
347 L2:      poland (+) //polish//
348 L12:   *             //poland// (+) poland was con//trolled// by german <hh>
349 L2:                                          //yeah ok//
350 L12:   * then <h> they (+) they still  (+) remember we:ll (+) what (+) wha:t (+)
351        * happened what was (+) what given  (+) to the polish people
352 L2:      uh //huh//
353 L12:   *    //du//ring second world war <hh> and (+) also french people believe
354        * (+) knew  <hh> they: (++) I think they probably french people don't[s]
355        * that's uh like uh german people (+) because it also german <hh> (hhh)
356 L15:     (hhh)=
357 L12:   * =they don't (huh) it's (+) german (+) want to make a bi::g german
358        * (+)
359 L2:      uh
360 L12:   * country,
361 L2:      ((unintelligible))
362 L12:   * then they (1) the army <h> face (+) into the world (++) get into the fran-
363        * france? (++) and it- probably (+) he afraid of <hh> it will be happen
364        * agai::n, (+) stro:ng germany have a <hhh> hhh (+) a s- (+)
365        * //try to// <hh> yeah-
366 L15:     //empire//
367 L12:   * e//mpi:re// or //try//: //to// <hh>//conquer a//  con(h)quer a
368 L15:     //empi:re//     //to//   //oh//     //conquer the//
369 L15:     a
370 L12:   * (huh huh huh huh)
371 L15?:    all over europe?
372 L12:   * yeah (+) uh do you think so? right?
373 L15:   * maybe he's think that conquer the economy or what-
```

```
374 L2:    not (+) not //all the//
375 L15:                //every//
376 L12?:  o- economy
377 L15:   oh=
378 L12:   =oh so (+) it got (+) political yeah,
379L15:    political, (+) oh
380        (1)
           (NM: Class 2, Phase 1, Group 4)
```

Unfortunately, it becomes clear from the subsequent excerpts of Auschwitz-related talk that occur during Phase 1 that L15 has still not understood the larger significance of Auschwitz in Grass' argument. For example, at lines 460 and 462–464 of Excerpt 8.4, L15 initiates more definition talk on this topic, but this time, she identifies the entire phrase "We cannot get by Auschwitz," rather than the single lexical item "Auschwitz," as the real problem.

Excerpt 8.4

```
460 L15:  * we cannot get by auschwitz ((reading))
461 L12:    what,
462 L15:  * why (+) meaning we cannot get by auschwitz (+) I mean (+) what it (+)
463       * what does it (+) this- (+) I mean (+) what is (++) we cannot get by
464       * auschwit[ʃ] (1.3) uhm
            (NM: Class 2, Phase 1, Group 4)
```

In Excerpt 8.5, after the teacher asks the learners at lines 530–535, 537, and 550 to form new groups to do the information exchange task that constitutes Phase 2, L15 clearly states at lines 539, 541, and 548 that she still does not understand why Auschwitz constitutes a barrier to German reunification.

Excerpt 8.5

```
530 T:    * yeah ok <h> what I want to do (+) is form groups (+) I'd like to separate
531       * you no:w (+) into groups I don't (++) care what group you get into (+) as
532       * long as there's no member of your pair or your (+) threesome (+) ok just
533       * (+) <h> you're going to take your information to the new group (+) ok?
534       * (+)
535       * because you're all reading different things. <h> so:
536 L2:     did you //each answer the question,//
537 T:    *            //split up //and// form a group//
538 L12:                       //how//
539 L15:  * what,
540 L2:     we got an idea how to answer the question,
541 L15:  * (hhhh) <hh) I don't yet (+) no, (+) unclear to me(h)
            ...
548 L15:  * I cannot do it? (hhhh)
            ...
```

550 T: * so (+) let's get <u>three</u> groups (1) <u>three</u> groups. ok?
          (NM: Class 2, Phase 1, Group 4)

During Phase 2, L15 is supposed to tell her new group partners
(L6, L7, and L14) why Auschwitz might be significant in a discussion
about the pros and cons of German reunification. Clearly, however,
L15 is not in a position to do this. Not surprisingly, therefore, L15
initiates further work with her new conversational partners to try to
resolve this problem. In Excerpt 8.6, which is a schismatic
conversation between L7 and L15 (that is, L7 and L15 form one
conversational pair while L6 and L14 form another; the two pairs are
simultaneously talking about different topics), L15 again initiates some
definition talk about the Auschwitz topic. Thus, at lines 93–94, 96,
and 99, L15 identifies her problem as the entire phrase, "We cannot
get by Auschwitz." As a result, L7 and L15 begin to do some
preliminary definition work at lines 101–108, which initially focuses
on the word "Auschwitz."   More specifically, L7 and L15
cooperatively construct the information that Auschwitz is a place
name at lines 101–108. Tantalizingly, L7's turn at line 103 is almost
unintelligible, but based on L15's claim of understanding at line 104,
whatever L7 says at line 103 seems not to be new information for
L15.

Excerpt 8.6 (schism)

93   L15: * excuse me ((L7's name)) do you understand what's this (+) we cannot get
94   * by auschwit[ʃ] ((reading)) I don't understand what we can't get by (1.5)
95   L7:   oh <hh> (+) uh we-
96   L15: * we can't get by I'm not su- I don't understand what is the meaning
97   L7:   we have every reason to be afraid of ((unintelligible)) ((L7 is reading; her
98   turn trails off into an unintelligible mutter))
99   L15: * we cannot get by (+) what's the meaning ((L15's turn overlaps the end of
100   L7's turn))
101 L7:   * (+) what is auschwitz (+) it is a::
102 L15: * I think it's a place because::
103 L7:   * ((unintelligible)) a ((unintelligible)) right,
104 L15: * yeah I guess that (+) I already understand that
105 L7:   * //concentra//tion camp,
106 L15: * //((unintelligible))//
107   (+)
108 L7:   * is that the one
             (NM: Class 2, Phase 2, Group 2)

At line 109, L15 expands the focus of the definition talk by
highlighting the phrasal verb "get by" as potentially problematic. This
expansion triggers a number of glosses of this verb by L7; for example,
at lines 110–112, L7 defines the meaning of "get by" as "you cannot

s:kip" and "you have to go through it." At line 114, L15 claims to have understood these glosses but at lines 115 and 117, L15 further refines her question by again asking why the phenomenon of Auschwitz poses a problem for the reunification of Germany. As shown by the change of state token "oh" produced by L7 at line 118, this clarification leads L7 to explain at lines 119–120 and 122 what happened at Auschwitz. Furthermore, at lines 124–125, L7 links this information to the larger question posed by L15 by glossing "get by" as "we never will forget about this."

Excerpt 8.6 (schism) (continued)

```
109 L15:  * yeah it cannot get by what is this
110 L7:   * we cannot get by ((reading)) <h> I think (+) you cannot s:kip like you
111       * cannot (+) you have to go through it, (+) you cannot get by (+) like (+)
112       * you  have to go through it, say (+) we cannot get by <hh> 'cause
113         (1)
114 L15:  * yes I understand
115       * //you (+) why he would <hh> because uh (++) the reason why//
116 L7:     //have every reason to be afraid of ((unintelligible))//
117 L15:  * he doesn't want t- a united germany is //be//cause that
118 L7:   *                                        //oh//
119 L7:   * because (+) you know the concentration camp, (+) then hitler he he tried
120       * to kill (+) in nazi germany,
121 L15:    yeah?
122 L7:    * ok (+) and the jewish (+) //right,//
123 L15:                               //yeah?//
124 L7:    * ok (+) so (+) say (+) he: he said we cannot get by that we- we never will
125       * forget about this (+) //to the end//
126 L15:                          //he says it's// (+) history:
            (NM: Class 2, Phase 2, Group 2)
```

On the surface, this explanation seems to be useful to L15. More specifically, at lines 128–129, L15 seems to understand that Grass is arguing that Auschwitz poses a serious moral problem for the proponents of German reunification. Indeed, at line 137, L15 latches L7's previous turn at line 136, so that the two participants cooperatively construct the following definition: L7: "we cannot get (+) by (+) Auschwitz <hh> this means that <hh> he=" L15: "=we can't forget we can't forget."

Excerpt 8.6 (schism) (continued)

```
127 L7:     uh huh (+) see, (+) //says this is really terrible//
128 L15:  *                     //says it's-it's like-// he doesn't wa:nt to: (+)
129       * //a u//nited germany
130 L7:     //I mean//
131 L15:    like=
132 L7:     =I guess (+) he says (+) this is  terrible
```

```
133 L15:      oh=
134 L7:       =a lot (+) they killed a lot of people right,
135 L15:      uh=
136 L7:    *  =we cannot get (+) by (+) auschwitz <hh> this means that <hh> he=
137 L15:   *  =we can't forget we can't forget
138 L7:       yeah and say (+) it's uh (+) this is really (1) big historical //eve//nt
139 L15:                                                                    //yeah//
140 L7:       nobody
141 L7:       could (+) forget about it, you know
              (NM: Class 2, Phase 2, Group 2)
```

Finally, at line 142, L7 checks that L15 has understood. At line 144, L15 not only claims understanding but, at line 149, even repairs L7's incipiently incorrect conclusion at lines 147–148 that Grass supports reunification. L7 accepts this repair as correct at lines 150–151 and further substantiates this interpretation by saying at line 155 that Germans cannot get by Auschwitz because Hitler killed a lot of people, statements with which L15 seems to agree at lines 152, 154, and 157.

Excerpt 8.6 (schism) (continued)

```
141 L15:      oh yeah //yeah//
142 L7:    *          //get// by (+) d'you- do you get that, (+)
143           //I think that ((unintelligible))//
144 L15:   *  //I think so// because uh (+) you know <hh> as (+) //it's//
145 L7:                                                           //so//
146 L15:   *  very (into) history and to (+) //into//
147 L7:    *                                 //uh huh// so this (+) does this guy: (+) agree
148        *  with uh (+) that
149 L15:   *  no (+) usually (+) against (+) //the german//
150 L7:    *                                 //again-// ok yeah <hh> oh- I- I guess uh
151        *  'cause I <h> if you ever been to a u uh- united germany right,
152 L15:      yeah
153 L7:    *  you cannot get (+) go by (+) auschwitz right, (+) this //is//
154 L15:                                                             //yeah//
155 L7:    *  really important he killed (+) a lot of people who cannot
156           ((unintelligible))
157 L15:   *  oh right
              (NM: Class 2, Phase 2, Group 2)
```

It seems as if Excerpt 8.6 might fulfill the same breakthrough function as Excerpt 7.5 does in chapter 7 when L10 understands what *coral* means. However, as shown by Excerpt 8.7, the conclusion that L15 has finally understood what "We cannot get by Auschwitz" means in the context of Grass' article proves unfounded. As shown by lines 217–220 and 223–225, L15 is still unable to explain the meaning of this phrase to the entire group of learners, L6, L7, L14 and L15.

Excerpt 8.7

```
217 L15:  *  ... my article is about (+) what auschwit[ʃ] or what (++) gu:h
218       *  (+) duh duh (1) this guy doesn't want a united germany because what
219       *  will we (+) he say can't by auschwit[ʃ] and I d(h)on't (h)understand what
220       *  is <hh>
221 L6:      I'm- I'm sorry I didn't //un//derstand what you said
222 L15:                            //we//
223 L15:  *  no (+) we cannot get by auschwit[ʃ] ((reading)) do you know- do you- do
224       *  you know what is the meaning- meaning I don't understand it (1.3) it's
225       *  something like the auschwit[ʃ] and what ab(h)out i(h)t
             (NM: Class 2, Phase 2, Group 2)
```

In Excerpt 8.8, more evidence appears that corroborates the analysis that L15 has still not understood this phrase. During this excerpt, the learners are producing a written summary of their conclusions on an overhead transparency, so that they can share their information with the rest of the class at a later date. L14 is the secretary of the group and is writing up the information. More specifically, at lines 256 and 259, L14 is summarizing Grass' position. At lines 271 and 276, L14 asks for specific information concerning why Grass considers Auschwitz to be a barrier to German reunification. At line 278–279, L15 attempts to provide the reason but is quickly forced to admit at lines 282 and 285–286 that she does not really understand why Auschwitz is such a problem for reunification, even though at line 285–286 she recycles information culled from Excerpt 8.6 that it has something to do with German history.

Excerpt 8.8

```
256 L14:  *  <h> hh grass is (+) <h> strongly, (1) <h> against ((L14 is writing as
257          he speaks))
258 L7:       against, (+) this guy is kind of a
259 L14:  *  <h> the unification ((L14 is writing as he speaks))
             ...
271 L14:  *  so what's- what's with the auschwit[ʃ] (+) au[s] ((whisper))
             ...
276 L14:  *  s- so why- why was it so important in the title (+) to the article
277 L6:       he's (+) what,
278 L15:  *  why:, (1) (huh hh) yeah (+) this is the reason why he doesn't want (+) a
279       *  united germany
280          (+)
281 L14:      because (+) of au//sch[v]itz?//
282 L15:                    //((unintelligible))// (it does)=I//:: not sure//
283 L6:                                          //he's afraid// of u:h (+) what
284          happened in ausch[v]itz might happen again?
285 L15:  *  I don't know (+) I don't know but (+) I think that it it (+) history of uh
286       *  (+) it would (+) au[switʃ]
             (NM: Class 2, Phase 2, Group 2)
```

Further talk on this topic ensues between lines 287 and 323, which are not reproduced here. At lines 324 and 327–328, however, L15 again explicitly states that she does not understand what "We cannot get by Auschwitz" means, at which point L6 calls on the teacher to break the deadlock at lines 331, 334 and 336:

Excerpt 8.8 (continued)

```
324 L15:  *  a:nd, (+) //I don't understand what// is (+) we can't get by
325 L6:                      //then we are-//
326 L6:      w::- we're listening
327 L15:  *  uh (+) I mean (+) and I s- (+) I till (+) I tol- I tell you that <h> I don't
328       *  understand what is the meaning we cannot get by auswit[ʃ] (hh) (++)
329 L6:      ok
330 L15:     <hhh>
331 L6:   *  there is a problem here she //doesn't// underst(h)and
332 L15:                                 //(huh h)//
333 L7:      (huh)
334 L6:   *  and we don't understand what <h> //what means exactly this//
335 L15:                                       //why we can't get auswit[ʃ]// (+) oh
336 L6:   *  we cannot get by ausch[v]itz
             (NM: Class 2, Phase 2, Group 2)
```

It is worth making three points about the talk that ensues from lines 336–358. First, with the exception of two unimportant turns at lines 338 and 351, L15 does not actively participate in any of the interaction that occurs in the presence of the teacher. Second, whereas L6 attempts at lines 339–340 to explain the phrase "We cannot get by Auschwitz" in terms of the larger debate on German reunification, the teacher focuses more narrowly on glossing the phrasal verb "get by" at lines 357–358 as "you can never forget." Unbeknownst to the teacher, this is precisely how L7 had previously defined this verb at lines 124–125 of Excerpt 8.6. Furthermore, it is also how L7 and L15 had cooperatively defined this verb at lines 135–136 of the same excerpt (see the previous analysis of this excerpt). Consequently, the teacher's intervention in Excerpt 8.8, which provides us with a classic example of the structure of unequal power discourse getting in the way of learning (Pica, 1987), does not give L15 any new information.

Excerpt 8.8 (continued)

```
336 L6:      we cannot get by ausch[v]itz
337 T:       ok (+) what d'you think it might mean
338 L15:  *  (uh huh) (+) (uh huh //h)//
339 L6:   *                     //it// might [b]ean (+) probably u::h we::: (+) cannot
340       *  have another ausch[v]itz again if uh germany unites
```

341   o:r maybe <hh>
342 T: does it mean <u>that</u>?
343 L6:   I- I //[ni:]-//
344 L14:   //do//es it-
345 L6:   I didn't read it
346 L14:   does //it-//
347 L6:   ////I[z]-// I don't know//
348 T: //what do you think//
349 L14:   does it-
350 T: o h
351 L15:   *   //no//
352 L14:   //do//es it mean that u:hm //<hh>//
353 L6:   //I didn't read it//
354 L14:   that if the uni- if (+) the germany unite again <h> the ausch[v]it might
355   exist, <hhh>
356   (+)
357 T: *   yeah. that's ba- we. can't- when you can't get by something that's <hh>
358   *   you can never forget.
359 L14:   right.
360   (+) ((T moves away from the group))
361 L6:   oh (+) 'cause
362   (1.3)
363 L15:   well (+) all right (+) all right (hh)
364 L6:   does it make sense?
365 L15:   yeah it's makes sense
                 (NM: Class 2, Phase 2, Group 2)

Finally, the coda of student–student talk that occurs at lines 360–364, when T has moved away from the group, also suggests that L15 still does not understand what "We cannot get by Auschwitz" means. Note that in the question–answer adjacency pair that occurs at lines 363–364, L15's claim of understanding is extracted from her almost under duress by L6's previous turn. More specifically, given that L6 has just gone out on a limb on L15's account and has publicly lost face vis-a-vis the teacher and his peers as a result of his intervention, L15 is under great pressure to say that she has finally understood what this problem phrase means. However, L15 does not offer any independent information of her own to demonstrate to L6 (and therefore to analysts) that she has understood what "We cannot get by Auschwitz" means. Furthermore, her immediately preceding conversational behavior at lines 361–362 is extremely tentative. More specifically, she is silent for 1.3 seconds following L6's turn at line 360 and then produces a very ambivalent turn at line 362 marked by a prefatory "well," two pauses and a laughter token.

To summarize, although L15 is able to gloss "Auschwitz" as a "concentration camp" and "get by" as "not forgetting" Auschwitz, there is no positive evidence (e.g., the unambiguous comprehended input and output that L10 got and produced in Excerpts 5 and 8 of appendix B), that L15 has understood what a concentration-camp-as-symbol-of-Nazism is. Similarly, there is an equal lack of observable evidence that L15 has understood the larger question of why Auschwitz might therefore be considered a problem for German reunification.[2] In contrast, there is a wealth of negative evidence that she has not understood the metaphorical meaning of the phrase "We cannot get by Auschwitz."

More specifically, L15 has difficulty in formulating precisely what her problem is to her various interlocutors during the two phases of group work. For example, in Excerpts 8.1–8.5, she seems to focus principally on the word "Auschwitz" only, whereas in Excerpts 8.6–8.8, she mostly focuses on the entire phrase, "We cannot get by Auschwitz." Consequently, L15's conversational partners spend a lot of time trying to explain this phrase in terms of its constituent linguistic elements, alternately switching back and forth between a focus on the word "Auschwitz" and the whole phrase "We cannot get by Auschwitz" throughout the eight excerpts of definition talk on this topic. Although there is evidence that L7 has correctly understood during Excerpt 6 that L15's problem may not be primarily linguistic, this insight gets lost in subsequent excerpts. Most importantly, this information never becomes available to the teacher, who focuses exclusively on linguistic meaning in Excerpt 8.8.

If L15's problem in understanding the metaphorical meaning of this phrase is not linguistic, then what is the nature of her problem? There is no evidence in all of the Auschwitz-related collection that L15 ever draws on the kind of schematic knowledge of the world that L10 used so successfully in the coral-related collection. An explanation that is consistent with the data is that L15 does not know anything about the history of the Holocaust. For this reason, she is not able to make the link between Auschwitz-as-symbol-of-Nazi-genocide and objections to the reunification of East and West Germany.

As already noted, unlike L10 in Excerpt 5 of appendix B, L15 never elaborates on a previous speaker's talk by volunteering new information about what Auschwitz is. She always stays within the bounds of information she receives from others or from the source reading. Furthermore, as shown in Excerpts 8.1, 8.3, and 8.6, L15 also fleetingly displays to her interlocutors on several occasions that she is uninformed about the Holocaust. For example, in response to L12's turn at lines 117–119 of Excerpt 8.1 — which, incidentally, contains L12's elaboration that it was Hitler who put the Jews in Auschwitz — L15 says that she does not know or remember anything about Auschwitz at lines 128 and 130 respectively.

Excerpt 8.1

```
117  L12: *  ... ausch[v]itz it's (2) probably during world war two: <hhh> that hh
118       *  (++) ah I can't draw (1) straw. (1) hit- gathered the jewish (+)
119       *  in (+) one place?
120  L15:    yeah,
121  †T:     write your answers on the //paper because you'll be separating// ...
122  L12:                                //that's a building? and that means//
123           ausch[v]itz?
124  L15:    oh the building?
125  L12:    yeah
126  L15:    oh
127  L12:    do you think so? did you remember that?
128  L15: *  no I don't kno(h)w
129  L12:    oh h
130  L15: *  I don't remem//ber//
131  L12:             //I// think so
          (NM: Class 2, Phase 1, Group 4)
```

Of course, this hesitancy on L15's part may be due to the fact that she does not understand what L12 is trying to tell her at this particular juncture in the discourse — a logical possibility since the information that Auschwitz was a building is hardly very useful in this context. The trouble-indicating pause at line 306 of Excerpt 8.3, combined with the rising intonation with which L15 says "what" at line 307, both suggest that L2's information in lines 304–305 concerning the existence of death camps is new to L15.

Excerpt 8.3

```
304 L2:  *                    ... remember (+) when there is second world war one
305      *  (+) there is the death camps,
306      *  (+)
307 L15: *  what,
          (NM: Class 2, Phase 1, Group 4)
```

In a similar vein, the high rising intonation with which L15 says "yeah" at lines 121 and 123 of Excerpt 8.6 again suggests that the information about Hitler attempting to exterminate the Jews (contained in L7's turns at lines 119–120 and 122) is at the very least quite surprising to L15.

Excerpt 8.6

```
119 L7:  *  because (+) you know the concentration camp, (+) then hitler he he tried
120      *  to kill (+) in nazi germany,
121 L15: *  yeah?
```

122 L7:   * ok (+) and the jewish (+) //right,//
123 L15: *   //yeah?//
        (NM: Class 2, Phase 1, Group 4)

      I therefore maintain that the most likely reason for L15's otherwise unexplainable lack of comprehension is that, although she may have understood the individual words that make up the phrase "We cannot get by Auschwitz," she did not understand their larger discoursal and cultural significance. I now link the empirical findings of this conversation analysis to broader issues in SLA.

8.4. CONNECTING CA WITH BROADER ISSUES IN SLA STUDIES

The collection analyzed in this chapter raises some interesting methodological and theoretical issues for SLA researchers. I argue that CA is a powerful methodological resource for SLA studies. In terms of SLA theory construction, I suggest that SLA specialists might revisit with profit how learners' problems are categorized, and how the role that comprehended input plays in the acquisition of L2s is conceptualized.

8.4.1. Methodological Issues: The Power of CA

As I argued in chapter 2, CA methodology should be:

- based on empirically-motivated, emic accounts of members' interactional competence in different speech exchange systems;
- based on collections of relevant data that are excerpted from complete transcriptions of communicative events.
- capable of exploiting the analytical potential of fine-grained transcripts;
- capable of identifying both successful and unsuccessful learning behaviors, at least in the short term;
- capable of showing how meaning is constructed as a socially distributed phenomenon, thereby critiquing and recasting cognitive notions of comprehension and learning.

      Given that until now there has been a lack of empirical evidence to substantiate theoretical claims that comprehension and production gains lead directly to acquisition (Pica, 1987), these are rather ambitious goals, particularly the one encapsulated in bullet #4. However, the conversation analyses carried out in this and the preceding chapter demonstrate that CA methodology is capable of identifying not only the behaviors that suggest that a learner has understood and learned new language (at least in the short term) as a result of social interaction but also those behaviors that imply the contrary result.

These are significant achievements, whose methodological and theoretical importance transcends what might wrongly be argued to be the limited nature of individual learning acts. More specifically, to go back to the photographic analogy with which I began this book, CA successfully fills in important details of the SLA landscape that other methodologies would otherwise have left blank. Furthermore, I claim that there is currently no other methodology available to SLA researchers that is either so methodologically conservative or so well-suited to simultaneously demonstrating (a) whether specific acts of understanding and learning occur or do not occur as a result of learners engaging in specific communicative events, (b) when breakthroughs in understanding occur or do not occur during the course of talk-in-interaction, (c) how learners achieve or do not achieve such breakthroughs as a result of learners engaging in specific communication strategies, and (d) why learners are ultimately successful or unsuccessful in their attempts to learn. At the same time, it is clear that embracing a CA methodology to pinpoint understanding and learning behaviors problematizes a number of theoretical questions in SLA. It is to these issues that I now turn.

8.4.2. Theoretical Issues: On the Categorization of Learners' Problems

It is abundantly clear from the data analyzed in this and the preceding chapter that the participants in both classes conceptualized the problem items to be solved as lexical in nature. This member analysis is key to understanding how the participants set about trying to resolve these problems. In the data discussed in chapter 7, this analysis was correct. However, even in this relatively simple case, the kinds of linguistic resources that L10 and her co-participants had to deploy in order for her first to understand this word and then produce the elaborated comprehended output documented in the last excerpt of the *coral* collection drew simultaneously on discoursal, syntactic, morphological, and phonological levels of language.

In the "Auschwitz"-related collection, however, the issues are far more complex. Although the participants try to treat the issue of what "We cannot get by Auschwitz" means as a lexical problem, they clearly have a great deal of trouble specifying the precise nature of this problem. Consequently, they explore at some length different syntactic and semantic formulations of the problem. Indeed, in

Excerpt 6 of this collection, they even briefly explore the historical, cultural, and symbolic significance of the problem phrase.

In short, although the ultimate results of L10 and L15's efforts are not the same, it is rather striking that members in both classes consistently integrate linguistic resources from all levels of language in their attempts to solve the problems with which they are faced. Furthermore, the range of linguistic resources and communicative strategies that members deploy in their attempts to resolve these two problems is unexpectedly rich. These findings suggest that although L2 learners may ascribe particular importance to vocabulary in terms of what they explicitly notice as problematic in the flow of talk-in-interaction, they probably learn far more than individual words as a result of a focus on lexis. These results also suggest that further study of the range of linguistic resources and communicative strategies that members deploy would likely provide other interesting insights into how members' folk categorizations of the problems they encounter during talk-in-interaction facilitate or impede behaviors that promote understanding and learning. Research of this kind would also develop, in ethnomethological terms, Slimani's (1992) ethnographic work on these issues.

8.4.3. Theoretical Issues: On the Role of Comprehended Input for SLA

Whereas the data analyzed in chapter 7 provide substantial micro-analytic confirmation of the importance of negotiated comprehended input as a resource for SLA, the data presented in this chapter are much more ambiguous. Although L10 and L15 engage in similar tasks and employ many similar problem-solving strategies, L15 ultimately does not enjoy the same level of success in understanding her problem item as L10 does in understanding hers. Part of the reason for this variability has to do with the fact that L10 is trying to understand a single concrete noun, whereas L15 is dealing with a phrase with complex symbolic associations (for a review of psycholinguistic factors thought to be involved in the acquisition of new vocabulary, see Ellis, 1994). Nonetheless, this variability raises important questions that speak to the issue of whether and how repair functions as a resource for SLA. More specifically, the data in these two chapters strongly suggest that although repair-as-a-source-of-negative-evidence may be necessary, it is not sufficient to promote language learning (see also Long, 1996).

Why is this so? First, in both collections of data, there is strong behavioral evidence that (for problems that members define in lexical terms, at least) participants are unable to make profitable use of the information they get as a result of repairing each other's talk unless these repairs connect at some point with what they already know about the world. In other words, the mechanical resource of repair is, by itself, insufficient to promote language learning because interactional and systemic knowledge must combine with schematic knowledge in order to develop lexical knowledge.

Second, as I noted in chapter 6, although appropriate repair is a resource for maintaining intersubjectivity, it is also a potentially face-threatening, and therefore dispreferred, activity, both for others and for current speaker. This is especially true when it is done to excess (Aston, 1986). In such a situation, the social imperative of maintaining intersubjectivity may at times take precedence over the achievement of language-learning goals, even in a language classroom. One manifestation of this phenomenon entails members avoiding initiating any repair work at all. As I have shown in my analysis of the "Auschwitz"-related collection in this chapter, there is observable evidence that L15 allows other learners (L12 in Excerpts 8.1 and 8.3 and L6 in Excerpt 8.8) to initiate repairs with the teacher on her behalf. An explanation for this behavior that would be consistent with the data is that, as she engages in more and more repairs on the same problem item, the more embarrassed L15 becomes at having to make repeated, public displays of her ignorance.[3] Thus, a structural reason why repair cannot be sufficient to promote successful language acquisition is that engaging in repair can at times lead to participants looking foolish in the eyes of their fellow members. And when learners lose face in this way (what Krashen, 1982 termed the negative effects of a *raised affective filter*), they are unlikely to risk engaging in further risky repair behavior. It may further be speculated that this line of research may provide interesting insights into the phenomenon of fossilization.

The data in this and the preceding chapter also complexify what it means to understand input. One dimension of this complexity is that comprehension is not a simple all-or-nothing construct. Even when breakthrough moments in understanding occur, as in Excerpt 7.5, this behavior is contextualized in a matrix of other talk, all of which may contribute tiny but ultimately relevant micro-moments of understanding to an overall change in cognitive state (see, e.g., how L10 reassembles different words and phrases taken from previous excerpts to construct her final definition of *coral* in Excerpt 7.8).

This point highlights another aspect of the complexity of the construct of understanding. Even when focus is on the efforts of one particular individual to comprehend new language, understanding is not solely an act of individual cognition but a behavior that is collaboratively constructed by members as an act (or, more accurately, a series of acts) of socially distributed cognition. Thus, even though L10 and, to a much lesser extent, L15 both undergo changes of state in their levels of understanding of previously unknown language, they do so as a direct result of the contributions of their more knowledgeable conversational partners (see Excerpts 7.5 and 8.6 for particularly clear examples of co-constructed meaning).

Finally, another important dimension of the complexity of this construct is encapsulated in the phrase "levels of understanding" (Gass, 1997). L15 arguably understands the constituent parts of "We cannot get by Auschwitz." However, her failure to understand the more important symbolic meaning of this phrase shows that comprehension is a process that cannot always be reduced to parsing the phrase structure of a problem clause, as the problem that has to be solved entails a lack of schematic, not systemic knowledge.

8.5. CONCLUSIONS

I have demonstrated the kinds of insights that SLA researchers can gain into language-learning processes by using the micro-analytic methodology of CA. More specifically, I have attempted to lay out how CA methodology can be used to show whether, when, how, and why understanding and learning occur as conversational behavior. I have then shown how the results of such an analysis can be related to current thinking in SLA about the possible role of negotiated talk in acquiring new language. In so doing, I stress that I am not proposing yet another theory of SLA. Rather, I am proposing an alternative way of confirming the social interactionist hypothesis.

The alternative I am proposing may at times sound heretical. However, as Kasper (1997) argued, heresy can sometimes illuminate what orthodoxy finds obscure.

> To conclude on a heretic note, if the excellent microanalytic tools of CA were incorporated into a language socialization approach to SLA, we might be able to reconstruct links between L2 discourse and the acquisition of different aspects of communicative competence that have been largely obscure so far. (p. 311)

Although I have not chosen to link the use of CA to a language-socialization approach to SLA, it is clear that using CA methodological techniques may in fact be the only viable means of successfully implementing important aspects of Long's (1985a) research program into the role that conversational modifications play in promoting SLA. To the extent that this research program has been, and continues to be, one of the most productive in the recent history of SLA studies, the incorporation of insights from CA has the potential to make further significant contributions to the field.

NOTES

1. Of course, this is not to say that the acquisition of vocabulary has not been studied. See for example, Coady and Huckin (1997) and Harley (1995). However, as Ellis (1994) pointed out, there has been almost no research on the incidental acquisition of vocabulary as a result of modified conversational input.

2. It might be suggested that it would be appropriate at this point to use an ethnographic retrospective talking-aloud protocol to find out what L15 understands. However, given how much trouble L15 has with understanding this phrase, there is no guarantee that the use of such a protocol would elicit a correct assessment of her state of knowledge at the time that she produces the talk (see appendix C).

3. Although L15 gets the benefit of the subsequent public feedback that L12 and L6 receive (see Slimani, 1992, on the psycholinguistic utility of such talk), it is important to note that most of this feedback (particularly that given during the talk reproduced in Excerpt 8.8) is off the mark.

Appendix A:
Transcription Conventions

Transcription conventions are abridged and adapted from Atkinson and Heritage (1984b, pp. ix–xvi).

Identity of speakers

T:	teacher
L1:	identified learner (Learner 1)
L:	unidentified learner
L3?:	probably Learner 3
LL:	several or all learners simultaneously

Simultaneous utterances

L1: //yes//
L2: //yeh//   simultaneous, overlapping talk by two speakers

L1: //huh?//oh// I see//
L2:   //what//
L3: //I dont get it//   simultaneous, overlapping talk by three (or more) speakers

Contiguous utterances

=   a)   turn continues at the next identical symbol on the next line
                     b)   if inserted at the end of one speaker's turn and the beginning of the next speaker's adjacent turn, it indicates that there is no gap at all between the two turns

Intervals within and between utterances

(+) (++) (1)   (+) = a pause of between .1 and .5 of a second;
                     (++) = a pause of between .6 and .9 of a second;
                     (1) (2) (3) = pauses of one, two or three seconds respectively.

Characteristics of speech delivery

?	rising intonation, not necessarily a question
!	strong emphasis, with falling intonation
yes.	a period indicates falling (final) intonation
so,	a comma indicates low-rising intonation suggesting continuation
go:::d	one or more colons indicate lengthening of the preceding sound; each additional colon represents a lengthening of one beat
no-	a hyphen indicates an abrupt cut-off, with level pitch
bec<u>au</u>se	<u>underlined</u> type indicates marked stress
SYLVIA	capitals indicate increased volume
°the next thing°	degree sign indicates decreased volume
<hhh>	in-drawn breath
hhh	exhaled breath
(hhh)	laughter tokens

Commentary in the transcript

((coughs))	comment about actions noted in the transcript, including non-verbal actions
((unintelligible))	indicates a stretch of talk that is unintelligible to the analyst
. . . . (radio)	single parentheses indicate unclear or probable item

Other transcript symbols

†T:	† indicates talk (in this case, by T) from a parallel conversation to the one in which current speakers are engaged
includ[ə]s	brackets indicate phonetic transcription
*	an asterisk in the margin of a transcript draws attention to a particular phenomenon the analyst wishes to discuss
at the bottom of the sea,	bold font shows material which is subsequently re-used in later talk
(NM: Class 1, Group 1)	Initials after an excerpt identify the source of the transcript being quoted

Appendix B: "Coral" Collection

Excerpt 1
(Group work phase)

```
163 L10:   <hh> hhhh what is th- what is the (+) coral (+) what's ((whisper)) (+) I
164        don't know (h)
165 L11:   just- look at it (+) as a (+) an m- material that's all (+)
166 L9?:   uhm don't worry about it
167        (+)
           (NM: Class 1, Group 3)
```

Excerpt 2
(Group work phase)

```
187 L10:   excuse me what is c-o-r-a-l
188        (+)
189 T:     can I: (+) open //(h)// <h> (++) get an idea (+) see where's that <h>
190 L10:              //(h)//
191 L10:   I don't know whether the-
192        (+)
193 T:     corals (+) does anyone know? (+) where you find corals?
194 L9:    corals (+) u- underwater //you mean? under the-//
195 T:                             //uh huh,//
196        (+)
197 T:     that's right yeah some-
198 L9:    //under// the sea? //in the sea//
199 T:     //down-//
200 L10:              //oh hh//
201 T:     ex- counting some shells o//:r I don't// know s-
202 L9:                            //shells yeah//
203        (+)
204 L10:   at the bottom of the of the s- (+) sea?
205        (+)
206 T:     yeah
207        (+)
208 L9:    at the bottom
209 L10:   o:h
210 L9:    //yes//
211 L10:   //oh// ok oh I see (+) thank you <h>
212        (1)
213 T:     have you divided this up into (+) sections between you
           (NM: Class 1, Group 3)
```

Excerpt 3
(Group work phase)

```
312 T:     ok when you're explaining that to the: uh to the
313 L9:    uh
```

314 T: class or (+) whoever is <h> probably //you'll// have to say (+) what
315 L9:   //((unintelligible whisper))//
316 T: corals (+) are //=because//
317 L10:   //what is// corals
318 T: yeah give a definition of //uh of corals//
319 L10:   //oh okay what// is corals maybe uh
320   (+)
321 L10:   or say-
322 T: or give an example say //for// instance in //austra://lia (+) around
323 L9:   //((unintelligible whisper))//
324 L10:   //oh yeah,//
325 T: australia you get lots of barrier reefs
326 L9:   (barrier reefs)
327 T: //o//therwise people might not kno:w (+) might not be
328 L10:   //oh//
329 T: //familiar with that word//
330 L10:   //oh okay, okay **coral reefs**//
331   (1)
332   (NM: Class 1, Group 3)

Excerpt 4
(Group work phase)

337 L10:   what is uh corals I don't know
338 L11:   did you read (in) about corals
339 L9?:   no
340   (++)
            (NM: Class 1, Group 3)

Excerpt 5
(Group work phase)

376   ((L10 is reading her article to herself)
377 L10:   coral. what is corals
378   (4)
379 L9:   <hh> do you know the under the sea, under the sea,
380 L10:   un-
381 L9:   there's uh::
382   (+)
383 L9:   //how do we call it//
384 L10:   //have uh some coral//
385 L9:   ah yeah (+) coral sometimes
386   (+)
387 L10:   eh includ[ə]s (+) uh includes some uh: somethings uh-
388   (++)
389 L10:   //the corals,// is means uh: (+) s somethings **at bottom of**
390 L9:   //((unintelligible))//
391 L10:   //**the**// **sea**
392 L9:   //yeah,//
393 L9:   **at the bottom of the sea,**

394 L10: ok uh:m also is a food for is a food for fish uh and uh
395   (+)
396 L9:   food?
397   (+)
398 L10: foo-
399 L9:   no it is not a food it is like a stone you know?
400 L10: oh I see I see I see I see I see I know I know (+) I see (+) a whi- (+) a kind of
401   a (+) white stone <h> //very beautiful//
402 L9:   //yeah yeah// very big yeah
403   //sometimes very beautiful and// sometimes when the ship moves
404 L10: //I see I see I ok//
405 L9:   //ship tries ((unintelligible)) I think it was the ((unintelligible; the final
406   part of this turn is overlapped by L10's next turn))
407 L10: //oh I see (+) I see the chinese is uh (+)// sanku
408   (++)
409 L11: unh?
410 L10: sanku
411   (+)
412 L9:   what
413 L10: c//orals//
414 L11:   //corals//
415 L9:   corals oh okay
416 L10: yeah
         (NM: Class 1, Group 3)

Excerpt 6 (simplified)
(Group work phase)

41 9 L10: **fissel** (++) **fissel** ((whisper)) (+) <h> **I think (+) the coral is also is a** °**fis**°
420   (("fis" is whispered)) **is a fi-** f:: ((unintelligible whisper))
421 L9:   fi-shing?
422 L10: if- (1) how to s-   how to spell <hhh>
423   (1)
424 L10: //**fis**-//
425 L9:   //**foss**//**il** (+) **f**//**ossil**//
426 L10:   //**fossil?**// how to F U ? ((L9 and L10 spell the word
427   "fossil" together))
428 L9:   f- F-O
429 L10: F-o
430   (+)
431 L9:   //**f-o-S-S-I-L**//
432 L10: //**f-o-S-S-**//**I-L**
433   (+)
434 L9:   **fossil is a**
435 L10: **I-**
436 L9:   //**fossil is uhm**//
437 L10: //**I also think**// **of the- coral (+) is a is a kind of fossil**
         ...
         (NM: Class 1, Group 3)

Excerpt 7 (simplified)
(Group work phase)

```
520 L11:   ok (+) excuse me (+) uh: what what does it mean hab- (+) habi-
521        (+)
522 T:     habitats
523 L11:   habitats
524 T:     yeah (+) you had that word as well (+) what do you think it means
525        (++)
526 L10:   <hhh>//hh//
527 T:              //you// all spoke about habitats didn't it
528 L10:   uh:m
529 T:     the //m//ost important (1) habitat
530 L10:        //I//
531        (++)
532 L10:   I think (+) the habitats is the:[əm] (+) e//nvironment uh// and the
533 L9:                                            //environment//
534 L10:   environment and uh (1) uhm
535        (++)
536 L9:    is it is //it the: nearest environment//
537 L10:           //for for (+) for the fish// you (mea be:) (hh)
538 T:     <h> yeah what would be another word for a habitat then (+) it's like
539        (1)
540 T:     //it's hli-//
541 L11:   //I ha//ve no idea ((in an exasperated tone))
542 L9:    //situation//
543 T:     //'s like the whole// (+) situation (+) //home//
544 L10:                                             //home//
           (NM: Class 1, Group 3)
```

Excerpt 8
(Whole class oral discussion phase)

```
923 L10:   ... <h> in my section I think the main point is the: <hh> raising of
924        the sea (+) sea level <hh> we are accompanied uh global
925        tempera increasing <hh> (+) so these (+) put he co[l]al (+) at
926        [l]isk. <h> I think the co[l]al is the kind of fossil (+) <h>
927        fossil at the: botto of the sea. <hh> the: co[l]al reef
928        you are one of the imp- very important, <hh> habitats (+)
929        fo:r fish that support th[']:m more than (+) <h> one (+) more
930        than one third of topic- topical species. <hh> the habitats
931        is the: home (+) is the home for animal living <hh> so this is
932        very important (+) very important <hhh> so: now, the
933        conversationalist uh want to find some [v]ay: (+) to save
934        these uh (+) to: (+) solve this problem.
           (NM: Class 1, Whole class)
```

Appendix C:
"We Cannot Get by Auschwitz"
Collection

Excerpt 1

081 L12: yeah this qu//estion// (++) so (+) what d'you think.
082 L12:   //ok//
083 L12: uh (1.3) could you tell me what is ausch (+) //ausch[v]it//
084 L15:   //that- don't// have it-
085   you kno(h)w (+) <hh> (hhh)
086 L12: ausch[v]it
087   (+)
088 L15: I can't get that ausch[v]itz (++) they don't want to know (1) maybe (2)
089   maybe that's german way (2) they didn't ((unintelligible whisper))
090   (1)
091 L12: <h> ((T's name))
092 T: yeah
093 L12: what's the meaning of (+) ausch[v]itz?
094 T: d- uhm does anybody here know what auschwitz was?
095 L6:   yeah
096 T: //you want to explain it//
097 L6:   //concentration camp//
098   (+)
099 T: //explain it to her//
100 L6:   //ausch[v]itz//
101 T: explain it to ((L12's name))
102   (+)
103 L6:   uh its a concentration camp, and (+) uh they would send some uh (+) jews
104   there, to (++) to <u>gas</u> them to kill them (++) uh during the world war two
105   (+) in germany (1) //I don:'t kno:w I'm// not (+) quite sure
106 L12:   //for (+) jews,//
107 L6:   if uh auschwitz ausch[v]itz (+) was in germany or in in uh
108 L11: //no (+) it's in poland//
109 L1:   //no it was poland//
110 L6:   poland ok
111   (+)
112 L11: in germany it's dachau for example it's: (+) near munich
113   (2)
114 L12: you understand, (+) ausch[v]itz,
115   (1)
116 L15: n://o//
117 L12:   //au//sch[v]itz it's (2) probably during world war two: <hhh> that hh
118   (++) ah I can't draw (1) straw. (1) hit- gathered the jewish (+)
119   in (+) one place?
120 L15: yeah,
121 †T: write your answers on the //paper because you'll be separating// ...
122 L12:   //that's a building? and that means//
123   ausch[v]itz?

124 L15:   oh the building?
125 L12:   yeah
126 L15:   oh
127 L12:   do you think so? did you remember that?
128 L15:   no I don't kno(h)w
129 L12:   oh h
130 L15:   I don't remem//ber//
131 L12:   //I// think so
132 L15:   can you give me
133 L12:   I don't know (+) <hh>
134 L15:   ((L15 reads in an unintelligible mutter))
135 L12:   ausch[v]it I::: ((L12 reads in an unintelligible mutter; she overlaps L15's
136   turn after .3 second)) I don't (+) I don't understand it's never going to
137   ((unintelligible)) I'm ashamed to know ((reading))
           (NM: Class 2, Phase 1, Group 4)

Excerpt 2

211 L12:   did he solve (+) af- (+) this also solve (+) like uh (+) afraid of (++)
212   strong germany? (+) in europe?
213 L15:   where,
214 L12:   did he <h> afraid of (1) f- ok (+) why
215 L15:   he- (+) yeah- he h (+) //he//
216 L12:   //why// he against
217 L15:   he is against a united germany for (+) why oh
218 L12:   //why
219 L15:   becau:se,
220 L12:   why//
221 †T: //we have to tape it (+) put it this to you here? (++) and that goes like that
222   h ok.//
223 L15:   I think you see we have a reason <hh> (1) we cannot get hh (+) we
224   shouldn't even trust (au[ʃəʃiʃ]) ((L15 is reading from the article from "we
225   cannot get" onward))
226 L12:   <h> the:n (+) she:
227   (+)
228 L15:   I think
229   (+)
230 L12:   she: (1) she will no- (+) he's a- (+) he is afraid of that uh <hhh> u:::h (++)
231   <hh> is a stron:g germany in:: (++) d- (+) during second world war but
232   before second world war (+) this is uh
233 L15:   (world //war,)//
234 L12:   //like-// so <hh> h uh we cannot get by ausch[v]i (+)
235   ausch[v]it ((reading)) <hhh> ((unintelligible)) we try: (++) ((reading)) I
236   think we already ((unintelligible)) because ausch[v]itz belong (++)
237   <hu:::> (1) go:d ((high pitch on the in-drawn breath; L12 sounds very
238   surprised))
239   (1) (bad) (1.3) we finally are ourselves
240   (+)
241 L15:   ((unintelligible muttered reading)) we can't get by au[s]witz
           (NM: Class 2, Phase 1, Group 4)

Excerpt 3

272 L12:	so hh ((whisper)) (1) do you know (++) //that means//
273 L15:	//I can't understand// why? (+) he
274	(+) <h> (+) why he doesn't want (+) united germany (+) I mean (1.3) we
275	can't get (1) hhh
276	(1)
277 L12:	we can't get (10) <hh> hh (+) ((T's name))
278 T:	yeah?
279 L12:	I still
280	(+)
281 T:	I have uhm (+) ((L2's name)) reading your article.
282 L12:	uh huh,
283 T:	((L2's name)) have you finished?
284	(1)
285 L2:	yeah just (1) I'm in the last sentence
286 T:	o//k.// (+) could you move here with,
287 L12:	//ok//
288	(+)
289 L12:	yeah
290	(+)
291 T:	'cause they're having trouble with the article and I think you may be able
292	to clear something up h
293 L2:	ok
294 L12:	yeah ausch- ausch[v]itz is a building?
295 L2:	<h> auschwitz ((whisper))
296 T:	no its a- uhm ((L2's name)), (++) you know what's auschwitz is
297	don't you.
298 L2:	yeah
299 T:	ok could ////you// explain it//// to ((L12's name))
300 L12:	//ok//
301 L2:	//the death camps//
302 L12:	(uhh) (1) I think <h> is where[zə] they keep (huh)
303 L15:	yeah (h)
304 L12:	(keep why there) this //article//
305 L2:	//remem//ber (+) when there is second world war one
306	(+) there is the death camps,
307	(+)
308 L15:	//what,//
309 L2:	//that// hitler killed like <h> six million uh
310 L12:	uh huh yeah
311 L2:	jews so (+) they were taken to the: (+) the most important uh
312	concentration uh death camp <h> when (+) where he killed all those
313	people (+) was ausch- auschwit- au- //whatever I'm saying//
314 L15:	//is that the name of the// place,
315 L2:	yeah
316 L15:	ok
317 L2:	yeah (+) that was the (+) the name of the death camp
318 L12:	place, (+) oh and //uh//
319 L2:	//au//schwitz
320 L12:	<hh> and uh (+) he draw a (+) german has a very strong idea <hh> we

```
321              are very (++) goo:d nation in the world (+) like a (+) strong german and
322              we wi- (+) we will be ((unintelligible)) we are very s- (+) intelligen:t (+)
323              goo:d <h> (1) people in the world (+) they believe (+) then, <hhh> they
324              killed jewish
325  L15:        uh
326  L12:        during second world wa:r <h> then <h> I think< (+) he <h> he (+) he
327              was afraid of that <hh> too much a strong germany (+) do you think so?
328  L2:         <hh>
329  L12:        why (+) why he
330  L15:        we- well he
331  L12:        against ////a// united// <h> yeah (+) germany
332  L15:                    //so//
333  L2:                 //a united germany//
334  L2:         I don't (+) I don't (1) h I don't get the an//swer to that question//
335  L15:                                              //yeah (+) I// can't get any-
336              why (+) he (+) strongly against it (+) I mean
337              //<hh> you can't get-// (+) sh //hhh// ((sigh))
338  L12:        //<hh> you know//              //hhh// ((sigh)) (1) yeah it's uh (++) you
339              know (+) I had a chance to talk with (+) polish <hhh> she was so (+) she
340              don't like (+) deutsch (+) deut- (+) deutsche? (+) german people?
341  L2:         uh huh
342  L12:        <hh> yeah? (+) because uh (++) because (+) ausch[v]itz wa- (+) by hitler?
343  L2:         uh //huh//
344  L15:           //uh// huh
345  L12:        <hhh> polish was (++) uh h (+) controlled
346  L2:         poland (+) //polish//
347  L12:                   //poland// (+) poland was con//trolled// by german <hh>
348  L2:                                          //yeah ok//
349  L12:        then <h> they (+) they still (+) remember we:ll (+) what (+) wha:t (+)
350              happened what was (+) what given (+) to the polish people
351  L2:         uh //huh//
352  L12:           //du//ring second world war <hh> and (+) also french people believe
353              (+) knew <hh> they: (++) I think they probably french people don't[s]
354              that's uh like uh german people (+) because it also german <hh> (hhh)
355  L15:        (hhh)=
356  L12:        =they don't (huh) it's (+) german (+) want to make a bi::g german
357              (+)
358  L2:         uh
359  L12:        country,
360  L2:         ((unintelligible))
361  L12:        then they (1) the army <h> face (+) into the world (++) get into the fran-
362              france? (++) and it- probably (+) he afraid of <hh> it will be happen
363              agai::n, (+) stro:ng germany have a <hhh> hhh (+) a s- (+)
364              //try to// <hh> yeah-
365  L15:        //empire//
366  L12:        e//mpi:re// or //try//: //to// <hh>//conquer a// con(h)quer a
367  L15:        //empi:re//    //to//   //oh//    //conquer the//
368  L15:        a
369  L12:        (huh huh huh huh)
370  L15?:       all over europe?
371  L12:        yeah (+) uh do you think so? right?
372  L15:        maybe he's think that conquer the economy or what-
```

```
373 L2:     not (+) not //all the//
374 L15:                  //every//
375 L12?:   o- economy
376 L15:    oh=
377 L12:    =oh so (+) it got (+) political yeah,
378 L15:    political, (+) oh
379         (1)
            (NM: Class 2, Phase 1, Group 4)
```

Excerpt 4

```
460 L15:    we cannot get by auschwitz ((reading))
461 L12:    what,
462 L15:    why (+) meaning we cannot get by auschwitz (+) I mean (+) what
463         it (+) what does it (+) this- (+) I mean (+) what is (++) we cannot get by
464         auschwit[ʃ] (1.3) //uhm//
465 L12:              //((unintelligible))// <h> I think (+) he:[m] (1) <h> u::h (+) I
466         got (1) <h> we cannot repea:t such history.
467 L15:    je-
468 L12:    re//pea:t// (+) repea:t
469 L15:       //repeat the history,//
470 L15:    can't get //by auswi-//
471 L12:                //agai:n//
472 L15:    oh (++) oh (++) they- (+) they ((unintelligible))
473         (3)
474 L12:    if: (2.3) we shouldn't even try that ((reading)) (+) then (+) they grade (+)
475         then (++) germans shouldn't even try: to <hhh> (+) have a idea (1) about
476         (+) ausch[v]itz, or what.
477 L15:    u:hm
478 L12:    they got (+) very stron:g
479 L15:    u:h,
480 L12:    they could (+) control (+) the whole  country and its surrounding country
481         <hhh>
482         (++)
483 L15:    oh
484         (+)
485 L12:    did- did- we should (+) not even try:
486         (1.3)
            (NM: Class 2, Phase 1, Group 4)
```

Excerpt 5

```
530 T:      yeah ok <h> what I want to do (+) is form groups (+) I'd like to separate
531         you no:w (+) into groups I don't (++) care what group you get into (+) as
532         long as there's no member of your pair or your (+) threesome (+) ok just
533         (+) <h> you're going to take your information to the new group (+) ok?
534         (+)
535         because you're all reading different things. <h> so:
536 L2:     did you //each answer the question,//
537 T:                //split up //and// form a group//
538 L12:               //how//
```

539 L15:   what,
540 L2:   we got an idea how to answer the question,
541 L15:   (hhhh) <hh> I don't yet (+) no, (+) unclear to me(h)
542 L2:   uh huh,
543   (1.3)
544 T: u:hm just (+) the only thing I don't you want you to do is be in a group
545   with ((L5's name)) (+) and ((L6's name)).
546 L6:   ah hah
547 T: you can pick any group you want as long as you're not together.
548   (+) 'cause
549   you've all got the same information
550 L15:   I cannot do it? (hhhh)
551 LL: ((unintelligible))
552 T: so (+) let's get <u>three</u> groups (1) <u>three</u> groups. ok?
           (NM: Class 2, Phase 1, Group 4)

Excerpt 6 (schism)

093 L15:   excuse me ((L7's name)) do you understand what's this (+) we cannot get
094   by auschwit[ʃ] ((reading)) I don't understand what we can't get by (1.5)
095 L7:   oh <hh> (+) uh we-
096 L15:   we can't get by I'm not su- I don't understand what is the meaning
097 L7:   we have every reason to be afraid of ((unintelligible)) ((L7 is reading; her
098   turn trails off into an unintelligible mutter))
099 L15:   we cannot get by (+) what's the meaning ((L15's turn overlaps the end of
100   L7's turn))
101 L7:   (+) what is auschwitz (+) it is a::
102 L15:   I think it's a place because::
103 L7:   ((unintelligible)) a ((unintelligible)) right,
104 L15:   yeah I guess that (+) I already understand that
105 L7:   //concentra//tion camp,
106 L15:   //((unintelligible))//
107   (+)
108 L7:   is that the one
109 L15:   yeah it cannot get by what is this
110 L7:   we cannot get by ((reading)) <h> I think (+) you cannot s:kip like you
111   cannot (+) you have to go through it, (+) you cannot get by (+) like (+)
112   you have to go through it, say (+) we cannot get by <hh> 'cause
113   (1)
114 L15:   yes I understand
115   //you (+) <u>why</u> he would <hh> because uh (++) the reason why//
116 L7:   //have every reason to be afraid of ((unintelligible))//
117 L15:   he doesn't want t- a united germany is //be//cause that
118 L7:   //oh//
119 L7:   because (+) you know the concentration camp, (+) then <u>hitler</u> he he tried
120   to kill (+) in nazi germany,
121 L15:   yeah?
122 L7:   ok (+) and the jewish (+) //right,//
123 L15:   //yeah?//
124 L7:   ok (+) so (+) say (+) he: he said we cannot get by that we- we never will
125   forget about this (+) //to the end//

```
126 L15:              //he says it's// (+) history:
127 L7:   uh huh (+) see, (+) //says this is really terrible//
128 L15:                 //says it's-it's like-// he doesn't wa:nt to: (+)
129       //a u//nited germany
130 L7:    //I mean//
131 L15:  like=
132 L7:   =I guess (+) he says (+) this is  terrible
133 L15:  oh=
134 L7:   =a lot (+) they killed a lot of people right,
135 L15:  uh=
136 L7:   =we cannot get (+) by (+) auschwitz <hh> this means that <hh> he=
137 L15:  =we can't forget we can't forget
138 L7:   yeah and say (+) it's uh (+) this is really (1) big historical //eve//nt
139 L15:                                                       //yeah//
140 L7:   nobody could (+) forget about it, you know
141 L15:  oh yeah //yeah//
142 L7:         //get// by (+) d'you- do you get that, (+)
143       //I think that ((unintelligible))//
144 L15:  //I think so// because uh (+) you know <hh> as (+) //it's//
145 L7:                                                    //so//
146 L15:  very (into) history and to (+) //into//
147 L7:                          //uh huh// so this (+) does this guy: (+) agree
148       with uh (+) that
149 L15:  no (+) usually (+) against (+) //the german//
150 L7:                       //again-// ok yeah <hh> oh- I- I guess uh
151       'cause I <h> if you ever been to a u uh- united germany right,
152 L15:  yeah
153 L7:   you cannot get (+) go by (+) auschwitz right, (+) this //is//
154 L15:                                                     //yeah//
155 L7:   really important he killed (+) a lot of people who cannot
156       ((unintelligible))
157 L15:  oh right
          (NM: Class 2, Phase 2, Group 2)
```

Excerpt 7

```
217 L15:         ... my article is about (+) what auschwit[ʃ] or what (++) gu:h
218       (+) duh duh (1) this guy doesn't want a united germany because what will
219       we (+) he say can't by auschwit[ʃ] and I d(h)on't (h)understand what
220       is <hh>
221 L6:    I'm- I'm sorry I didn't //un//derstand what you said
222 222 L15:               //we//
223 L15:  no (+) we cannot get by auschwit[ʃ] ((reading)) do you know- do you- do
224       you know what is the meaning- meaning I don't understand it (1.3) it's
225       something like the auschwit[ʃ] and what ab(h)out i(h)t
226 L7:   is it auschwitz //or// concentration camp //you're// talking about
227 L15:             //yeah//
228 L6:                                        //yeah//
229 L6:    //yeah//
230 L15:  //uh//
2321     (1)
```

```
232 L6:    yeah uh (+) it was uh (+) a terrible one
233 L7:    uh huh yeah
234 L15:   //yeah// that's why he doesn't wa//:::nt// (+) a united germany
235 L6:    //во//                          //retrace,// ((mutter))
236        (4)
           (NM: Class 2, Phase 2, Group 2)
```

Excerpt 8

```
242 L7:                                                  ... ok (+) my
243        my //(article) is that germans are terrible//
244 L15:      //like he doesn't want a united germany because//
245 L7:    anx//ious//
246 L15:       //I// //don't know//
247 L6:              //he's afraid// of- of auschwitz,
248        (2)
249 L14:   germany's
250 L15:   //(huh huh)// (huh) //<h//hh>//
251 L6:    //yeah//      //it's//     //it's// hard to say
252        (1.3)
253 L15:   u:h ((high pitch))
254 L6:    (huh huh huh) <hh>
255        (5)
256 L14:   <h> hh grass is (+) <h> strongly, (1) <h> against ((L14 is writing as he
257        speaks))
258 L7:    against, (+) this guy is kind of a
259 L14:   <h> the unification ((L14 is writing as he speaks))
260        (+)
261 L7:    he (+) is against the unification but somehow <h> he doesn't even want
262        (to the word be) (+) you know
263 L14:   <hh>
264 L7:    so he said
265 L14:   why-
266 L7:    german should be united
267 L14:   //<hhh>// hhh ((sigh))
268 L6:    //ok//
269 L14:   what-
270 L6:    o k
271 L14:   so what's- what's with the auschwit[ʃ] (+) au[s] ((whisper))
272 L6:    ausch[v]itz
273        (+)
274 L14:   oh ausch[v]itz
275 L15:   ausch[v]i[ʃ]
276 L14:   s- so why- why was it so important in the title (+) to the article
277 L6:    he's (+) what,
278 L15:   why:, (1) (huh hh) yeah (+) this is the reason why he doesn't want (+) a
279        united germany
280        (+)
281 L14:   because (+) of au//sch[v]itz?//
282 L15:                //((unintelligible))// (it does)=I//:: not sure//
283 L6:                                  //he's afraid// of u:h (+) what
```

284   happened in ausch[v]itz might happen again?
285 L15:   I don't know (+) I don't know but (+) I think that it it (+) history of uh
286   (+) it would (+) //au[s//wit∫]
287 L6:   //sorry//
288   (++)
289 L15:   re-
290   (+)
291 L6:   yeah I read //that// (+) I read that //but// u:h
292 L15:   //yeah//   //(hh)//
293   (+)
294 L15:   it's curious what he's saying we can't get by au[swit∫]
295 L7:   is that- (+) means he cannot f:
296 L6:   yeah but uh I- I gue//ss he means// u:h (++) tha:t he wishes (+) there
297 L7:   //go through it,//
298 L6:   is no: ausch- ausch[v]itz again
299 L7:   yeah (++) great well can we say (+) if he- (+) the german can united (+) do
300   it (1) go by
301 L6:   let's see the questions
302 L7:   ausch[v]itz
303 L6:   grass speaks out strongly //against a ni-// united germany <h> why
304 L15:   //against a united germany yes//
305 L6:   (+) do you think these views are [more eyt (+) //stri:m//] ((reading))
306 L14:   //more// extreme
307   (++)
308 L6:   I mean why do you //think// these views ((reading))
309 L7:   //why//
310   (+)
311 L15:   I mean this is the oth//er// question
312 L6:   //yeah//
313 L15:   //because why (+) why//
314 L14:   ////do you think it's moderate// or extreme//
315 L6:   //do you think his views are// (+) more ex(+)treme
316 L15:   well is she strong against a united germany (hh) //why//
317 L6:   //yeah// u:hm
318 L15:   (huhh,)
319 L6:   it's a hard task you read it
320   (+)
321 L15:   yeah I read it
322 L14:   uh huh ((mutter))
323 L6:   //ok//
324 L15:   //a:nd,// (+) //I don't understand what// is (+) we can't get by
325 L6:   //then we are-//
326 L6:   w::- we're listening
327 L15:   uh (+) I mean (+) and I s- (+) I till (+) I tol- I tell you that <h> I don't
328   understand what is the meaning we cannot get by auswit[∫] (hh) (++)
329 L6:   ok
330 L15:   <hhh>
331 L6:   there is a problem here she //doesn't// underst(h)and
332 L15:   //(huh h)//
333 L7:   (huh)
334 L6:   and we don't understand what <h> //what means exactly this//
335 L15:   //why we can't get auswit[∫]// (+) oh

336 L6:   we cannot get by ausch[v]itz
337 T: ok (+) what d'you think it might mean
338 L15:   (uh huh) (+) (uh huh //h)//
339 L6:   //it// might [b]ean (+) probably u::h we::: (+) cannot
340   have another ausch[v]itz again if uh germany unites
341   o:r maybe <hh>
342 T: does it mean <u>that</u>?
343 L6:   I- I //[ni:]-//
344 L14:   //do//es it-
345 L6:   I didn't read it
346 L14:   does //it-//
347 L6:   ////I[z]-// I don't know//
348 T: //what do you think//
349 L14:   does it-
350 T: oh
351 L15:   //no//
352 L14:   //do//es it mean that u:hm //<hh>//
353 L6:   //I didn't read it//
354 L14:   that if the uni- if (+) the germany unite again <h> the ausch[v]it might
355   exist, <hhh>
356   (+)
357 T: yeah. that's ba- we can't- when you can't get by something that's
358   <hh> you can never forget.
359 L14:   right.
360   (+) ((T moves away from the group))
361 L6:   oh (+) 'cause
362   (1.3)
363 L15:   well (+) all right (+) all right (hh)
364 L6:   does it make sense?
365 L15:   yeah it's makes sense
            (NM: Class 2, Phase 2, Group 2)

References

Abelson, R. (1967). Definition. In P. Edwards (Ed.), *The encyclopedia of philosophy* (Vol. 2, pp. 314–324). London and New York: MacMillan and Free Press.

Aljaafreh, A. & Lantolf, J. P. (1994). Negative feedback as regulation and second language learning in the zone of proximal development. *The Modern Language Journal, 78,* 465–483.

Allwright, R. (1980). Turns, topics, and tasks: Patterns of participation in language learning and teaching. In D. Larsen-Freeman (Ed.), *Discourse analysis in second language research* (pp. 165–187). Rowley, MA: Newbury House.

Anderson, A. & Lynch, T. (1988). *Listening.* Oxford: Oxford University Press.

Aston, G. (1986). Trouble-shooting in interaction with learners: the more the merrier? *Applied Linguistics, 7,* 128–143.

Atkinson, J. M. & Heritage, J. (Eds.) (1984a). *Structures of social action.* Cambridge: Cambridge University Press.

Atkinson, J. M. & Heritage, J. (1984b). Transcript notation. In J. M. Atkinson & J. Heritage (Eds.), *Structures of social action* (pp. ix–xvi). Cambridge: Cambridge University Press.

Bachman, L. (1990). *Fundamental considerations in language testing.* Oxford: Oxford University Press.

Banbrook, L. & Skehan, P. (1990) Classrooms and display questions. In C. Brumfit & R. Mitchell (Eds.), *Research in the language classroom* (pp. 141–152) *(ELT Documents 133).* London: Modern English Publications in association with the British Council.

Beebe, L. M. & Giles, H. (1984). Speech accommodation theories: A discussion in terms of second language acquisition. *International Journal of the Sociology of Language, 46,* 5–32.

Benson, D. & Hughes, J. (1991). Method: Evidence and inference for ethnomethodology. In G. Button (Ed.), *Ethnomethodology and the human sciences* (pp. 109–136). Cambridge: Cambridge University Press.

Bilmes, J. (1992). Dividing the rice: A microanalysis of the mediator's role in a Northern Thai negotiation. *Language in Society, 21,* 569–602.

Bilmes, J. (1993). Ethnomethodology, culture, and implicature: Toward an empirical pragmatics. *Pragmatics, 3,* 387–409.

Boden, D. & Zimmerman, D. H. (Eds.) (1991). *Talk and social structure.* Cambridge: Polity Press.

Bolinger, D. (1975). Meaning and memory. *Forum Linguisticum, 1,* 2–14.

Brock, C. A. (1986). The effects of referential questions on ESL classroom discourse. *TESOL Quarterly, 20,* 47–59.

Button, G. (Ed.) (1991). *Ethnomethodology and the human sciences.* Cambridge: Cambridge University Press.

Button, G. & Lee, R. E. (Eds.) (1987). *Talk and social interaction.* Clevedon, England: Multilingual Matters.

Bygate, M. (1988). Units of oral expression and language learning in small group interaction. *Applied Linguistics, 9,* 59–82.

Canale, M. & Swain, M. (1980). Theoretical bases of communicative approaches to second language teaching and testing. *Applied Linguistics, 1,* 1–47.

Carlsen, W. S. (1991). Questioning in classrooms: A sociolinguistic perspective. *Review of Educational Research, 61,* 157–178.

Carroll, S. & Swain, M. (1993). Explicit and implicit feedback. An empirical study of the learning of linguistic generalizations. *Studies in Second Language Acquisition, 15,* 357– 386.

Celce-Murcia, M. (1990a). Data-based language analysis and TESL. In J. Alatis (Ed.), *Linguistics, language teaching and language acquisition: The interdependence of theory, practice and research.* (pp. 245–259). Washington, DC: Georgetown University Press.

Celce-Murcia, M. (1990b). Discourse analysis and grammar instruction. *Annual Review of Applied Linguistics, 11,* 135–151.

Celce-Murcia, M. Dörnyei, Z. & Thurrell, S. (1995). Communicative competence: A pedagogically motivated model with content specifications. *Issues in Applied Linguistics, 6,* 5–35.

Chaudron, C. (1982). Vocabulary elaboration in teachers' speech to L2 learners. *Studies in Second Language Acquisition, 4,* 170–180.

Chomsky, N. (1965). *Aspects of the theory of syntax.* Cambridge, MA: MIT Press.

Chomsky, N. (1975). *Reflections on language.* New York: Pantheon.

Chomsky, N. (1980). *Rules and representations.* New York: Columbia University Press.

Chomsky, N. (1986). *Knowledge of language: Its nature, origin, and use.* New York: Praeger.

Cicourel, A. (1992). The interpenetration of communicative contexts: Examples from medical contexts. In A. Duranti & C. Goodwin (Eds.), *Rethinking context: Language as an interactive phenomenon* (pp. 291–310). Cambridge: Cambridge University Press.

Coady, J. & Huckin, T. (Eds.) (1997). *Second language vocabulary acquisition: A rationale for pedagogy.* Cambridge: Cambridge University Press.

Coughlan, P. J. (1995). Conversations with Vovo: A case study of child second language acquisition and loss. *Issues in Applied Linguistics, 6,* 123–136.

Crookes, G. (1989). Planning and interlanguage variation. *Studies in Second Language Acquisition, 11,* 367–383.

Crookes, G. (1990). The utterance, and other basic units for second language discourse analysis. *Applied Linguistics, 11,* 189–199.

Davidson, J. (1984). Subsequent versions of invitations, offers, requests, and proposals dealing with potential or actual rejection. In J. M. Atkinson & J. Heritage (Eds.), *Structures of social action* (pp. 102–128). Cambridge: Cambridge University Press.

Dillon, J. T. (1981). Duration of response to teacher questions and statements. *Contemporary Educational Psychology, 6,* 1–11.

Dillon, J. T. (1988). The remedial status of student questioning. *Journal of Curriculum Studies, 20,* 197–210.

Doughty, C. & Pica, T. (1986). Information gap tasks: Do they facilitate second language acquisition? *TESOL Quarterly, 20,* 305–325.

Douglas, D. & Selinker, L. (1994). Research methodology in context–based second language research. In E. Tarone, S. Gass, & A. Cohen (Eds.), *Research methodology in second language acquisition* (pp. 119–131). Hillsdale, N.J: Lawrence Erlbaum.

Drew, P. (1984). Speakers' reportings in invitation sequences. In J. M. Atkinson & J. Heritage (Eds.), *Structures of social action* (pp. 129–151). Cambridge: Cambridge University Press.

Drew, P. & Heritage, J. (1992). Analyzing talk at work: An introduction. In P. Drew and J. Heritage (Eds.), *Talk at work: Interaction in institutional settings* (pp. 3–65). Cambridge: Cambridge University Press.

Drew, P. & Heritage, J. (Eds.) (1992a). *Talk at work: Interaction in institutional settings.* Cambridge: Cambridge University Press.

Du Bois, J. (1991). Transcription design principles for spoken discourse research. *Pragmatics, 1,* 71–106.

Duff, P. A. (1986). Another look at interlanguage talk: Taking task to task. In R. Day (Ed.), *Talking to learn: Conversation in second language acquisition* (pp. 147–181). Rowley, MA: Newbury House.

Duranti, A. & Goodwin, C. (Eds.) (1992). *Rethinking context: Language as an interactive phenomenon.* Cambridge: Cambridge University Press.

Edwards, J. A. (1992). Transcription of discourse. In W. Bright (Ed.), *International encyclopedia of linguistics* (pp. 367–371). New York: Oxford University Press.

Edwards, J. A. & Lampert, M. D. (1993). *Talking data.* Hillsdale, NJ: Lawrence Erlbaum.

Ellis, R. (1990). Researching classroom language learning. In C. Brumfit and R. Mitchell (Eds.), *Research in the language classroom* (pp. 54–70) *(ELT Documents 133).* London: Modern English Publications in association with the British Council.

Ellis, R. (1994). Factors in the incidental acquisition of second language vocabulary from oral input: A review essay. *Applied Language Learning, 5,* 1–32.

Faerch, C. & Kasper, G. (1982). Phatic, metalingual and metacommunicative functions in discourse: Gambits and and repairs. In Enkvist, N. E. (Ed.), *Impromptu speech* (pp. 71–103). Åbo: Åbo Akademi.

Faerch, C. & Kasper, G. (1986). The role of comprehension in second language learning. *Applied L:inguistics, 7,* 257–274.

Fanselow, J. (1977). Beyond Rashomon – conceptualizing and describing the teaching act. *TESOL Quartely, 11,* 17–39.

Firth, A. (1995). Talking for a change: Commodity negotiating by telephone. In A. Firth (Ed.), *The discourse of negotiation* (pp. 183–222). Oxford: Pergamon.

Firth, A. (1996).   The discursive accomplishment of normality: On "lingua franca" English and conversation analysis. *Journal of Pragmatics, 26,* 237–259.

Firth, A. & Wagner, J. (1997).   On discourse, communication, and (some) fundamental concepts in SLA research.   *The Modern Language Journal, 81,* 285–300.

Firth, A. & Wagner, J. (1998).   SLA property: No trespassing!   *The Modern Language Journal, 82,* 91–94.

Flowerdew, J. (1991) Pragmatic modifications on the "representative" speech act of defining.   *Journal of Pragmatics, 15,* 253–264.

Flowerdew, J. (1992).   Definitions in science lectures.   *Applied Linguistics, 13,* 202–221.

Foster, P. (1998).   A classroom perspective on the negotiation of meaning. *Applied Linguistics, 19,* 1–23.

Foster, P. & Skehan, P. (1996).   The influence of planning on performance in task-based learning.   *Studies in Second Language Acquisition, 18,* 299–324.

Garfinkel, H. (1952).   *The perception of the other: A study in social order.*   Unpublished doctoral dissertation, Harvard University.

Garfinkel, H. (1967).   *Studies in ethnomethodology.*   Englewood Cliffs, N.J: Prentice Hall.

Garfinkel, H. (1974).   The origins of the term ethnomethodology.   In R. Turner (Ed.), *Ethnomethodology* (pp. 15–18). Harmondsworth, England: Penguin.

Garfinkel, H. (1984).   *Studies in ethnomethodology.*   Cambridge: Polity Press.

Garfinkel, H. & Sacks, H. (1970).   On formal structures of practical actions.   In J. C. McKinney & E. A. Tiryakin (Eds.), *Theoretical sociology* (pp. 338–366).   New York: Appleton-Century-Crofts.

Gaskill, W. (1980).   Correction in native speaker-non-native speaker conversation.   In D. Larsen-Freeman (Ed.), *Discourse analysis in second language research* (pp. 125–137). Rowley, MA: Newbury House.

Gass, S. M. (1993).   Second language acquisition: Past, present and future. *Second Language Research, 9,* 99–117.

Gass, S. M. (1997).   *Input, interaction and the second language learner.* Mahwah, NJ: Lawrence Erlbaum.

Gass, S. M. (1998).   Apples and oranges: Or, why apples are not oranges and don't need to be. A response to Firth and Wagner. *The Modern Language Journal, 82,* 83–90.

Gass, S. M. & Selinker, L. (1994). *Second language acquisition: An introductory course.* Hillsdale, NJ: Lawrence Erlbaum.

Gass, S. M. & Varonis, E. M. (1984). The effect of familiarity on the comprehensibility of non–native speech. *Language Learning, 34,* 65–89.

Gass, S. M. & Varonis, E. M. (1989). Incorporated repairs in NNS discourse. In M. Eisenstein (Ed.), *The dynamic interlanguage* (pp. 71–86). New York: Plenum Press.

Gass, S. M. & Varonis, E. M. (1985a). Task variation and non-native/nonnative negotiation of meaning. In S. M. Gass & C. G. Madden (Eds.), *Input in second language acquisition* (pp. 149–161). Rowley, MA: Newbury House.

Gass, S. M. & Varonis, E. M. (1985b). Variation in native speaker speech modification to non–native speakers. *Studies in Second Language Acquisition, 7,* 37–57.

Gass, S. M. & Varonis, E. M. (1989). Incorporated repairs in NNS discourse. In M. Eisenstein (Ed.), *Variation and second language acquisition* (pp. 71–86). New York: Plenum.

Gass, S. M. & Varonis, E. M. (1994). Input, interaction and second language production. *Studies in Second Language Acquisition, 16,* 283–302.

Geertz, C. (1983). *Local knowledge.* New York: Basic Books.

Goffman, E. (1967). *Interaction ritual. Essays in face-to-face behaviour.* New York: Anchor Books.

Goffman, E. (1974). *Frame analysis.* New York: Harper and Row.

Goodwin, C. (1979). The interactive construction of a sentence in natural conversation. In G. Psathas (Ed.), *Everyday language: Studies in ethnomethodology* (pp. 97–121). New York: Irvington Publishers.

Goodwin, C. (1981). *Conversational organization: Interaction between speakers and hearers.* New York: Academic Press.

Goodwin, C. (1984). Notes on story structure and the organization of participation. In J. M. Atkinson & J. Heritage (Eds.), *Structures of social action* (pp. 225–246). Cambridge: Cambridge University Press.

Goodwin, C. (1999). Action and embodiment within situated human interaction. *Journal of Pragmatics,* 32.

Green, J., Franquiz, M. & Dixon, C. (1997). The myth of the objective transcript: Transcribing as a situated act. *TESOL Quarterly, 31,* 172–176.

Gregg, K. R. (1984). Krashen's monitor and Occam's razor. *Applied Linguistics, 5,* 79–100.

Gregg, K. R. (1993). Taking explanation seriously; or, let a couple of flowers bloom. *Applied Linguistics, 14,* 276–294.

Gregg, K. R. (1996). The logical and developmental problems of second language acquisition. In W. C. Ritchie & T. K. Bhatia (Eds.), *Handbook of second language acquisition* (pp. 49–81). New York: Academic Press.

Gregg, K. R., Long, M. H., Jordan, G. & Beretta, A. (1997). Rationality and its discontents in SLA. *Applied Linguistics, 18,* 538–558.

Hall, J. K. (1993). The role of oral practices in the accomplishment of our everyday lives: The sociocultural dimension of interaction with implications for the learning of another language. *Applied Linguistics, 14,* 145–166.

Hall, J. K. (1995a). "Aw, man, where we goin?" Classroom interaction and the development of L2 interactional competence. *Issues in Applied Linguistics, 6,* 37–62.

Hall, J. K. (1995b). (Re)creating our worlds with words: A sociohistorical perspective of face-to-face interaction. *Applied Linguistics, 16,* 206–232.

Hall, J. K. (1997). A consideration of SLA as a theory of practice: A response to Firth and Wagner. *The Modern Language Journal, 81,* 301–306.

Halliday, M. A. K. (1973). Towards a sociogical semantics. In M. A. K. Halliday, *Explorations in the functions of language* (Chapter 4, pp. 72–102). London: Edward Arnold. Extracts reprinted in C. J. Brumfit & K. Johnson (Eds.), (1979) *The communicative approach to language teaching* (pp. 27–45). Oxford: Oxford Univerity Press.

Harley, B. (Ed.) (1995). *Lexical issues in language learning.* Ann Arbor/Amsterdam/Philadelphia: John Benjamins.

Harris, Z. (1951). *Methods in structural linguistics.* Chicago: University of Chicago Press.

Hatch, E. (1978). Discourse analysis and second language acquisition. In E. Hatch (Ed.), *Second language acquisition: A book of readings* (pp. 402–435). Rowley, MA: Newbury House.

Hatch, E. (1979). Apply with caution. *Studies in Second Language Acquisition, 2,* 123–143.

Hatch, E. (1983). *Psycholinguistics: A second language perspective.* Rowley, MA: Newbury House.

Hatch, E., Shirai, Y. & Fantuzzi, C. (1990). The need for an integrated theory: Connecting modules. *TESOL Quarterly, 24,* 697–716.

Hawkins, B. (1985). Is an 'appropriate' response always so appropriate? In S. M. Gass and C. Madden (Eds.), *Input in second language acquisition* (pp.162–178). Rowley, MA: Newbury House.

Heritage, J. (1984). A change-of-state token and aspects of its sequential placement. In J. M. Atkinson & J. Heritage (Eds.), *Structures of social action: Studies in conversation analysis* (pp. 299–345). Cambridge: Cambridge University Press and Paris: Editions de la Maison des Sciences de l'Homme.

Heritage, J. (1987). Ethnomethodology. In A. Giddens & J. H. Turner (Eds.), *Social theory today* (pp. 224–272). Stanford, CA: Stanford University Press.

Heritage, J. (1988). Current development in conversation analysis. In D. Roger & P. Bull (Eds.), *Conversation* (pp. 21–47). Clevedon, England: Multilingual Matters.

Heritage, J. & Greatbatch, D. (1986). Generating applause: A study of rhetoric and response at party political conferences. *American Journal of Sociology, 92,* 110–157.

Heritage, J. & Roth, A. L. (1995). Grammar and institution: Questions and questioning in the broadcast news interview. *Research on Language and Social Interaction, 28,* 1–60.

Hopper, R. (1988). Conversation analysis and social psychology as descriptions of interpersonal communication. In D. Roger & P. Bull (Eds.), *Conversation* (pp. 48–65). Clevedon, England: Multilingual Matters.

Hopper, R. (Ed.) (1990/1991). Special section: Ethnography and conversation analysis after *Talking Culture. Research on Language and Social Interaction, 24,* 161–387.

Hopper, R., Koch, S. & Mandelbaum, J. (1988). Conversation analysis methods. In D. G. Ellis & W. A. Donohue (Eds.), *Contemporary issues in language and discourse processes* (pp. 169–186). Hillsdale, N.J: Lawrence Erlbaum.

Hymes, D. H. (1972). On communicative competence. In J. B. Pride & J. Holmes (Eds.), *Sociolinguistics* (pp. 269–293). Harmondsworth: Penguin.

Itoh, H. (1973). *A Japanese child's acqusition of two languages.* Unpublished master's thesis, University of California, Los Angeles.

Jacobs, S. (1986). How to make an argument from example. In D. G. Ellis & W. A. Donohue (Eds.), *Contemporary issues in language and discourse processes* (pp. 149–167). Hillsdale, N.J: Lawrence Erlbaum.

Jacobs, S. (1987). Commentary on Zimmerman: Evidence and inference in conversation analysis. *Communication Yearbook, 11,* 433–443.

Jefferson, G. (1974). Error correction as an interactional resource. *Language in Society, 2,* 181–199.

Jefferson, G. (1978). Sequential aspects of story-telling in conversation. In J. Schenkein (Ed.), *Studies in the organization of conversational interaction* (pp. 219–248). New York: Academic Press.

Jefferson, G. (1987). On exposed and embedded correction in conversation. In G. Button & R. E. Lee (Eds.), *Talk and social interaction* (pp.86–100). Clevedon, England: Multilingual Matters.

Jefferson, G. (1988). Preliminary notes on a possible metric which provides for a 'standard maximum' silence of approximately one second in conversation. In D. Roger & P. Bull (Eds.), *Conversation* (pp. 167–196). Clevedon, England: Multilingual Matters.

Jefferson, G. & Schenkein, J. (1978). Some sequential negotiations in conversation: Unexpanded and expanded versions of projected action sequences. In J. Schenkein (Ed.), *Studies in the organization of conversational interaction* (pp. 155–172). New York: Academic Press.

Johnson, K. (1982). Five principles in a "communicative" exercise type. In K. Johnson (Ed.), *Communicative syllabus design and methodology* (pp. 163–175). Oxford: Pergamon.

Jones, E. E. & Gerard, H. B. (1967). *Foundations of social psychology.* New York: Wiley.

Kasper, G. (1985). Repair in foreign language teaching. *Studies in Second Language Acquisition, 7,* 200–215.

Kasper, G. (1997). "A" stands for acquisition: A response to Firth and Wagner. *The Modern Language Journal, 81,* 307–312.

Koshik, I. (1999). *Teacher question sequences in ESL writing conferences.* Unpublished doctoral dissertation, University of California, Los Angeles CA.

Krashen, S. D. (1977). Some issues relating to the Monitor Model. In H. Brown, C. Yorio, & R. Crymes (Eds.), *On TESOL '77* (pp. 144–158). Washington, DC: TESOL.

Krashen, S. D. (1980). The input hypothesis. In J. E. Alatis (Ed.), *Current issues in bilingual education* (pp. 168–180). Washington, D. C: Georgetown University Press.

Krashen, S. D. (1981). *Second language acquisition and second language learning.* Oxford: Pergamon.

Krashen, S. D. (1982). *Principles and practice in second language acquisition.* Oxford: Pergamon.

Lantolf, J. P. (1994a). Sociocultural theory and second language learning. Introduction to the special issue. *The Modern Language Journal, 78,* 418–420.

Lantolf, J. P. (Ed.) (1994b). Sociocultural theory and second language learning. *The Modern Language Journal, 78,* 4.

Lantolf, J. P. & Appel (Eds.) (1994). *Vygotskian approaches to second language research.* Norwood, NJ: Ablex.

Larsen-Freeman, D. (1976). An explanation for the morpheme acquisition order of second language learners. *Language Learning, 26,* 125–134.

Larsen-Freeman, D., & Long, M. H. (1991). *An introduction to second language acquisition research.* London and New York: Longman.

Lerner, G. H. (1991). On the syntax of sentences-in-progress. *Language in Society, 20,* 441–458.

Lerner, G. H. (1993). Collectivities in action: Establishing the relevance of conjoined participation in conversation. *Text, 13,* 213–245.

Lerner, G. H. (1994). Responsive list construction: A conversational resource for accomplishing multifaceted social action. *Journal of Language and Social Psychology, 13,* 20–33.

Lerner, G. H. (1995). Turn design and the organization of participation in instructional activities. *Discourse Processes, 19,* 111–131.

Levinson, S. (1983). *Pragmatics.* Cambridge: Cambridge University Press.

Liddicoat, A. (1997). Interaction, social structure, and second language use: A response to Firth and Wagner. *The Modern Language Journal, 81,* 313–317.

Long, M. H. (1980). *Input, interaction and second language acquisition.* Unpublished doctoral dissertation, University of California, Los Angeles.

Long, M. H. (1981). Input, interaction and second language acquisition. In H. Winitz (Ed.), *Native language and foreign language acquisition: Annals of the New York Academy of Sciences, 379,* 259–278.

Long, M. H. (1983a). Inside the "black box": Methodological issues in classroom research on language learning. In H. W. Seliger and M. H. Long (Eds.), *Classroom oriented research in second language acquisition* (pp. 3–35). Rowley, MA: Newbury House.

Long, M. H. (1983b). Linguistic and conversational adjustments to non–native speakers. *Studies in Second Language Acquisition, 5,* 177–193.

Long, M. H. (1983c). Native speaker/non–native speaker conversation and the negotiation of comprehensible input. *Applied Linguistics, 4,* 126–141.

Long, M. H. (1985a). Input and second language acquisition theory. In S. M. Gass & C. Madden (Eds.), *Input in second language acquisition* (pp. 377–393). Rowley, MA: Newbury House.

Long, M. H. (1985b). A role for instruction in second language acquisition: Task–based language training. In K. Hyltenstam & M. Pienemann (Eds.), *Modelling and assessing second language acquisition* (pp. 77–99). Clevedon, England: Multilingual Matters.

Long, M. H. (1989). Task, group, and task–group interactions. *University of Hawai'i Working papers in ESL, 8,* 1–26.

Long, M. H. (1991). Focus on form: A design feature in language teaching methodology. In K. de Bot, R. B. Ginsberg, & C. Kramsch (Eds.), *Foreign language research in perspective* (pp. 39–51). Amsterdam/Philadelphia: John Benjamins.

Long, M. H. (1996). The role of the linguistic environment in second language acquisition. In W. C. Ritchie & T. K. Bhatia (Eds.), *Handbook of second language acquisition* (pp. 414–468). New York: Academic Press.

Long, M. H. (1997). Construct validity in SLA research: A response to Firth and Wagner. *The Modern Language Journal, 81,* 318–323.

Long, M. H. (in press). *Task–based language teaching.* Oxford: Blackwell.

Long, M. H. & Porter, P. A. (1985). Group work, interlanguage talk and second language acquisition. *TESOL Quarterly, 19*, 207–228.

Long, M. H. & Sato, C. J. (1983). Classroom foreigner talk discourse: Forms and functions of teachers' questions. In H. W. Seliger & M. H. Long (Eds.), *Classroom oriented research in second language acquisition* (pp. 268–285). Rowley, MA: Newbury House.

Mackey, A. (1999). Input, interaction and second language development: An empirical study of question formation in ESL. To appear in *Studies in Second Language Acquisition. 21,* 557-587.

Markee, N. P. P. (1994). Toward an ethnomethodological respecification of second language acquisition studies. In E. Tarone, S. M. Gass, & A. Cohen (Eds.), *Research methodology in second language acquisition* (pp. 89–116). Hillsdale, N.J: Lawrence Erlbaum.

Markee, N. P. P. (1995). Teachers' answers to students' questions: Problematizing the issue of making meaning. *Issues in Applied Linguistics, 6,* 63–92.

Marriot, H. (1995). 'Deviations' in an intercultural business negotiation. In A. Firth (Ed.), *The discourse of negotiation* (pp. 247–268). Oxford: Pergamon.

McLaughlin, B. (1987). *Theories of second language learning.* London: Edward Arnold.

McLaughlin, M. (1988). The analysis of action sequences in conversation: Some comments on method. In D. G. Ellis & W. A. Donohue (Eds.), *Contemporary issues in language and discourse processes* (pp. 187–200). Hillsdale, NJ: Lawrence Erlbaum.

McHoul, A. (1978). The organization of turns at formal talk in the classroom. *Language in Society, 7,* 183–213.

McHoul, A. (1990). The organization of repair in classroom talk. *Language in Society, 19,* 349–377.

Mehan, H. (1978). Structuring school structure. *Harvard Educational Review, 48,* 32–64.

Mehan, H. (1979). *Learning lessons: Social organization in the classroom.* Cambridge, MA: Harvard University Press.

Mehan, H. (1982). The structure of classroom events and their consequences for student performance. In P. Gilmore & A. Glatthorn (Eds.), *Children in and out of education: Ethnography and education* (pp. 59–87). Washington, DC: Center for Applied Linguistics.

Mehan, H. (1993). Beneath the skin and between the ears: A case study in the politics of representation. In S. Chaiklin & J. Lave (Ed.), *Understanding practice* (pp. 241–268). Cambridge: Cambridge University Press.

Mehan, H. & Wood, H. (1975). *The reality of ethnomethodology.* New York: Wiley Interscience.

Merrit, M. (1976). On questions following questions in service encounters. *Language in Society, 5,* 315–357.

Moerman, M. (1988). *Talking culture: Ethnography and conversation analysis.* Philadelphia: University of Pennsylvania Press.

Ochs, E. (1979). Transcription as theory. In E. Ochs & B. Schieffelin (Eds.), *Developmental pragmatics* (pp. 43–72). New York: Academic Press.

Ohta, A. S. (1995). Applying sociocultural theory to an analysis of learner discourse: Learner-learner collaborative interaction in the zone of proximal development. *Issues in Applied Linguistics, 6,* 93–121.

Oliver, R. (1995). Negative feedback in child NS-NNS conversation. *Studies in Second Language Acquisition, 17,* 459–481.

Ortega, L. (1999). Planning and focus on form in L2 oral performance. *Studies in Second Language Acquisition, 21,* 109–148.

Pawley, A. & Syder, F. (1983). Two puzzles for linguistic theory: Nativelike selection and nativelike fluency. In J. C. Richards & R. Schmidt (Eds.), *Language and communication* (pp. 191–226). London: Longman.

Payne, G. & Hustler, D. (1980). Teaching the class: The practical management of a cohort. *British Journal of Sociology of Education, 1,* 49–66.

Peck, S. (1978). Child–child discourse in second language acquisition. In E. Hatch (Ed.), *Second language acquisition: A book of readings* (pp. 383–400). Rowley, MA: Newbury House.

Peck, S. (1980). Language play in child second language acquisition. In D. Larsen-Freeman (Ed.), *Discourse analysis in second language research* (pp. 154–164). Rowley, MA: Newbury House.

Pica, T. (1983a). Adult acquisition of English as a second language under different conditions of exposure. *Language Learning, 33,* 465–497.

Pica, T. (1983b). The article in American English: What the textbooks don't tell us. In N. Wolfson & E. Judd

(Eds.), *Sociolinguistics and second language acquisition* (pp. 222–233). Rowley, MA: Newbury House.

Pica, T. (1987). Second language acquisition, social interaction and the classroom. *Applied Linguistics, 8,* 3–21.

Pica, T. & Doughty, C. (1985). The role of group work in classroom second language acquisition. *Studies in Second Language Acquisition, 7,* 233–248.

Pica, T., Doughty, C., & Young, R. (1986). Making input comprehensible: Do interactional modifications help? *International Review of Applied Linguistics, 72,* 1–25.

Pica, T. & Long, M. H. (1986). The linguistic and conversational performance of experienced and inexperienced teachers. In R. R. Day (Ed.), *Talking to learn: Conversation in second language acquisition* (pp. 85–98). Cambridge, MA: Newbury House.

Pica, T., Young, R. & Doughty, C. (1987). The impact of interaction on comprehension. *TESOL Quarterly, 21,* 737–758.

Pica, T., Holliday, L. Lewis, N., & Morgenthaler, L. (1989). Comprehensible output as an outcome of linguistic demands on the learner. *Studies in Second Language Acquisition, 11,* 63–90.

Pica, T., Kanagy, R. & Falodun, J. (1993). Choosing and using communication tasks for second language instruction. In G. Crookes and S. M. Gass (Eds.), *Tasks and language learning: Integrating theory and practice* (pp. 9–34). Clevedon, England: Multilingual Matters.

Plough, I. & Gass, S. M. (1993). Interlocutor and task familiarity: Effects on interactional structure. In G. Crookes and S. M. Gass (Eds.), *Tasks and language learning: Integrating theory and practice* (pp. 35–56). Clevedon, England: Multilingual Matters.

Pomerantz, A. (1975). *Second assessments: A study of some features of agreements/disagreements.* Unpublished doctoral dissertation, University of California, Irvine.

Pomerantz, A. (1978a). Attributions of responsibility: Blamings. *Sociology, 12,* 115–121.

Pomerantz, A. (1978b). Compliment responses: Notes on the cooperation of multiple constraints. In J. N. Schenkein (Ed.), *Studies in the organization of conversational interaction* (pp. 79–112). New York: Academic Press.

Pomerantz, A. (1984a). Agreeing and disagreeing with assessments: Some features of preferred/dispreferred turn shapes. In J. M. Atkinson & J. Heritage (Eds.), *Structures of social action* (pp. 152–163). Cambridge: Cambridge University Press.

Pomerantz, A. (1984b). Pursuing a response. In J. M. Atkinson & J. Heritage (Eds.), *Structures of social action* (pp. 57–101). Cambridge: Cambridge University Press.

Porter, P. (1986). How learners talk to each other: Input and interaction in task–centered discussions. In R. R. Day (Ed.), *Talking to learn: Conversation in second language acquisition* (pp. 200–222). Rowley, MA: Newbury House.

Preston, D. (1982). 'Ritin folklower daun 'rong. *Journal of American folklore, 95,* 304–326.

Preston, D. (1985). The Lil' Abner syndrome: Written representations of speech. *American Speech, 60,* 328–336.

Psathas, G. (1986). Some sequential structures in direction-giving. *Human Studies, 9,* 231–246.

Richards, J. C. (1990). The dilemma of teacher education in second language teaching. In J. C. Richards & D. Nunan (Eds.), *Second language teacher education* (pp. 3–15). Cambridge: Cambridge University Press.

Roberts, C. (1997). Transcribing talk: Issues of representation. *TESOL Quarterly, 31,* 167–171.

Roger, D. & Bull, P. (1988). Introduction. In D. Roger & P. Bull (Eds.), *Conversation* (pp. 21–47). Clevedon: Multilingual Matters.

Sacks, H. (1974). An analysis of the course of a joke's telling. In R. Bauman & J. Sherzer (Eds.), *Explorations in the ethnography of speaking* (pp. 337–353). Cambridge: Cambridge University Press.

Sacks, H., & Schegloff, E. A. (1979). Two preferences in the organization of reference to persons and their interaction. In G. Psathas (Ed.), *Everyday language: Studies in ethnomethodology* (pp. 15–21). New York: Irvington.

Sacks, H., Schegloff, E. A., & Jefferson, G. (1974). A simplest systematics for the organization of turn-taking in conversation. *Language, 50,* 696–735.

Sato, C. (1986). Conversation and interlanguage development: Rethinking the connection. In R. R. Day (Ed.), *Talking to learn: Conversation in second language acquisition* (pp. 23–45). Rowley, MA: Newbury House.

Savignon, S. (1972). *Communicative competence: An experiment in foreign language teaching.* Philadelphia: Center for Curriculum Development.

Scarcella, R. (1983). Discourse accent in second language performance. In S. M. Gass & L. Selinker (Eds.), *Language transfer in language learning* (pp. 306–326). Rowley, MA: Newbury House.

Scarcella, R. & Higa, C. (1981). Input and age differences in second language acquisition. In S. D. Krashen, R. Scarcella, & M. H. Long (Eds.), *Child–adult differences in second language acquisition* (pp. 175–201). Rowley, MA: Newbury House.

Schegloff, E. A. (1968). Sequencing in conversational openings. *American Anthropologist, 70,* 1075–1095.

Schegloff, E. A. (1972). Sequencing in conversational openings. In J. J. Gumperz & D. H. Hymes (Eds.), *Directions in sociolinguistics* (pp. 346–380). New York: Holt, Rhinehart and Winston.

Schegloff, E. A. (1979). The relevance of repair to syntax-for-conversation. In T. Givon (Ed.), *Syntax and semantics: Vol. 12. Discourse and Syntax* (pp. 261–286). New York: Academic Press

Schegloff, E. A. (1980). Preliminaries to preliminaries: "Can I ask you a question?" *Sociological Inquiry, 50,* 104–152.

Schegloff, E. A. (1987). Between macro and micro: Contexts and other connections. In J. Alexander, B. Giesen, R. Munch, & N. Smelser (Eds.), *The micro-macro link* (pp. 207–234). Berkeley: University of California Press.

Schegloff, E. A. (1990). On the organization of sequences as a source of "coherence" in talk-in-interaction. In B. Dorval (Ed.), *Conversational organization and its development* (pp. 51–77). Norwood, NJ: Ablex.

Schegloff, E. A. (1991a). Conversation analysis and socially shared cognition. In L. R. Resnick, J. M. Levine, & S. D. Teasley (Eds.), *Socially shared cognition* (pp. 150–171). Washington, DC: American Psychological Association.

Schegloff, E. A. (1991b). Reflections on talk and social structure. In D. Boden & D. Zimmerman (Eds.), *Talk and social structure* (pp. 44–70). Cambridge: Polity Press.

Schegloff, E. A. (1992a). On talk and its institutional occasions. In P. Drew & J. Heritage (Eds.), *Talk at work* (pp. xxx). Cambridge: Cambridge University Press.

Schegloff, E. A. (1992b). Repair after next turn: The last structurally provided defense of intersubjectivity in conversation. *American Journal of Sociology, 97,* 1295–1345.

Schegloff, E. A. (1993). Reflections on quantification in the study of conversation. *Research on Language and Social Interaction, 26,* 99–128.

Schegloff, E. A. (1996). Turn organization: One intersection of grammar and interaction. In E. Ochs, E. A. Schegloff, & S. Thompson (Eds.), *Interaction and grammar.* Cambridge: Cambridge University Press.

Schegloff, E. A. (in press). Third turn repair. In G. R. Guy, J. Baugh, & D. Schiffrin (Eds.), *Toward a social science of language: A festschrift for William Labov.* Cambridge: Cambridge University Press.

Schegloff, E. A., Jefferson, G., & Sacks, H. (1977). The preference for self-correction in the organization of repair in conversation. *Language, 53,* 361–382.

Schegloff, E. A., & Sacks, H. (1973). Opening up closings. *Semiotica, 8,* 289–327.

Schiffrin, D. (1991). Conversation analysis. *Annual Review of Applied Linguistics, 11,* 3–16.

Schmidt, R. (1990). The role of consciousness in second language learning. *Applied Linguistics, 11,* 17–46.

Schmidt, R. (1993). Awareness and second language acqusition. *Annual Review of Applied Linguistics, 13,* 206–226.

Schmidt, R. & Frota, S. (1986). Developing basic conversational ability in a second language: A case study of an adult learner. In R. R. Day (Ed.), *Talking to learn: Conversation in second language acquisition* (pp. 237–326). Rowley, MA: Newbury House.

Schumann, J. H. (1976). Social distance as a factor in second language acquisition. *Language Learning, 26,* 391–408.

Schwartz, J. (1980). The negotiation for meaning: Repair in conversations between second language learners of English. In D. Larsen-Freeman (Ed.), *Discourse analysis in second language research* (pp. 138–153). Rowley, MA: Newbury House.

Selinker, L. & Douglas, D. (1985). Wrestling with context in interlanguage theory. *Applied Linguistics, 6,* 75–86.

Selinker, L. & Douglas, D. (1989). Research methodology in contextually-based second language research. *Second Language Research,* 5, 93–126.

Sharwood Smith, M. (1991). Second language acquisition and the cognitive enterprise. Plenary presented at Second Language Research Forum, Los Angeles, CA.

Sinclair, J. & Coulthard, M. (1975). *Towards an analysis of discourse.* Oxford: Oxford University Press.

Sinclair, J. & Coulthard, M. (1992). Towards an analysis of discourse. In M. Coulthard (Ed.), *Advances in spoken discourse analysis* (pp. 1–34). London: Routledge.

Skehan, P. (1998). *A cognitive approach to language learning.* Oxford: Oxford University Press.

Slimani, A. (1992). Evaluation of classroom interaction. In J. C. Alderson and A. Beretta (Eds.), *Evaluating second language education* (pp. 197–220). Cambridge: Cambridge University Press.

Slobin, D. I. (1982). Universal and particular in the acquisition of language. In E. Wanner & L. Gleitmann (Eds.), *Language acquisition: State of the art* (pp. 128–170). Cambridge: Cambridge University Press.

Stubbs, M. (1983). *Discourse analysis.* Oxford: Basil Blackwell.

Swain, M. (1985). Communicative competence: Some roles of comprehensible input and comprehensible output in its development. In S. Gass amd C. Madden (Eds.), *Input in second language acquisition* (pp. 235–253). Rowley, MA: Newbury House.

Swain, M. (1995). Collaborative dialogue: Its contribution to second language learning. Plenary paper presented at the Annual American Association of Applied Linguistics Conference, Long Beach, CA.

Swain, M. & Lapkin, S. (1998). Interaction and second language learning: Two adolescent French immersion students working together. *The Modern Language Journal, 82,* 320–327.

Taylor, T. J. & Cameron, D. (1987). *Analyzing conversation.* Oxford: Pergamon.

Tsui, A. B. M. (1989). Beyond the adjacency pair. *Language in Society, 18,* 545–564.

Tsui, A. B. M. (1994). *English conversation.* Oxford: Oxford University Press.

Ulichny, P. (1996). Performed conversations in an ESL classroom. *TESOL Quarterly, 30,* 739–764.

van Lier, L. (1988). *The classroom and the language learner.* London: Longman.

van Lier, L. (1996). *Interaction in the language curriculum.* London: Longman.

Varonis, E. M. & Gass, S. M. (1985). Non-native/non-native conversation: A model for negotiation of meaning. *Applied Linguistics, 6,* 71–90.

Wagner, J. (1996). Foreign language acquisition through interaction: A critical review of research on conversational adjustments. *Journal of Pragmatics, 23,* 215–235.

Wagner–Gough, J. & Hatch, E. (1975). The importance of input data in second language acquisition studies. *Language Learning, 25,* 297–307.

Watson, R. (1985). Towards a theory of definition. *Journal of Child Language, 12,* 181–197.

Wesche, M. & Paribhakt, S. (Eds.) (1999). Special issue on Incidental Vocabulary Acquisition: Theory, current research, and instructional implications, *Studies in Second Language Acquisition, 21.*

White, L. (1987). Against comprehensible input: The input hypothesis and the development of second language competence. *Applied Linguistics, 8,* 95–110.

White, L. (1989). *Universal grammar and second language acquisition.* Amsterdam: John Benjamins.

White, J. & Lightbown, P. M. (1984). Asking and answering in ESL classrooms. *Canadian Modern Language Review, 40,* 228–244.

Wilson, T. P. (1991). Social structure and the sequenmtial organization of interaction. In D. Boden & D. H. Zimmerman (Eds.), *Talk and social structure* (pp. 22–43). Cambridge: Polity Press.

Wilson, T. P. & Zimmerman, D. H. (1986). The Structure of silence between turns in two-party conversation. *Discourse Processes, 9,* 375–390.

Woken, M. & Swales, J. (1989). Expertise and authority in native-non–native conversations: The need for a variable account. In S. M. Gass, C. Madden, D. Preston, & L. Selinker (Eds.), *Variation in second language acquisition: Discourse and pragmatics* (pp. 211–227). Clevedon, England: Multilingual Matters.

Young, R. (1997). Interactional competence. Paper presented at the Second Language Acquisition and Teacher Education Colloquium Series, University of Illinois, Urbana-Champaign.

Zimmerman, D. H. (1987). On conversation: The conversation analytic perspective. *Communication Yearbook, 11,* 406–432.

Zuengler, J. (1989). Performance variation in NS–NNS interactions: Ethnolinguistic difference or discourse domain? In S. M. Gass, C. Madden, D. Preston, and L. Selinker (Eds.), *Variation in second language acquisition: Discourse and pragmatics.* Clevedon, England: Multilingual Matters.

Zuengler, J. & Bent, B. (1991). Relative knowledge of content domain: An influence on native-non-native conversations. *Applied Linguistics, 12,* 397–415.

Author Index

Subject Index

F

G